The 1930s House Manual

Published in September 2005
Reprinted in 2007, 2008, 2011, 2012 and 2014

British Library Cataloguing in Publication Data:
A catalogue record for this book is available from the British Library

ISBN 978 0 85733 819 8

Published by Haynes Publishing,
Sparkford, Yeovil, Somerset BA22 7JJ, UK
Tel: 01963 442030 Fax: 01963 440001
Int. tel: +44 1963 442030 Int. fax: +44 1963 440001
E-mail: sales@haynes.co.uk
Website: www.haynes.co.uk

Haynes North America Inc.
861 Lawrence Drive, Newbury Park,
California 91320, USA

Printed in the USA by Odcombe Press LP,
1299 Bridgestone Parkway, La Vergne, TN 37086

Acknowledgements

Photos: Ian Rock and Ian MacMillan, except where credited and acknowledged below.
Editing, technical advice and step by steps Ch 6 & Ch 12: Ian MacMillan
Thanks also to:- Louise McIntyre, project manager and Ian Heath, copy editor

For assistance with photos and research: Paul Hackett at P&R Roofing, Oxford; Greg Stevenson at Under The Thatch; Peter Clements at Clement Windows Group Ltd; Cordula Zeidler and Ian at the Twentieth Century Society; Mike Hammet at the Brick Development Association; Phil and Fran Davies; Neil Curling at Halifax General Insurance; Minchinhampton Architectural Salvage Co; Debbie Taylor and Rosie Kinneir at Countrywide Surveyors; Howard Joynes and Phil Parnham at Sheffield Hallam; Clive Flisher; Sigrid Albers and Mr Annison; John Templeman; J. and S. Ferrier; Jeff Stott; Paul Swarbrick; Tim Ollier; Elizabeth Kirkpatrick; Steve Lees; Amanda Peacock; Mr and Mrs Simpson; Brown & Merry Estate Agents, Wendover; Hamnet Hayward Estate Agents, Princes Risborough; Mr Stark at The Blue House, Ashridge; Andrew Abbott at TRADA; Mike Parrett at dampbuster.com; Stephen Cobb at AngelPlastics.co.uk; E. G. Books; and Margaret Steele at Freeman Dawson & Co.

Many thanks to the following chartered surveyors: Tony Blay at Esurv, John O' Neil, Adrian Russell, Phil Drummond, Ian Burden, Andrew Lister, Adrian Shippey, Christopher Wallin, Folke Pope, Chris Schofield, Norman Barrett, Phil Sellors, Bill Greenfield, Vince Clifford, and D. Rapley.

The 1930s House Manual

Ian Alistair Rock MRICS

Edited by **Ian R. MacMillan** FRICS

CONTENTS

INTRODUCTION

You have chosen well. Most 1930s houses were of comparatively modern construction, yet could still display genuine character and style.

After so many years, however, a lot of these properties are now in need of 'essential repairs'. Problems such as cavity wall-tie failure, bowed roofs, collapsed drains, and subsidence are well known – but otherwise how can you tell if your house has significant defects or is just typical for its age? This Haynes manual shows what to check and where to look, what's 'normal' and what isn't, and how to remedy common defects. Many homes have also suffered from inappropriate DIY 'improvements', so we show how you can add real value by restoring some of the original character. You may still need to call in the professionals, but there's a lot you can do yourself.

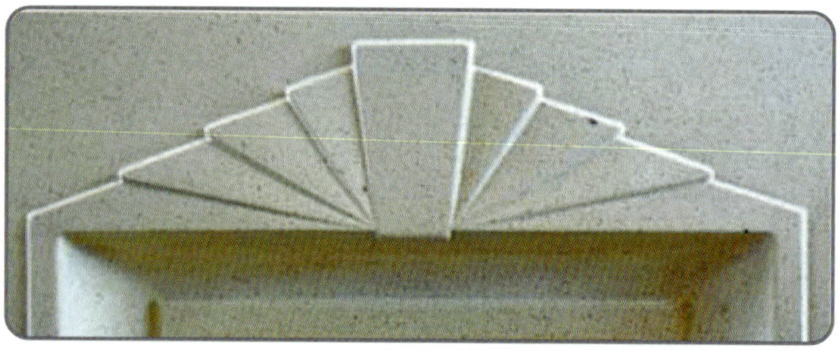

About this book

This Haynes manual is designed to be easy to read and is written broadly in the format of a homebuyers' survey. However, each chapter could easily have made an entire book in itself, so, inevitably, some aspects – like architecture and history – are only touched on very briefly. Because of the sheer number of possible defects in houses of this age, the Haynes **'defect, cause, solution'** format makes it quick and easy to look up the causes of technical problems and immediately see how to fix them. There are also some useful **Projects** giving detailed practical guidance on how to add value with popular improvements. And our classic **step-by-step** photo guides show how to repair and maintain your house – in easy stages.

This Haynes manual will tell you considerably more than the average house survey. But if you need to know more, full details of Building Regulations, planning issues, specialist craftsmen, and suppliers of materials for 1930s houses can be found at www.ThirtiesHouse.co.uk.

How 'thirties' is your house?

In terms of construction technology, most 1930s houses were a major departure from the old Victorian building methods that had soldiered on into the 1920s. In fact, their modern design proved so popular that the general layout as well as the methods and materials of construction remained largely unchanged until long after the Second World War. Some estates started in the late 1930s were completed as late as the 1950s. So if your house was built any time between the late 1920s and the 1950s, the technical data in this manual should be relevant.

Before you start

There are two key things to consider before embarking on the projects described here: that you are not putting yourself at risk of injury or death; and that you are not about to unwittingly commit a criminal offence.

A pair of typical 1930s semis – but styles actually varied considerably.

HEALTH AND SAFETY

Serious injury is a real risk when working on buildings – especially from lack of care when using power tools, ladders, and electrical equipment, as well as from less well-known causes such as trench collapse. So before you begin it makes sense to reduce the risk of serious injury by taking sensible precautions:

- Wear gloves, eye protectors, dust masks, and gloves, particularly when using power tools or chemical sprays.
- For roofing jobs and any work at a high level use access towers or scaffolding. Roof ladders or 'wheel ridge hook' ladder adaptors can be used by those experienced with them, but ladders must always be well secured so that they are stable and level.
- Use an RCD electrical safety cut out adaptor.
- Angle grinders and electric saws are notorious. A disk under load may shatter, or a blade may snap, so always wear protective safety clothing and a mask when using power tools.
- Keep hands well behind the edges of cutting tools.
- If you're unfamiliar with hired equipment or any tool, always read the instructions.
- Skips on roads must have nightlights.
- Never rush a job, and don't be too proud to call in a tradesman if a job turns out to be harder than anticipated.

If in doubt always seek professional advice.

__NB__ Every year about 70 fatalities and 5,000 serious injuries are caused by falls from a height. Health and Safety legislation now requires anyone who could potentially fall more than 2m (6.5ft) to use a fall protection system, so it's worth investing in a full body harness and safety helmet (available from most DIY stores).

Art deco fireplace. (Photo: c20fires)

The Law:

BUILDING REGULATIONS AND PLANNING

All structural alterations must be carried out with **Building Regulations** consent. This includes works such as taking down internal walls, making openings in walls, removal of chimney breasts and alterations to the roof structure (but not minor roof repairs). You will need to submit your plans in advance, possibly with engineers' calculations, and the building inspector will visit at key stages to check the works. Also, most DIY electrical work is now prohibited. The full documents can be seen at www.ThirtiesHouse.co.uk.

Planning law is concerned with development, external features, and changes of use. In Britain's 10,000 conservation areas it is safest to assume that any external changes visible from the street – even to fences, railings, and trees – are likely to require consent. For listed buildings even internal changes are strictly controlled.

Otherwise, subject to location, you can normally build small side or rear extensions without planning permission. Like for like re-roofing and the adding of skylights are also normally exempt. Porches qualify if they are less than $3m^2$ in floor area, less than 3m high, and more than 2m back from a road. The best advice is to consult your friendly Local Authority Planning Officer at the outset, or check the website for more information. Other legal issues, such as the Party Wall Act, are referred to in the appropriate chapters.

GETTING TO KNOW YOUR HOUSE

This was the age of the dream home – the decade of 'thirties chic', when millions moved out to better lives in fashionable, technologically-advanced new houses on the outskirts of town. These bright, labour-saving homes with gardens and garages were an exciting new way of living – a modern world of fantasy retro interiors combined with the convenience of the latest technologies; the first all-electric homes with the luxury of plumbed-in bathrooms with instant hot water.

The modern world

The 1930s witnessed nothing less than the biggest building boom ever seen in the UK (before or since), with around 300,000 new houses being built every year by the middle of the decade, fuelled by cheap land with minimal planning and building control. Encouraged by low interest rates on readily available mortgages from building societies, many people became homeowners for the first time (previous generations had rented). To speed things along, mortgage applications were often processed by the builders. Yet this was also a decade of falling property values. Falling costs, and fierce competition between building firms, reduced the price of houses considerably.

Architecture

The 1930s house is an instantly recognisable design classic, yet its origins are found in the *Garden City* houses of the late 19th-century. It was forged from two radically conflicting styles, one from the past, one from the future. The traditional 'mock-Tudor' cottage style with its 'Olde Worlde' charm clashed head on with revolutionary new Continental

Sleek modernist architecture – in downtown Kettering.

Modern-Movement architecture – streamlined villas with flat roofs and wide, metal-framed windows. But the ideal of the newly married couple was the country cottage 'with all mod cons', and it was the traditional style that triumphed, although many houses adopted ideas from both extremes.

MOCK-TUDOR

Like a popular rewrite of Shakespeare, 1930s private builders enthusiastically borrowed from the 16th and early 17th centuries (the Tudor, Elizabethan, and Jacobean periods) to create the so-called 'Tudorbethan' or 'Jacobethan' styles. Pretend Tudor black-and-white cottages appeared with diamond leaded bay windows under steep tiled roofs with tall, thin chimneys. Pebbledashed or tile hung walls frolicked with herringbone brickwork panels and forbidding Jacobean oak doors studded with heavy iron nails and strap-hinges.

But much of this architectural gaiety wasn't entirely fresh thinking. The Edwardians and even the late Victorian 'Arts and Crafts' architects had started dipping into old rural vernacular styles, reviving in a small way forgotten traditional features such as half-timbering and pebbledashing. Massive gable roofs that swooped down almost to the ground to embrace bay windows and porches were already evident in the 1920s, while pebbledash, regarded as a quintessentially *thirties* feature (based on traditional 'harling'), was actually applied more sparingly than in the previous decade.

But the 1930s was really all about 'big time' development. Mainstream, mass-produced housing blossomed with every design trick in the builder's repertoire: large overhanging roof eaves, projecting Elizabethan style 'jettied' first floors resting on exposed beams, elaborate pseudo-Tudor chimney tops, traditional weather-boarded

cottages with integral garages, and even crow-stepped Dutch gables and romantic balconies.

The porch was an essential feature, usually recessed within the front wall or made from stout oak posts supporting a gabled roof. In larger houses the retro theme would sometimes continue inside, with dark Jacobean oak panelling, false beams, and cosy cottage inglenook fireplaces. Bay windows had become pretty much universal on private housing. Square sided 1920s-style bays evolved into round or angled ones nestling under huge gables, or supporting massive overhanging eaves with 'cottagey' wooden brackets or brick corbels.

'MODERNE'

Some developers risked building modern homes in the 'International style', much beloved by architects. These bright, white-painted houses would typically be cube-

shaped, with daring flat roofs and walls of smooth rendered brick (to simulate concrete). Wide, metal-framed windows, with horizontal glazing bars curving around the corners of the house, would vie for attention with jazzy glazed front doors or black marble-effect porches and columns of glass blocks. The design was evocative of speed, with strong lateral lines and curved walls. Elegant, streamlined balconies echoed progressive images of express trains, racing cars, and monoplanes.

The appeal of modernism was that it encapsulated the fashion for fresh air, health, and sunshine, so small pockets of 'moderne' or 'suntrap' housing sprang up in the suburbs, often sitting rather uneasily alongside their cottage-style neighbours, although there was rarely much difference internally.

But the modernist dream of moonlit ocean-liner balconies and sleeping under the stars on 'a whole floor of extra space' (the flat roof) never really caught on – Building Societies were wary of lending on anything non-conventional, and the soggy British climate put paid to exotic notions of sunbathing on the roof.

This lack of popularity resulted in part from other practical considerations – white rendering was

prone to cracking and required periodic repainting, and metal windows tended to rust. Within a year of their launch some modern flat-roofed estates had sprouted traditional pitched roofs, and the 'compromise style' was born. Red brick 'Tudor' cottages appeared incorporating streamlined 'moderne' features – curved glass and steel 'suntrap' windows, sleek white bands of render, and maybe a porthole or deco coloured glass window.

ART DECO AND 'HOLLYWOOD MODERNE'

To this already eclectic mix was added a pinch of film studio glamour – popular culture in the form of art deco *machine age* style. Think Odeon cinemas and Agatha Christie's Poirot – zigzag lines in green, black and orange, jazzy stepped fireplaces and curved walls. Rising sun motifs with spreading rays appeared on front gates, gable ends, and garage doors, the appeal of art deco's sun-worshipping Egyptian, Central American, and Oriental influences perhaps being explained by the new fashion for sunbathing and popular interest in archaeological tomb-raiding.

Hollywood moderne architecture appeared just before the Second World War: large, white-rendered houses with dark metal windows and exotic green or blue pantiled roofs – just like in the movies.

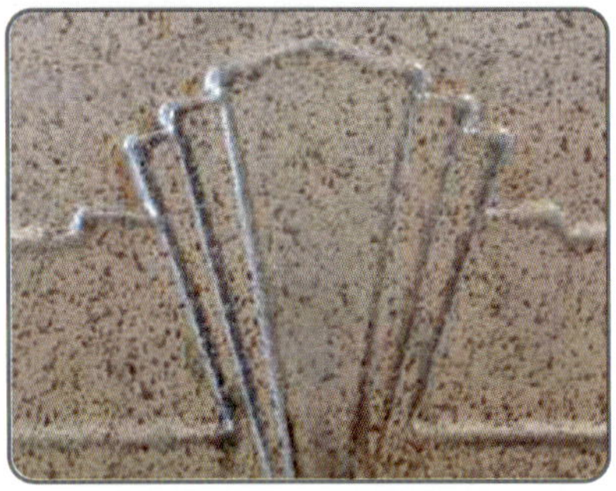

The bungalow, which had been around in small numbers as Indian-style seaside retreats since the last century, also became suddenly all the rage, thanks to films emanating from Hollywood where it was already a popular building form. Inspired by such glamorous images, entire suburban estates of detached and semi-detached bungalows spread across the landscape, the chalet bungalow variant growing a couple of additional loft bedrooms.

COUNCIL HOUSING

Meanwhile, Local Authorities were erecting large estates of unfashionable plain brick terraces and 'no frills' semis. To preserve the unity of the front elevations of the short rows of terraced houses, access to back gardens was normally through shared passageway 'tunnels' in mid terrace.

About a quarter of new inter-war houses were Council built. Designed for low maintenance, the design dispensed with 'frivolous' popular features such as bay windows, but often included outdated multi-paned sash windows. Some houses had small storm porches of reinforced concrete over the front doors and flat-roofed brick stores/WCs to the rear. This basic Council semi and terraced house design continued to be constructed into the 1960s.

ABOVE: Privately built flats – 'cottage on steroids' architecture, London W5.

LEFT: Fashionable 'ocean-going' private flats.

Whilst Council architects produced designs which stressed uniformity, it was the desire of private owner-occupiers to display some individuality. Owners of privately-built suburban semis looked down on neo-Georgian council estates, some even building giant walls across the street in an effort to enhance the tone of the area by keeping the hoi polloi out of sight!

Many privately-built apartment blocks developed at this time – often named 'Courts' or 'Gardens' – had fashionable balconied elevations in brick and render, displaying cool art deco motifs and modern metal windows. The equivalent council flats were typically larger four or five storey blocks usually of a quite different style. Many were utilitarian developments in heavy dark brick *neo-Georgian* style, with forbidding concrete staircases and outside 'deck access' built around an inner courtyard – a design that was both dark and noisy.

LAYOUT

The 1930s house was designed to suit smaller modern families. The new houses needed to be manageable and labour-saving with fewer rooms than pre-war homes, designed for housewives without resident servants (although a *daily help* might still pop in).

The archetypal 1930s house is a two-storey, three bed semi, but the typical rectangular layout was remarkably consistent in most house types. The front door, sheltered within a porch, would open into the main entrance hall, which was important for giving the right impression to visitors. Halls were now wider than most Victorian hallways, perhaps allowing the stairs to turn at the bottom to display 'Jacobethan' newel posts or fashionable panelled-in bannisters.

Ground floor accommodation typically comprised a front bay-windowed 'drawing room' (a.k.a. the living room, lounge, or front parlour) and a rear dining room with French doors to the garden. The front reception was still kept 'for

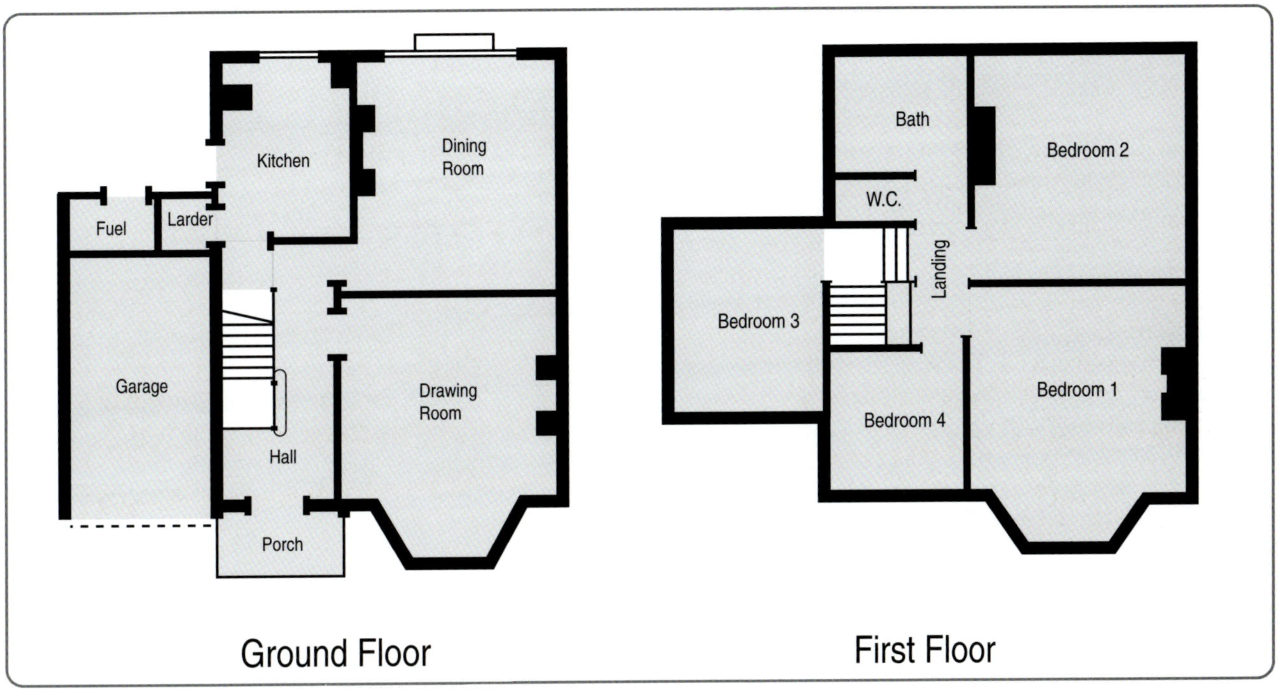

best', so it was the dining room that was normally the centre of family life. Separate access to each reception room was considered essential, but the Victorian fondness for dividing doors between the two rooms had died out. The small kitchen allowed mums to keep an eye on children playing in the back garden, but the cooker and sink had to be crammed into corners to leave space for the boiler, the garden door, and access to the larder etc. A serving hatch to the dining room could help save valuable space. An alternative arrangement was the combined 'parlour-kitchenette', a single back room with the cooker and sink placed along the side wall, partially screened off by a partition wall either side. From a modern perspective, it is the restrictive kitchen space that is probably the biggest single drawback to 1930s house design, and explains why so many have subsequently been extended.

Upstairs most houses had two double bedrooms above the reception rooms and a smaller front 'baby' boxroom over the hall. The bathroom at the rear would normally have a separate adjacent WC. The more expensive version shown in the illustration has an attached garage and store with a fourth bedroom above. A major plus point of this type of house for many of today's owners is the cavernous roof space that, with a little floorboarding, can become a useful den, or, with more extensive work, can prove suitable for a full-blown loft conversion.

The main departure from this layout is found in Council houses, which often omitted the second reception room and placed the bathroom and WC downstairs. Also deviating from the established pattern were bungalows, some with a central front door surrounded by a bay-windowed front bedroom on one side and living room on the other, some with the main door and entrance hall accessed from the side in the 'moderne' style.

Although 1930s houses were generally smaller than pre-war, the plots on which they were built were wider and usually deeper. Each privately-built house stood within its own gardens set back from the road, many with a shared driveway.

The rise of the semi

A staggering three million homes were built in the 1930s and most of these were semi-detached, comprising more than one in eight UK houses today. Most were built for sale by private developers, who funded each project with the profits from the disposal of previous buildings. Smaller firms would generally build houses in batches of as few as ten at a

time, so it was essential that the types of houses they built satisfied the market.

Though the ideal home may have been a detached house, the cheaper semi became by far the most popular form. This provided a breath of fresh air after the damp and dingey rooms of high density Victorian inner city housing. It was no longer fashionable to live in terraced houses, which were largely phased out in the 1920s, but some small blocks – typically of four or six houses – were still built at cheaper prices than the semi, often with the same imitation timber styling and leaded glass bay windows.

The suburban semi was now mostly owned rather than rented, and had to express a degree of individuality without being too different from its neighbours; buyers also wanted it to be easily distinguishable from its Council house equivalent. 'No two houses the same' therefore became the proud boast of many developers. In truth, each pair of semis was usually identical, the symmetry of the pair being important to the balance of the whole. But the individuality of each property on the same development was provided by numerous permutations of detailing – small variations in the half-timbering or in the leaded glass patterns of tile-hung or rendered bay windows, different stained glass images, and assorted porch treatments.

Even detached homes were sometimes built to the plans of a semi, to the extent that some appear to have lost their other half.

The semi-detached design allowed for a tradesman's entrance and in a few cases an attached garage, or at least the space for one – few buyers were expected to be able to afford a car as well as a mortgage!

Sounds of the suburbs

Take a drive out of the city and travel through time. Clusters of Georgian terraces soon give way to swathes of Victorian and Edwardian housing, in turn eclipsed by the inter-war suburbs. Now seen as a peculiarly 1930s phenomenon, the concept of city suburbs was actually inspired by earlier *garden suburbs* such as Hampstead and Letchworth.

Major new road and rail construction was opening up vast areas of green belt land around large towns and cities, introducing the new concept of commuting and attracting new factories, which in turn required new estates for workers. 'Sub-urban' housing made it possible for city workers to live in fresh, spacious, leafy surroundings away from the grimy Victorian inner city. 'In the country – close to town', 'Living In the Country', and 'Room to breathe', were the enticing sales slogans.

The dream of escaping from the polluted city to the clean suburban fringe was marketed partly on health grounds – fatal diseases like TB were aggravated by urban smog. But the motorcar had already begun to play an ever-increasing role in British life, and the reality for many was sprawling 'ribbon development' along major new approach roads to big towns, between jazzy modern factories and new roadhouse pubs and garages.

So what was new?

This was a real break with the past. Gone were the endless Victorian terraces built fronting the street; gone were the long, dark hallways, draughty high-ceilinged rooms, decrepit rear extensions, and damp basements.

New architectural styles deserved new materials and new technology. In came technical improvements such as modern cavity walls, decent damp-proof courses, and mains electricity supplies. New stronger, lighter, labour-saving materials appeared – breeze blocks, plasterboard, reinforced concrete, Portland cement, concrete roof tiles, asbestos cement sheeting, pre-manufactured lintels, and steel windows. Exciting new interior materials like chromed tubular steel, Bakelite plastic handles and fittings, veneered oak, and steam-bent plywood announced the arrival of the efficient new 'machine age'.

A large part of the appeal for homebuyers was the modern plumbing and the well equipped kitchens, with up-to-date freestanding cookers, built-in fittings, and instant water heaters at the sink, as well as luxuries such as electric fires, hygienic tiled bathrooms, and internal upstairs WCs. However, many of the labour-saving appliances we take for granted today – fridges, washing machines, etc – were only just making an appearance and were generally too costly to be universally adopted. Only the most expensive properties would have advanced features such as central heating.

New technology was also transforming the construction process. Cement mixers, mechanical diggers, and even electric saws were now generally available to speculative builders, while many materials were bought-in and goods were available ready-finished, reducing the need for skilled craftsmen.

Building control

But some things never change. Increasing complaints about 'jerry-building' were voiced as some small estates were hurriedly constructed by jobbing builders, whose aim was to maximise profits in the shortest possible time. By today's standards these were unplanned, uncontrolled, and largely unregulated developments. And because of the speed of construction (often only four months per dwelling) and the limited number of inspectors, construction was often completed before any sub-standard work could be discovered.

'You know that builder you recommended…?'

In some cases the combination of rogue builders and the lack of practical building control lead to serious defects materialising soon after construction, such as cracked or damp walls, leaking roofs, warped and shrunken floorboards, jammed windows, and faulty electric cables.

Builders looking for economies were sometimes tempted to use the cheapest grades of brick, which they would cover with pebbledash or roughcast. This offered fairly adequate weather protection until it inevitably cracked. The best bricks were usually confined to the street frontage.

Non load-bearing internal walls were also built of the cheapest grades of brick or breeze blocks. And roof work offered opportunities for economy too: in less expensive houses the timber frame could be lightly made of cheap wood, and felting or boarding beneath the roof tiles was generally omitted.

Even expensive architect-designed modernist villas of this period could suffer from defects such as condensation, cold-bridging, and water penetration – problems derived from the relatively new materials and construction techniques, compounded by inadequate maintenance to aspects such as flat roofs, windows, render, and copings on parapet walls.

Fortunately, most suburban developments were large-scale projects run by well-organised firms. Materials were delivered by convoys of lorries, and some larger estates were developed over five years or more. Many house builders amalgamated, resulting in the emergence of several of today's large firms, including Laing, Wimpey, Costain, and Wates.

Whilst building control was still fairly rudimentary, the impact of town planning – the *garden suburb* movement in particular – was already dictating lower densities, open spaces, and gaps between buildings, all essential ingredients of 1930s suburbs. Although the Green Belt Act didn't arrive until 1938, road widths were set by planning requirements (or local byelaws) and consideration started to be given to estate layouts with winding roads, planted open spaces, and variations in architectural styles. Another *garden city* influence was that of 'rural' grass verges running alongside roads on new estates. New restrictions on development density were agreed at 12 houses per acre, which became the norm (although when ingeniously combined with new cul-de-sac layouts it turned out to be even more cost-effective than the old terraces).

Materials

The favoured material for the main walls was red brick, which was liked for its 'warmth' and vaguely Tudor connotations. Even in regions where stone had long been the traditional building material, new houses constructed entirely of local stonework were now rare, with stone often only appearing as panels within brick walls. But large expanses of brick were frowned upon, so first floor walls were often treated with pebbledash or white-painted plain render. Brickwork could also be tempered with traditional tile-hanging, but this was now largely restricted to bay windows and gables.

Other favourites on gables were timber weatherboarding and, of course, good old black-and-white 'mock-Tudor' half-timbering, suggestive of period timber-frame construction.

BRICKS

Most brickwork was now fairly anonymous and not a major architectural feature as it had been in Victorian times. The days of distinctive local bricks, hand-made in a wide variety of styles and vivid colours, were long gone, although local brickworks continued to provide the visually important facing bricks for many front walls. Otherwise, standardised 'Fletton' bricks had started to dominate. Attempts were made to manufacture some of them in a vaguely 'period' style, and these were used for some better quality housing. To add character, others were made with patterned surfaces, such as the popular light red wire-pressed 'wavy' variety.

BREEZE BLOCKS

In the late 1920s 'breeze blocks' started to be used, sometimes being manufactured on site using small presses. They were extremely cheap since they largely comprised waste derived from gas works or blast furnaces (like 'coke breeze' and 'black ash') combined with cement. They were used extensively in internal partition walls, but rather less so for the inner leaves of main cavity walls. In addition to their cheapness, the other advantages of blocks over bricks are that they can be laid much more quickly (one block is equivalent to six bricks, three high and two long) and have better insulating properties.

MORTAR AND RENDER

Modern Portland cement had generally superseded lime for use in concrete and bricklaying mortar. However, lime was still commonly mixed into cement render, which was applied as roughcast and pebbledash or, in more modern style, as smooth horizontal bands.

BELOW: exception to the general rule – houses clad in reconstituted stone in Swindon.

Its original colour was the creamy-beige tone of the self-coloured 'Snowcrete' waterproof render. Concrete made with *coke breeze* was often used for foundations and for some solid ground floors. Reinforced concrete was used more rarely, sometimes in flat roofs and for the floors in blocks of flats.

ROOFS

Plain red tiles, initially of clay and later of cheaper concrete, had largely replaced slates as the roofing material of choice. Larger interlocking Roman tiles and pantiles also enjoyed popularity. The big 'hipped' roof design was the predominant style, often combined with large front gables or hips over the bays.

TIMBER

1930s builders had naturally seasoned wood at their disposal, as opposed to the modern kiln-dried variety. Structural timber was commonly from softwood species such as Douglas fir, spruce, Scandinavian pine, and red deal. Items like casement windows were available in mass-produced form 'ready for fixing', and the sizes of joists and rafters were fairly standardised. Floors largely continued to be made from imported deal – suspended timber with pine boards. Hardwoods, particularly oak, were used for joinery and flooring in more expensive homes.

So much for history and architecture. Now let's take a look at each part of the property in turn to see what commonly goes wrong, what causes typical defects, and how to fix them.

ABOVE: 21st century 1930's revival ('mock, mock-Tudor').

BELOW LEFT: Original, left : anonymous, right.

BELOW: The proud owner of a newly constructed semi in 1930.

THE ROOF

There is a certain streamlined elegance to many roofs of this period. Here we look at the 1930's fashion for hipped roofs covered with plain tiles or colourful glazed pantiles – not forgetting those brave flat roof designs that never quite caught on in Britain.

But many roofs of this age are now reaching the end of their useful lives, and it is not unknown for unscrupulous builders and roofers to take advantage of homeowners' lack of specialist knowledge. What are the crucial signs of ageing to look for? And how long should different roof coverings last?

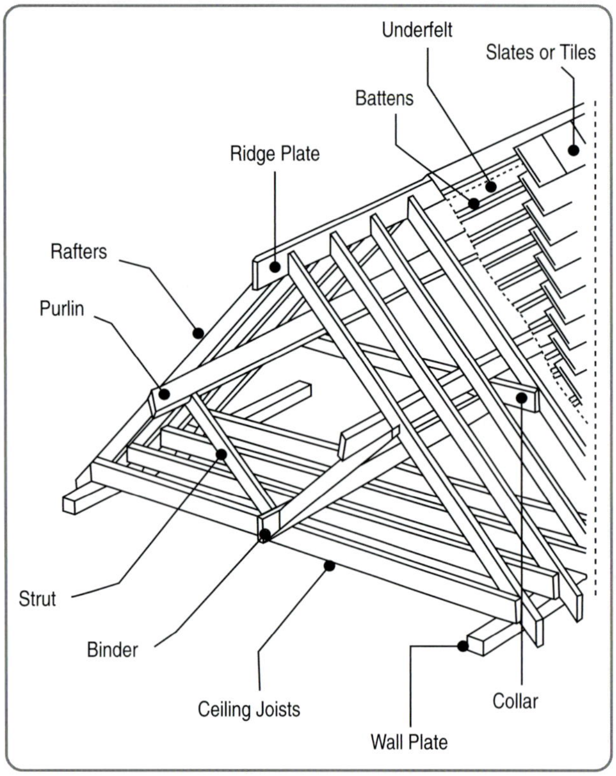

Roof structure

As everyone knows, a basic roof structure takes the form of a triangle: the front and rear roof slopes meet on top at the ridge, and at its base the triangle is coupled together by ceiling joists acting as 'collars'. But the predominant form of roof on 1930s houses was the more sophisticated 'hipped' roof. Here, in addition to the main front and rear roof slopes, there is a third roof slope over the side wall, making the whole thing look rather like a pyramid sliced down the middle. The hipped design was so fashionable that it was often complemented with another small hipped roof over the front bay window (as an alternative to a gable).

Hipped roof construction was of traditional cut timbers covered with tiles or slates fixed to battens running across the rafters. The 'corners' where the three roof slopes meet were made from special timber 'hip rafters' and were usually clad with round 'hip tiles' (similar to ridge tiles) or with cheekily upturned 'bonnet tiles'. Due to their weight, hip tiles normally required a protruding metal strip called a 'hip iron' at the base, to help prevent any loose ones slipping off.

The drawback with hipped roof structures is that they are

To most of us, roofs can be a little scary. When you're standing high up on a ladder, or the wind is howling around the scaffolding, you tend to develop a certain respect for the job in hand. And having to withstand the full force of the weather means that roofs are more likely to develop faults than just about any other part of the property. But weather isn't the only problem. Structural failures can occur, and repairs or additional support are sometimes needed.

But before embarking on any roofing work, you must first be certain that safe access has been provided – purpose-made roof ladders and platform towers or scaffolding are essential. In addition it is important to avoid damaging the tiles further (eg by walking on them). If in any doubt, or if you suffer from vertigo, don't go there!

BELOW LEFT: Classic hipped roof – in glazed pantiles.

RIGHT: Hip iron.

BELOW: Bonnet tiles.

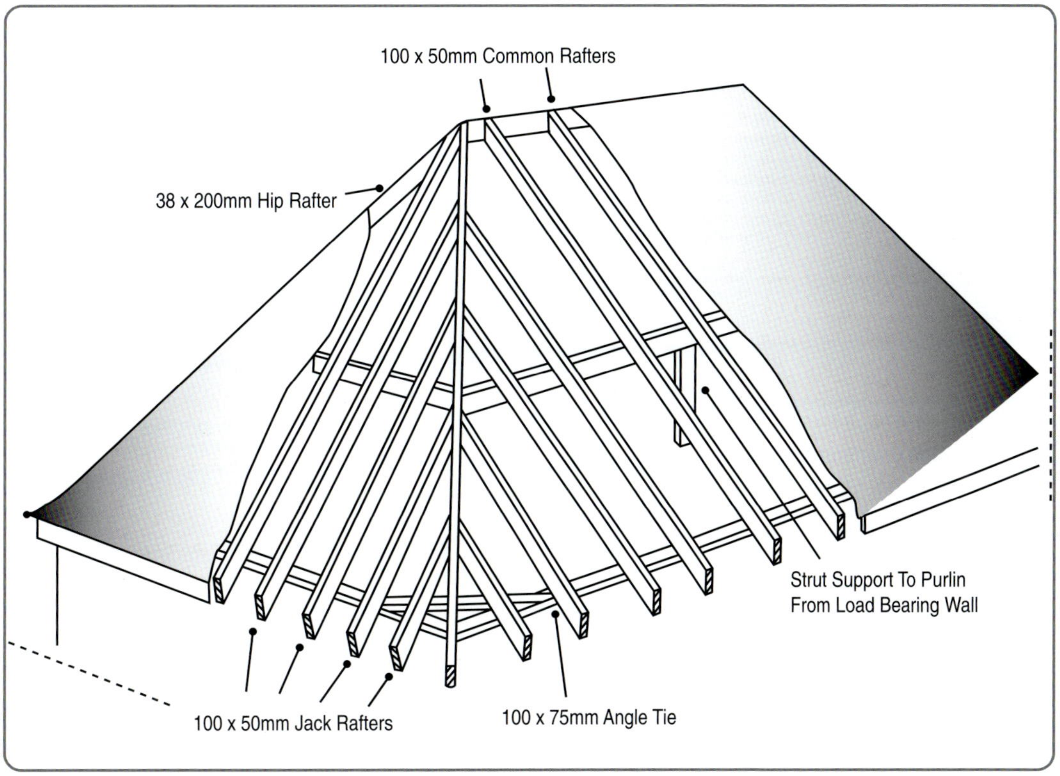

LEFT: Hipped roof structure.

BELOW LEFT: Rafters.

BELOW RIGHT: Collar, tying the front and rear purlins.

relatively complex to construct, requiring tricky angled cuts where the main roof timbers meet the side hip (the 'jack rafters'). So where the builders weren't fully competent or experienced with this type of structure, problems have sometimes arisen later.

RAFTERS

The roof slopes are constructed of timbers called rafters. Depending on the span of the roof, these are typically 100 x 50mm (4 x 2in) and are spaced about 400mm/16in, and not more than 600mm/2ft, apart. The rafters meet at the top at a timber 'ridge plate', which runs along from the party wall (in a semi or terraced house) to the side hip.

At their base, the rafters rest on a 'wall plate' (a wooden beam running along the top of the wall). To stop the rafters pushing outwards, they are tied in by the ceiling joists to make a strong and secure 'triangle'. The structure relies on adequate nailing between the feet of the rafters and the wall plate as well as secure bolting to the ceiling joists. The side hip roof slopes were designed to be tied in to the main roof with special angle ties known as 'dragon ties', but in practice these were usually omitted.

PURLINS, STRUTS, AND COLLARS

The rafters are normally supported by a large, horizontal timber beam known as a purlin, typically measuring about 175 x 75mm (7 x 3in), depending on the span. Purlins were fairly easy for builders to install in a typical Victorian terraced

LEFT: Belt and braces: purlin supported by a strut and also tied in with a horizontal collar.

BELOW LEFT: Battens.

BELOW RIGHT: Old horsehair blanket underlay, moulded away.

roof, as the they simply ran from side to side – from one party wall to the other (embedded in the masonry or resting on protruding brick corbels). But the problem facing 1930s builders with more complex hipped roof structures was that a third purlin was needed on the side slope, joining up the ends of those to front and rear.

Each purlin is normally supported by a central strut, with the loading ultimately taken by a bedroom wall below, sometimes via timber 'binders' that spread the load. An alternative to struts is the provision of collars, which are horizontal beams joining the two main purlins. Collars are more common on smaller roofs with shorter spans (as with some Council designs). Sometimes the 'belt and braces' school of construction employed collars as well as struts, just to be on the safe side.

BATTENS

Tiles are hung from traditional rough-sawn wooden battens running horizontally across the rafters. These typically measured 50 x 25mm or 38 x 25mm (2 x 1 or 1.5 x 1in) spaced apart according to the size and lap of the tiles and the pitch of the roof. Calculating batten spacing on a new or reclad roof can be quite complex, but tile manufacturers can normally help with the appropriate measurements.

FIREBREAK WALLS

The party walls in the roof spaces of semi-detached or terraced houses are known as a firebreak walls. They are normally of brickwork, although some may be of early concrete block construction. The two main chimney breasts are usually built up with the party wall, joining together at loft level into the main stack above. Where the party wall projects up above the roof it should be capped with coping stones or have tiles projecting out either side to disperse rainwater.

UNDERFELT

Since the 1950s, roofs have normally been built with underfelt fitted beneath the tiles. This provides a secondary line of defence against wind-driven rain, and until recently was typically made of black bituminised-hessian 'sarking felt'. But 1930s roofs were often built without any such underlay, so if you can see the underside of the tiles in the loft then the roof is likely to be original. Whilst there is more risk of rainwater or snow seeping through in severe weather conditions, the cost of stripping the tiles and battens to fit new underlay is not normally warranted, unless complete retiling is required anyway.

The sarking felt is supposed to sag slightly between the rafters and be carried down into the guttering to help

LEFT AND RIGHT: Timber 'featherboarding'. BELOW LEFT: mineral wool loft insulation.

disperse any water that may have been driven under the tiles. However, the problem with the bituminised variety of underlay was that it is impermeable, which could trap moisture in the loft and cause it to suffer from damp and mould. In addition it was often torn during installation. Since the mid-1990s modern vapour-permeable underlays have been used instead, which keep rainwater out but allow the roof to breathe without fitting extra vents.

Before the days of modern underfelt, some roof coverings were bedded with mortar or straw, or even had thin strips of timber lath underneath for added weatherproofing, but this could restrict ventilation and retain water, risking decay to the battens. Some 1930s properties had a primitive lining blanket under the tiles made from horsehair, but these will now be damp and in poor condition. Instead, many better quality roofs were built with timber 'featherboarding' (a.k.a. 'sarking timber'), which in most cases has proved surprisingly durable.

INSULATION AND VENTILATION

Insulation was not the strong suit of 1930s builders. The roofs of their houses were not normally insulated to any great extent, so living in them must have been a deeply chilly experience for the early occupants, and may explain the popularity of hot-water bottles at the time! But because uninsulated lofts are one of the biggest areas for heat-loss, most will now have had insulation fitted, albeit probably to a lesser depth than is currently recommended. Loft insulation should be 270mm (11in) deep laid over the ceiling joists, keeping the eaves clear to breathe. Where large bats of loft insulation have been stuck between the roof rafters instead, there is a risk that they might stop air circulating and trap moisture.

Traditionally, roofs were designed to be 'draughty', with lots of air passing through them in order to help maintain ventilation around the battens and roof timbers. This reduced the risk of decay, by allowing any moisture that got in to evaporate and dry out. So where old roofs have been reclad and underfelted problems from condensation and damp can occur unless ventilation has also been improved, as is now required by Building Regulations. Ventilation in the loft can be aided by clearing insulation at the edges by the eaves (there should be eaves vents externally, usually in the soffits) or by fitting special vents at the ridge tiles or to the roof slopes.

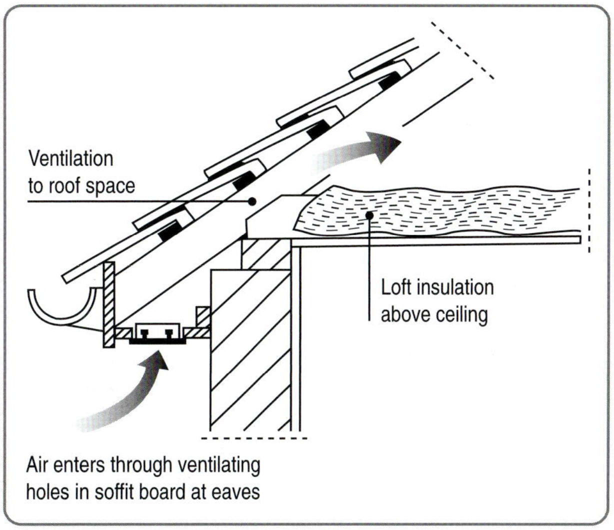

SPRAYED FOAM

Advertised in Sunday newspapers as a cheap solution for extending the life of old roofs, this is a controversial 'remedy'. The problem is that sprayed polyurethane foam encloses the (possibly still damp) battens and parts of the rafters, thereby preventing air circulation – a classic recipe for wood rot. It seals up the natural ventilation between the tiles or slates on older roofs, so damp can't evaporate away.

It also relies on the installer doing a good job fixing defects such as loose tiles and leaking flashings prior to spraying. But many roof spaces are less than ideal for access, and the temptation may be for the installer to cut corners. A roof that's already nearing the end of its useful life that is sprayed with foam internally must be suspect.

Another short-term measure sometimes used is to paint the surface of the slates or tiles (eg with bitumen or a cement wash), or to 'sheath' the roof with coated nylon mesh. This is not recommended. The only long-term solution is to have the roof stripped and reclad with new felt, battens, and coverings.

Roof coverings

Because the 1930s house was an economically-built, mass-produced structure, and hipped roofs were relatively complex to construct, roof timbers were sometimes used sparingly and some may be undersized by modern standards. Slight bowing is sometimes evident where timbers have settled under the weight of the tiles, or where original lightweight slate roofs have been replaced with large, heavy, concrete tiles, as was often done during the 1980s with grant assistance.

The earlier Victorian passion for slates at the expense of tiles was now completely reversed. Tiles had become highly fashionable and, being manufactured in huge quantities, were significantly cheaper than natural slate. They were also much easier to lay, and consequently had become the roofing material of choice.

But there are some similarities. Both tiles and slates are laid in rows (courses), starting at the bottom of the roof by the eaves and working upwards. Each course is laid so the tails overlap and cover the heads of the row below, the vertical joints being staggered, as in the bonding of brickwork, to protect the joints. The depth of the lap can be less for a steep roof (of say 50°) because the rain runs off more quickly. On shallow roofs the rainwater runs slower and tends to 'fan out', getting under the edges, so a greater lap is needed. The area most at risk is lower down near the eaves where the most water accumulates. Such *sprocket eaves* were formed with additional small rafters creating a shallower pitch in order to slow the rainwater for a safe landing in the gutter – a characteristic that gave so many 1930s roofs a fashionable 'pagoda' look.

When roofs are to be re-covered, some of the old clay tiles can often be salvaged and reused to achieve an authentic look. If using new materials, it is important to

nailed (in exposed windy areas, such as coastlines, tiles need to be double-nailed). Plain tiles were very popular in the 1930s, and were normally rectangular, very slightly curved, and about 13–24mm (0.5–1in) thick. A typical size would be 265 x 165mm (10.5 x 6.5in), but sizes vary (see technical data box at end of chapter). Being fairly small, the pitch of plain-tiled roofs could not normally be less than 35°, and they would typically need to be laid with a lap as deep as 88mm (3.5in).

These machine-made tiles have a fairly smooth surface and regular shape, unlike the rougher, traditional handmade clay tiles, which – except on some more expensive houses – had largely been superseded. The latter were sometimes known as 'sand-faced' tiles (the moulds were sanded to stop the clay sticking) and were tougher, being less prone to de-lamination and frost damage and having a lifespan of well over a hundred years. But both types can in time become porous, due to under-burning or from salts in the clay, and suffer from 'spalling', where they break down into flakes due to frost damage or thermal movement. They will then absorb moisture (from rain or from condensation inside the loft). This leads in turn to decay in the battens, which eventually results in the tiles slipping and leaving a hole in the roof.

If you can see several slipped or missing tiles on the roof, and there are white powdery deposits under the tiles around the nibs (visible from inside the roof space), the likely solution will be complete re-tiling, as the whole batch may be defective.

ensure that the correct size and type of tile has been selected for the angle of pitch, and that they have been laid to the correct lap, or else rainwater may track back underneath.

There are conflicting opinions as to whether moss and lichen on roofs should really be of any concern. These sometimes thrive on roofs exposed to damp and shady conditions. One view is that because they absorb moisture that freezes in winter, they can potentially damage the surface of tiles. Conversely, it is claimed that their minimal root systems should not damage sound tiles, and can even provide partial protection from frost. Confused? It is really a matter of degree. Large, extensive clumps are unsightly and can block gutters, but can be cleared using a high-pressure washer – as long as the roof is sound and you take great care!

PLAIN CLAY TILES

Traditional plain clay tiles were manufactured with projecting 'nibs' so they could be hung from battens, perhaps with only every fourth or fifth course needing to be

LEFT: Typical plain roof tiles showing signs of ageing – with rare original roof skylight.

BELOW: Tiles hung over battens by their nibs.

PLAIN CONCRETE TILES

It was during the 1930s that plain tiles manufactured from concrete, in sizes and styles to match traditional clay tiles, started to be used as a cheaper alternative. These were manufactured by firms like Marley and Redland, or were imported from continental Europe. Some original clay-tiled roofs will now have been patched or completely replaced with these small concrete tiles, which typically had a darker colour (when new) and a rougher surface. The main drawback with concrete tiles is that they have a shorter lifespan of only around 50–75 years and do not usually weather 'naturally' over the years, becoming pale and blotchy with age. Modern varieties have nevertheless achieved a very similar appearance to clay tiles when new.

PANTILES AND ROMAN TILES

Pantiles are traditional large tiles of Dutch origin with a wavy S-shaped profile. Glazed in striking greens or blues they were very much in vogue in 'Hollywood moderne' architecture, often laid with a pagoda-like shallow curve to the lower roof slopes. The overall effect is a series of ridges and furrows that produce an elegant roofscape. But because of the wavy profile, unsightly gaps could appear at the top course, where they met the straight line of the ridge tiles, so these were often filled with small inserts called 'dentil slips' set into mortar.

Pantiles are hung by their nibs like plain tiles but are lighter (per square metre) and can be laid to a shallower pitch – some as low as 17.5°. But the chief advantage of pantiles over plain tiles, apart from their dazzling appearance, was that they were easier and quicker to lay. Conventional plain tiles are laid side by side, so to prevent rainwater falling through the joints, they have to be completely overlapped by the tile above (double lap), or even lapped three times, to ensure watertightness. Pantiles, on the other hand, were designed to interlock and to overlap each other at the sides, thereby preventing water from penetrating. They therefore only need one short overlap from the row above (single lap). To construct a roof using regular plain tiles required 60 tiles per square metre, but with pantiles you only need about 15 tiles. The savings in weight and labour are self-evident.

Large clay 'Roman' tiles were also very popular in the 1930s. They are similar to pantiles but with a flatter profile. Typically of an orangey-red colour, they are fixed with conventional nibs or with clips. Some have a bold single 'roll' in the centre for a Mediterranean look; others are flat with smaller double channels on each side. This was an economical and stylish roof covering that, like pantiles, could be laid to a single lap, saving on labour. Cheap machine made interlocking clay tiles were imported in large numbers, mainly from Belgium and Holland.

INTERLOCKING TILES

In the 1980s some houses had their roofs reclad with large concrete tiles with interlocking side grooves. These low-profile tiles are similar to traditional 'Roman' tiles and are quick and easy to lay, but they are much heavier than the original slate coverings and impose substantially higher loads on the roof structure: without additional support, roofs can show signs of distress and may even ultimately collapse. Large concrete tiles are also difficult to adapt to angles, such as hipped areas over bay windows, and don't generally make

Original interlocking tiles.

Modern replacement concrete interlocking tiles (left).

a good replacement for original slates or plain tiles. However, they can be laid to a very shallow pitch, and if manufactured and fitted properly they should last well over 50 years.

NATURAL SLATES

Though slates took a back seat in the inter-war period they persisted in a few traditional slate regions, and despite their relative expense remained the material of choice for some local builders. There are several different sizes of slates, all with aristocratic pretensions – a 'Countess' being the commonly used 500 x 250mm (20 x 10in) standard size.

Slate is one of the most hardwearing of all roofing materials, being lightweight, frost resistant, and durable,

with a lifespan well in excess of a hundred years. Unlike tiles, which were mainly just hooked over the timber battens, slates had to be nailed through two holes, either in their centres or their heads (tops). The nails were of special copper, zinc, or galvanised iron, the last being prone to corrosion and having a shorter life. They would typically be laid to a 75mm (3in) lap, depending on the pitch, and in different grades of thickness, starting with the thinnest on top.

Failure is usually due to rusting of the nails ('nail sickness'), where the nails have become so corroded over the years that the slates fall loose. But slates are typically less affected than tiles by water penetration or by frost and thermal movement, although they can eventually de-laminate (or 'exfoliate'), absorbing moisture and becoming soft. Ideally an original slate roof should be reclad with new Welsh slate, but it's expensive. Recycled Welsh slate is a good compromise, as are new Canadian slates. You may well be able to salvage and reuse many of the old sound ones.

ARTIFICIAL SLATES

Modern composite slates have become a popular, cheaper alternative to natural slate for re-roofing. They can be laid to a very shallow pitch (some as low as 17.5°), and unlike concrete tiles they are lightweight and look authentic, if a little shiny. Most are even lighter than real slate, so to prevent

wind damage their tails may have to be laid with special metal rivets or ties. Early artificial slates contained asbestos-fibre reinforcement and were prone to discoloration and warp. Superseded in the 1980s by non-asbestos composite fibre slates, they are now the budget material of choice, although their lifespan may prove relatively short.

ASBESTOS TILES

Asbestos cement was the new wonder material of the inter-war years, used in many aspects of house construction right up until the 1980s. Fortunately, asbestos tiles are not very common, but they can still be seen on some 1920s and 1930s roofs, with their distinctive darkish pink squares often laid in a diagonal diamond pattern. Tiles of this age will now

require replacement, but the removal costs may be considerable and must be carried out by licensed contractors. And the replacement roof coverings will most likely be heavier, requiring the roof structure to first be strengthened.

Much more common is corrugated white asbestos cement sheeting, often found on outbuildings and garages (see Chapter 13). Asbestos cement sheeting is a thin, hard, lightweight material that can release dangerous fibres when broken or if subjected to continuous heavy weathering which causes deterioration. But if it's in good general condition there should be no significant hazard, other than its fragility. The important thing is to never try to sand, scrape, wire-brush, drill, or subject them to abrasion in any way – and never walk on these fragile roofs.

FLASHINGS

The biggest weak-point on most roofs is where they meet a wall, for example at porches and chimney stacks. Here you will find metal flashings or mortar fillets covering the joints. Cement mortar fillets at junctions have a short life as they tend to crack – a very common cause of leaks. They should be replaced with lead flashings. Metal 'soakers' are an additional way to protect a joint, with special strips of lead inserted under the tiles.

RIDGE AND HIP TILES

Probably the most exposed part of the roof is at the very top – the apex or 'ridge' – which therefore needs to be well protected and waterproofed. This was normally done by capping the ridges with special 'half-round' ridge or hip tiles.

Storm damage to ridge and hip tiles is quite common, the end ones often coming loose first, presenting a serious danger. Most rely simply on a bed of mortar to hold them down, often with some broken tiles inserted to reinforce the mix. But cracks can occur in the mortar for a number of reasons, eg if the mix was excessively strong with too much cement, or if the mortar dried too quickly as dry tiles sucked out the moisture, or due to different rates of expansion between the mortar and the tiles.

In any case, it is very common to find that the mortar pointing has badly eroded, and this should be pointed up before damp can penetrate, loosening the mortar and allowing the wind to dislodge the tiles. Hip irons at the base of hip corners should be periodically checked, as they help retain any loose hip tiles. For information on re-bedding see 'Defects' below. Modern ridge and hip tiles have overcome these traditional problems by being secured with special screws or a wire tied to the ridge timber below.

Valleys

Valleys are found where one roof joins another at an angle, typically where a bay roof meets the main roof. A major improvement in roof design in 1930s houses came with the adoption of manufactured pre-formed 'swept' valley tiles. However, some roofs still employed traditional 'open valleys' – a strip of lead or zinc sheeting (minimum width 100mm/4in) over a timber board base, with any gaps at the sides pointed up with mortar. Such valleys are a common weak point and a cause of water penetration and should be periodically cleared of moss and debris to prevent rainwater overflowing into the roof space. Modern purpose-made plastic (GRP) valley linings and flashings are a cheaper alternative to traditional lead.

Bays and porches

Bay windows were considered a highly desirable feature in the design of privately-built houses, and most had a two-storey bay. But, just like their Victorian predecessors, they could be problematic. See Chapter 7.

Bays were usually topped with large gabled or hipped roofs, or else were 'cut off' flat. A superior contemporary design was to tuck the bay under the big overhanging eaves of the main roof. As well as looking suitably streamlined, this neatly designed out the weak point at the valleys where bay roofs joined the main roof. But on bays with flat roofs (either single or two storey) there is another risk: the flat roof covering can perish, causing damp to the main front wall and rot to any nearby timbers, such as structurally crucial hidden lintels.

Porches were a similarly desirable feature for most private buyers. If not integral to the house, the front porch could comprise either a simple hood stuck to the front wall with 'cottagey' brackets underneath, or perhaps a larger gabled roof supported on big 'Jacobean' timber posts. The problem area of porch roofs is much the same as for bays – the vulnerable joints to the main house, which should be covered with lead flashings.

Eaves

The eaves are formed where the roof rafters project over the main walls to create a roof overhang that protects the upper walls from the weather. By the 1930s the adopted style was predominantly modern timber 'box eaves' with a soffit infill underneath. In modern houses the roof usually overhangs the walls by around 200mm (8in), but 1930s architecture revelled in the big eaves statement, with some displaying such extra detailing features as quaint carved timber 'supports' or corbelled eaves brackets made from layers of tiles.

Gables and verges

Big overhanging gables above front bays were a powerful 1930s architectural feature that had evolved from Edwardian architecture. These presented an irresistible opportunity for some 'jazzing up' with decorative half-timbering and render, tile hanging, or timber cladding. But the render may have been applied over no more than thin timber laths, which can be prone to damp and decay. Or the masonry behind the render may be very thin (of a single brick width, about 115mm/4.5in), and therefore potentially prone to damp penetration.

'Verges' are the sides of a roof slope, typically visible at gables or lean-to roofs. The edges of the roof were normally raised up or tilted inwards slightly to keep rainwater from spilling over. This was achieved by wedging a special course of tiles or slates (an 'undercloak') under the batten ends, bedded in mortar. The verges were then pointed up with mortar and often decorated with a wooden bargeboard ('vergeboard') fixed underneath. The verges normally overhang the wall below by between about 40 and 75mm (1.5–3in). Replacement 'cloaked' verge tiles, or verge coverings, are a modern 'maintenance-free' alternative but are not necessarily architecturally compatible on older buildings.

BELOW: Hipped roofs don't suffer from problems like this gable of rendered timber.

Dormer windows

Rooms built into roof spaces often have windows that project through the roof slopes. These dormer windows are particularly common on chalet bungalows and, like bays, they are often topped with small gabled or hipped roofs. Dormers were usually set back slightly, and built up from the rafters or floor joists with a framework of upright timber studs (rather than the Victorian preference for building the front straight up from the wall below).

The dormer sides (known as 'cheeks') were normally clad in zinc or lead sheet, or else hung with tiles. At the junctions to the roof there may be 'secret gutters' – soakers of sheet metal obscured by the tiles.

Common dormer failings are thin and poorly insulated walls and ceilings, prone to condensation and damp, leaks at defective side cheeks and blockages at roof joints (eg at valleys), and instability – some will have sagged inwards as the rafters have settled.

Flat roofs

Stylish 'modern movement' 1930s houses with radical 100 per cent flat roofs were the exception. Elsewhere, flat roofs were only ordinarily used for balconies, some bays and porches, and small rear additions, the term 'flat' typically meaning any slope less than about 10°. Construction was traditionally of timber in a similar style to that of floors, comprising joists covered with boards. For most houses, the choice of covering was either lead or zinc sheets. Superior copper sheet (normally identified by its light green patina) was too expensive for use on mainstream housing.

One drawback with flat roofs of this age is internal dampness to ceilings, either from leakage or from condensation.

ASPHALT

Bitumen-based asphalt was sometimes used as a finish to concrete roofs, or may have since been applied as a protective coat over metal roofs. It is normally laid hot in two layers to about 20mm (0.75in) thickness and covered with a solar reflective treatment such as stone chips, metal foil, etc. Typical asphalt defects include crazing, splitting and cracking, and ponding of water, but it should normally have a life of around 40 years. Small cracked and blistered areas can often be cut out and replaced, but if larger areas are affected complete re-covering will be required.

REINFORCED CONCRETE

Reinforced concrete was rarely used, other than on some flat roofs of 'moderne' houses and apartment blocks and some small storm porches. Over time, concrete can suffer from a number of debilitating ailments. One is 'carbonation', where carbon dioxide in the atmosphere reacts with the concrete and makes it porous, so that the steel reinforcement then rusts, causing cracking and, ultimately, disintegration. It can also be afflicted by 'concrete cancer', an internal chemical reaction with some kinds of aggregate in the mix, brought on by moisture. Protection of the surface (eg with asphalt) can help prevent such defects, unless erosion, cracking, or rust is already visible, in which case damaged areas need to be cut out and the roof treated – or in severe cases replaced.

ZINC

Zinc was a cheaper and thinner substitute for lead, normally of 0.8mm thickness ('14 gauge'). Though its lifespan is up to about 40 years, zinc has some major weaknesses. It is corroded by cat's urine, and cats love warm tin roofs! It is also badly affected by acid pollution, becoming brittle and crusted with carbonate over time. Consequently most original coverings will by now require replacement. Look for splits and pitting to the surface, or past attempts at coating with bitumen. Zinc-working is now a scarce skill and consequently zinc is rarely used. Replace with lead.

LEAD

Flat roofs on bays or porches of 1930s houses would typically be covered with sheets of milled lead. Today, lead is still specified by weight in pounds per square foot, varying between 4lb and 8lb psf ('Code 4' and 'Code 8'), the heavier the more durable; but Code 4 lead is the one builders tend to use unless instructed otherwise. Flashings should typically be made of Code 4 or 5 (1.8mm or 2.24mm thick) and valley gutters of thicker Code 5 or 6 (2.24mm or 2.65mm thick). Thickest of all is sheet roofing of Code 6, 7, or 8 (2.65mm, 3.15mm, or 3.55mm thick).

But lead is susceptible to two forms of corrosion: from alkaline conditions typically caused by eroding cement mortars, and from acidic conditions like rainwater from roofs affected by algae, moss, or lichen. In fact, acid rain and moss are the enemies of both lead and zinc, so watch for rainwater that runs off from other roofs of different materials. Lead and zinc mustn't be used together, as they can react and corrode, although the process is very slow. However, if you can see old splits, patch repairs, surface ripples, or impressions of the boarding below, then it's on its way out.

Lead is notoriously prone to expansion in hot weather, so any large areas without expansion joints will eventually cause splits and buckling. Sheets should therefore not exceed a length of 2.5m (code 7 lead). Expansion cracking can be prevented by building in 'rolls' and 'drips', 'rolls' being formed from a strip of lead wrapped around a wooden pole (rather like a broom handle) while 'drips' are basically steps in the flat roof covered with overlapping sheets. Lead is also prone to 'creep' – extremely slow movement downhill – so the roof pitch or 'fall' needs to be laid just right, between 25–75mm per 2.5m run (1–3in per 8ft). At joints with walls, the sheets should be turned up and lapped over by a separate lead flashing.

Technical data

Typical semi-detached house original roof timber dimensions are:

Common rafters 4 x 2in (100 x 50mm) or 3 x 2.5in (75 x 63mm)

Purlins 7 x 2.5in (175 x 63mm)

Ridge plate 6 x 1.25in (150 x 31mm)

Wall plates 4.5 x 3in (112 x 75mm)

Plain tile sizes varied between 250 x 150mm (10 x 6in) and 280 x 175mm (11 x 7in).

NB All stated laps and pitches are rough guides only. See www.Lafarge-roofing.co.uk for specific figures.

See www.ThirtiesHouse.co.uk for further advice on party walls, specialist materials, and contractors.

MODERN FLAT ROOFS

Many 1930s houses now have modern extensions with flat roofs made from timber decks covered with mineral felt. These roofs are often problematic, not least because of a lack of insulation. Typical defects include:

- The short life of felt coverings: 10–15 years is not unusual, depending on workmanship.
- Rot to decks: chipboard makes a poor quality deck, as it is prone to disintegrate when damp. Marine plywood is better.
- Insufficient slope: a fall of at least 1:40 is required or water will not easily disperse.
- Inner dampness: flat roof decks were often built without insulation, allowing condensation from the rooms below to penetrate up through the ceiling, causing dampness and rot. They should be insulated with polyurethane foam boarding above the deck (to create a 'warm' roof). Ceilings should be constructed with foil-backed plasterboard as a vapour-barrier.

Symptoms on the surface of felt roofs such as plant growth or the ponding of water into puddles, or black condensation mould on ceilings below, all indicate that replacement is necessary.

NB Before carrying out work on roof structures, Building Control must be consulted.

Defect: General dampness in loft but no signs of damage

SYMPTOMS

Damp ceilings with rotten laths; moist loft insulation and timbers.

Cause **Condensation due to lack of sufficient ventilation and insulation**

Warm moist air from the house seeps into the loft, eg through uninsulated ceilings or the loft hatch. The warm air hits cold roof coverings and condenses back into water, which then drips down onto the ceiling. Damp insulation loses its effectiveness.

Solution

- Upgrade loft insulation over ceilings to at least 270mm (11in) mineral wool, keeping eaves vents clear.
- Fill any holes in ceilings and insulate the loft hatch.
- Improve ventilation at eaves or fit vents to ridge or roof slopes or an airbrick to a side gable. Protect from bird ingress with mesh. Cut back any plant growth blocking vents.

Defect: Damp penetration in lead or zinc coverings

SYMPTOMS

Flat roofs with splits or holes in the surface; wrinkles in lead sheets; attempted sealing with bitumen paint; damp at valleys or hips.

Cause **Corrosion over time due to reaction with the wrong fixing nails, or moss growth and acid rain**

Cause **Lead sheets inadequately secured, or insufficient space for thermal expansion**

Solution *If the problem is extensive or if the metal is old and brittle, complete replacement with new lead sheets is needed. Use copper fixing nails. Sheets which have expanded should be shortened and new joints formed. Small defects can be repaired with soldered dots or patches of the same metal as a short-term measure.*

Leaks at valleys and hips may be due to loose mortar, which should be pointed and timbers checked for rot. Localised stripping and replacement of defective metal strips may be necessary, checking for rot to the timber base. Alternatively replace with purpose-made 'swept' valley tiles.

Defect: The roof sags

SYMPTOMS

The roof slopes aren't level, but show signs of 'dishing' or curvature; the roof seems bowed under the weight of the tiles. On semis and terraces the line of the party wall below the slates stands proud.

Movement to the roof structure has occurred. There are several possible causes:

Cause **Overloading**

Replacement concrete tiles are a very common cause of roof sagging because of their substantial weight, if the structure has not been strengthened.

Cause **Weak roof timbers**

Roof timbers cut: the result of bad DIY – such as a botched loft conversion, the removal of an old water tank, or the installation of roof windows without the existing rafters being strengthened.

Rafters: undersized or spaced too far apart when house was originally built.

Purlins: deflection due to:

- Undersized, split, or missing purlins, particularly to the side hip.

- No struts or collars to provide support.
- Feet of struts being unsupported: they often rely on an internal load-bearing wall, which may have settled or been removed, causing the struts and purlins to follow and the roof to sag.
- Purlin ends may have slipped on broken corbels or brackets on the party wall.

Solution *Strengthen the roof timbers.*

If movement is due to old historic settlement, it may have now stabilised and no repairs are required. Otherwise major remedial work may be needed:

- If the timbers are undersized or weakened it may be necessary to beef them up with additional support, such as extra purlins and struts to improve support to the rafters.
- If the load-bearing wall below has dropped causing the roof struts to follow, a structural engineer can advise how loadings may be transferred to the main walls or the wall may be strengthened.
- Missing or slipped purlins need to be strengthened or replaced, and can be supported on new metal hangers. Splits and poor jointing require the splicing of new timber alongside or bolting with metal plates.

Cause **Roof spread**

The rafters may push outwards, making the top of the main wall bulge out; the rafters then sink, causing the roof to dip in the middle.

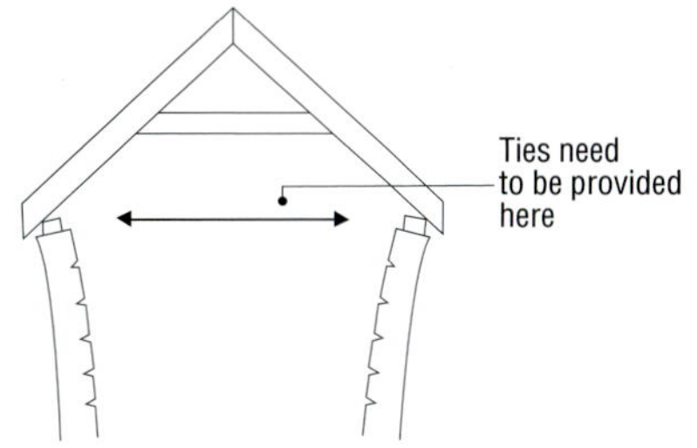

The roof structure has 'spread', pushing the walls out

Solution *The ceiling joists acting as collars normally restrain the roof rafters from pushing the walls out. If they are not properly secured, they will need to be tied in to prevent further movement.*

With hipped roofs there is often very little holding the side hip roof slope, which may not be tied in, particularly if the dragon ties were omitted. As a result the side walls can be particularly at risk from roof spread. In severe cases the tops of bowed walls will need to be rebuilt and tied in by the provision of collars or metal tie bars.

One method of preventing rafters from splaying out at the eaves is to fit timber 100 x 50mm (4 x 2in) bracing struts that tie each rafter to the ceiling joist below. These are connected with bolts and toothed washers about 600mm (2ft) from the base of the rafter to about 1m (3.3ft) from the end of the ceiling joist.

Cause **Rotten or beetle infested timbers**

Solution Roof timbers are a favourite place to find woodworm (beetle) bore holes, particularly around loft hatch openings. However, boreholes are rarely active (check for 'sawdust' around the holes) and may have been previously treated. See Chapter 6. Rotten or active beetle infested timbers must be treated, or cut out and replaced once the cause of the problem has been identified. Significant wet rot is not common in main roofs (although valley timbers can be prone to rot when damp) but is sometimes found at the top wall plate in lean-to roofs.

Defect: Water penetration

SYMPTOMS

Obviously damaged roof coverings; leaks and damp; wet rot to timbers where leaks have occurred over time.

The source of a leak is not always directly above the damp patch on the ceiling – water may run down rafters and along ceilings. A simple way to locate the source of a leak is to look in the loft space with the light off. Though there will normally be some small slivers of light evident through the tiles you can easily pinpoint any large gaps – often at flashings (see below).

Cause Slates or tiles broken, slipped, or missing as a result of damage or excessive weathering

On 1930s houses where old, redundant side and rear stacks have been taken down to below roof level, the 'patch' tiling laid over the former opening can often be uneven and prone to leakage.

Cause Surfaces of tiles are flaking (de-laminating) due either to age or poor quality of materials, allowing water to become absorbed, freeze, and expand

Solution *If there are only a few slipped or missing slates or tiles they can usually be refixed or replaced. If damage is extensive, or the coverings are obviously damaged, the whole roof may need re-covering.*

Creepers and climbing shrubs can invade eaves and dislodge slates or tiles, and must be regularly pruned or removed.

Tiles: these are prone to defects such as nibs breaking off, making them vulnerable to storm damage. To remove a broken tile, wedge up the two tiles above it with wooden wedges and use a bricklayer's trowel to lift the nib of the damaged tile off the batten and lift it out. The new tile can then be eased in and its nib hooked over the batten. See 'step-by-step'.

Timber: battens (or sarking boards) affected by leaks and damp can suffer from wet rot, causing them eventually to sag and fail to hold further nails. Stripping and re-battening will be required. Verges often need pointing up to prevent rot to batten ends. Where rot has affected small areas of roof timbers, localised parts can be treated. In more extensive cases, stripping and re-cladding the roof will be necessary. See Chapter 5.

Slates: although slates are long-lasting, check in the roof for blistering, de-lamination, and softness on the undersides, which is where the decay starts. Sulphates from acid rain pollution can react with carbonates in the slate, forming calcium sulphate that can eventually reduce slates to the consistency of cardboard. If they are easily scored with a knife, creating a powder, they are no longer of use. Normally, however, slates are very durable, but the old galvanised fixing nails may have corroded, causing them to slip. Refix using copper or aluminium alloy nails or, if just one or two are loose, refix using metal clips known as 'tingles'. But if a roof has more than about half-a-dozen tingles, it probably needs renewal. Replace like with like – try not to mix artificial with natural slates on the same slope.

Cause Missing or loose ridge or hip tiles

Neglected mortar pointing lets in damp, which affects the timber ridge plate and the tops of rafters. Falling tiles of any kind are a potentially lethal danger to passers-by, but loose ridge tiles are surprisingly common 'storm damage'.

Solution *Re-bed loose ridge or hip tiles and point up.*

Use mortar mix of 1:3 cement to sharp sand, with a small amount of PVA bonding to improve adhesion. The mix should be fairly stiff. Hip tiles need a 'hip iron' at the base to prevent slippage. Treat any timbers affected by damp.

Defect: Water penetration without obvious signs of damage

SYMPTOMS

Leaks and damp; decayed timbers. Roof coverings may have been painted.

Cause **Wind blowing rain under tiles**

Solution *If the problem is severe, complete re-roofing may be required: strip down to rafters, fit new underfelt and battens, and reclad with tiles or slates suitable for the roof's pitch. Painting an old roof to stop it leaking is a desperate short-term measure. Re-cladding is the best option.*

However, a little occasional water penetration may not be an issue. Original roofs were generally built without underfelt, so small amounts of rain or snow may enter roof spaces in severe weather, but should disperse through evaporation.

The type of roof covering should be appropriate for the degree of pitch of a roof, and must be sufficiently overlapped, otherwise rainwater can track back underneath the tiles, effectively running uphill. Slates and pantiles can cope with shallower pitches than small plain tiles, but if wrongly laid re-cladding will be needed.

Cause **Defective pipes or tanks**

Solution *Check all pipework and tanks for leaks. Pipe leaks are quite common in roofs where there is a lack of insulation, which allows pipes to freeze and burst in winter, particularly near the eaves. Drain down and repair.*

Cause **Cracked mortar fillets or defective flashings at junctions**

A major cause of damp penetration. See Chapter 3.

Solution *Replace flashings with new ones.*

Mortar fillets at joints are particularly prone to cracking (due to differential movement) and may only last a few years, particularly if the cement mortar mix was too strong. Original zinc or lead flashings may have corroded. Point up any eroded mortar joints to brickwork near the flashing.

In a semi or terrace you may also find problems where neighbouring roofs meet over party walls. Each house may by now have a different kind of roof covering, with inherent problems at the junctions. Some localised stripping will be required, and the provision of strips of lead sheet (soakers) under the joints. Any proposed work on party walls means that legal notices under the terms of the Party Wall Act may first need to be issued.

Defect: Nests and vermin

SYMPTOMS

Smells, droppings, and straw in loft; swarms of wasps or flies; chewed electric cables; damage to stored items.

Cause **Easy access routes into the roof space via gaps at eaves, broken tiles, open vents, plant growth, etc. Small wasps' nests are particularly common**

Solution *Carefully remove nests, taking appropriate precautions (beware of wasps!). Use traps and bait or hire pest control contractors.*

Clearly this situation is unhygienic and potentially dangerous (electric cables and even pipes can become damaged, or water tanks polluted), so future access should be checked by fitting wire mesh over any large holes that maintain good ventilation. Remember that bats are a protected species.

STEP BY STEP

Maintaining a tiled roof

Maintaining a single storey roof with a few slipped or broken plain clay tiles should be a feasible DIY project. Obviously great care must be taken on roofs – a common cause of cracked tiles is from people clambering on roofs without proper access equipment. Also, make sure no one is standing below!

All pictures courtesy P&R Roofing, Oxford

TOOLS REQUIRED

- Ladder with a stand-off bracket (to protect guttering)
- Roof ladder with a ridge hook (for two storey or higher use scaffolding or work-tower)
- Trowel
- Hammer
- Small timber wedges

MATERIALS

- Replacement tile(s)

1 Locate damaged tile.

2 Lift the tiles above the damaged tile with a trowel.

3 Hold the tiles above clear and insert trowel under damaged tile.

4 Ease the broken tile carefully away. These tiles are nibbed and are hooked over the batten. If tiles are nailed, rock them from side to side and prise off with the trowel.

5 Clear of all debris.

6 To fit matching replacement tile, wedge up the tiles above with timber wedges or trowel.

7 Slide in new tile and hook over batten.

8 If tiles have to be nailed, lift off additional courses above and nail to batten with 30mm (1.25in) galvanised nails.

CHAPTER 3 1930s House Manual

CHIMNEYS

Take a look down a typical street of 1930s houses, and the number and size of chimney stacks is quite striking. But stacks of this age can conceal serious threats to the wellbeing of the property and the occupants below. So here we investigate common problems such as dangerous leanings, crooked pots, mysterious leaks and damp patches, together with their likely causes and solutions. You should sleep easier assured by this knowledge!

Welcome to one of the most potentially dangerous parts of the property – and yet one of the most neglected: the lonely world of the chimney stack.

Close up, it's the sheer size of these structures that is so striking. And the bigger they stand the heavier they fall, so it's rather worrying that many are left in such a poor state of repair. Experienced surveyors will tell you that seriously eroded pointing and leaking flashings are extremely common defects on 1930s stacks – and that if neglected, dire problems may arise.

Hardly noticed from ground level (unless physically swaying in the breeze!), it helps to have a pair of binoculars handy in order to assess the condition of distant chimneys. If it does transpire that they are in need of attention, a major part of the cost of the repair works will be the erection of scaffolding, so it is normally cost-effective to plan any necessary roof works to be carried out at the same time.

High fliers

Architecturally, the general idea was for brick chimney stacks to emulate the elaborate styles found on Elizabethan houses. But the expense of ornately carved masonry was too great for most suburban houses, so the odd band of protruding brickwork was about as 'Tudor' as it got.

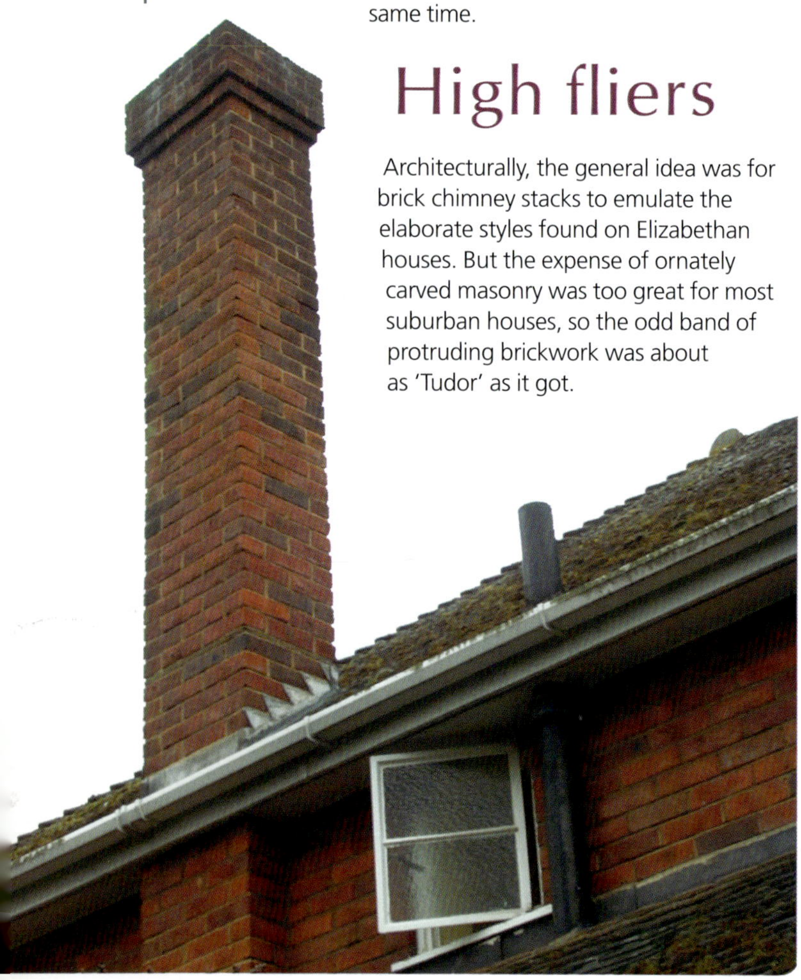

Spot the 'Tudor' detailing.

In a typical semi-detached house, the centrally located shared main stack normally serves the fireplaces in the reception rooms and main bedrooms and is built up the party wall, finally emerging through the roof at the ridge. This is a well-proven traditional design dating back many years.

But many 1930s houses have something of a split personality in the chimney department. These sturdy, reliable main stacks stand in sharp contrast to their wayward cousins, the unfeasibly thin perimeter stacks ascending to dizzying heights from the side or rear walls, seemingly defying the laws of nature. Such fashionably narrow stacks often served kitchen boilers and were sometimes built in a vaguely period style, with the chimney breasts projecting externally to save room space. But this is a feature that today can still cause serious structural concerns.

The fatal flaw in the design was its incompatibility with another design craze of the time – the hipped roof. The combination of the two meant that once these thin chimney stacks rose above gutter level, there was nothing there to tie them in and help stabilise them. Yet to overcome the downdraught (so that the fires could burn well) they needed to be taller than the highest part of the roof. The net result was that, over time, these stacks have displayed a tendency to lean inwards, aggravated by internal condensation problems (see below).

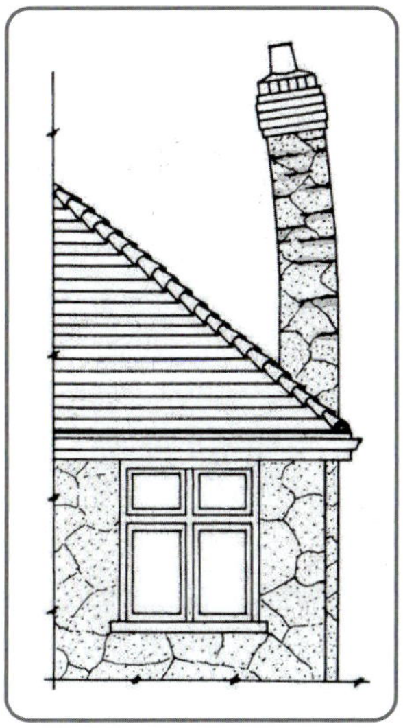

This problem is made even worse if the wall below happens to have been pushed outwards due to 'roof thrust' (see Chapter 5). Because such stacks have often wilted alarmingly with age, many have since had to be taken down and capped off.

LEFT: Inward lean aggravated by internal erosion.

Design

A stack should be built so that rain driving against it is deflected away onto the roof, so as not to cause damp in the structure below. Some good design features are:

- The top brick courses should project about 30mm so that they overhang sufficiently to throw rainwater clear of the main stack. The flaunching (the big lump of mortar at the base of the pots) should slope outwards.

- There should be lead flashings around the base to protect the joint where the stack meets the roof.
- There should be a damp-proof course (DPC) to prevent water soaking through the masonry and down into the roof structure.
- The chimney should terminate above the main roof ridge to avoid turbulence and 'smoke blow-back'.
- The pointing to the brick mortar joints should ideally be in a slanted 'weatherstruck' shape to help deflect rainwater outwards.

Chimney pots

The colourful days of ornate Victorian terracotta or clay pots were now long gone. Pots had become practical, stubby, and unobtrusive. To install the heavy pots over the wide opening of the stack below, the builders would bridge the gap at the top of the stack in the traditional manner, with tiles placed flat over the edges of the flues. The pots could then be lowered into position and bedded in mortar flaunching to a depth of at least 150mm (6in).

Masonry

Exposed for many years to driving rain, bitter winds, and frost, and under attack internally from chemical corrosion and intense heating and cooling, it's hardly surprising that some of the mortar joints (and the bricks themselves) may by now have become eroded.

Fortunately, 1930s brickwork was generally superior to that of earlier generations. Manufactured bricks were of more consistent quality and better burned. Also, mortar was now generally being made with stronger modern Portland cement instead of traditional lime. But the fashion for 'moderne' architecture meant that many stacks were rendered, which is not ideal technically due to its limited durability when exposed to expansion and contraction in stack brickwork plus the full force of the weather.

In addition the use of render presented less scrupulous builders with the temptation to conceal cheaper quality brickwork under it. To repair damaged render on an old stack, it is important that a render mix suitable for extreme conditions is used – see 'Defects' below.

Flues

Chimneys were typically built in traditional brick with 230 x 230mm (9in) flues. To protect the inner masonry and prevent gases escaping through mortar joints there would often be a layer of cement render, or old fashioned 'parging' – lime mortar traditionally mixed with cow dung or ox hair for reinforcement.

Over time, the toxic products of combustion from coal fires (tar acids, ammonia, sulphates, and water vapour) will have combined to eat away at the parging and the mortar joints, causing expansion and cracks. Tarry deposits and salts can then be carried through the bricks and plaster to damage internal decorations. See Chapter 10.

Another reason for the trademark sagging of those tall stacks is that chimneys built on outer walls are colder and more at risk than those built into party walls. The flue may be only one brick width (115mm/4.5in) away from the cold outer wall, and as a result the hot gases from the fire cool very rapidly, condensing into acidic water and corroding the masonry inside.

Eaten alive: damp acids slowly leeching out from the flue.

Technical data

Chimney pots should terminate a minimum of 1m (3.28ft) above the ridge of the roof. Minimum flue widths are 200mm (8in) for round fittings, 185mm (7.2in) for square.

Flashings should overlap each other by at least 100mm (4in).

Recommended dimensions of a back gutter flashing are:
Upstand at rear of stack 100mm (4in)
Length Width of stack + at least 225mm (9in) at each end
Sole of gutter At least 150mm (6in)
Extension piece for roof slope 225mm (9in)

The Building Research Establishment (BRE) 'official' limit of permitted lean to a stack is 1mm in 100mm.

For flues see Building Regulations approved document J at www.ThirtiesHouse.co.uk.

Chimneys on outer walls are colder – and more at risk.

Flashings

The joint at the base of a stack where it meets the roof is a major weak-point and a common cause of dampness to the rooms below. Lead is the best form of weatherproofing, but some inter-war houses have flashings made from zinc sheeting or, worse, just cement mortar fillets (often tiled). These are a cheaper and inferior form of jointing that is prone to cracking and leakage.

The enemy within

Anything hidden out of sight – such as flues – was often built by less skilled workers using cheaper materials, so the quality sometimes wasn't brilliant even when new. Add years of erosion from acrid gases and you may well have tired old flues full of gaps that let fumes into the rooms. The danger is that one person's fabulous living-flame gas fire is another's deadly carbon monoxide poisoning. Carbon monoxide is a toxic, invisible and odourless gas, and detectors should be fitted as a precaution – they are cheap and can save lives. See Chapter 10 for solutions to common flue problems.

Distinct leaning – eroded flues are often part of the problem.

Defect: A roof leak around the chimney

SYMPTOMS
Damp patches on walls, ceilings, and chimney breasts below.

Cause **Defective mortar fillets or flashings**

Solution *Replace with new lead flashings.*
Ideally flashings should be of lead, but some were of short-lived zinc which may, by now, have suffered from corrosion from acid solutions resulting from air pollution or moss growth – typically more of a problem in industrial cities. Mortar fillets are a common cheap alternative, comprising a thick covering of cement or lime mortar spread over the joint, sometimes tiled. Differential expansion between the stack and the roof causes the mortar to crack and lose its bonding. Rather than patch up defective mortar, it is always advisable to replace it with a modern lead flashing. See 'Renewing a flashing' project, below.

Cause **Insufficient or missing soakers under the tiles**
Soakers are special pieces of lead inserted under each tile to the sides of the stack (not necessary with interlocking tiles).

Solution *Provide new metal soakers to the side of the stack at every course of plain tiles, or fit new lead flashings.*

Cause **Metal flashing inadequately sealed to the brickwork**
'Back gutters' – the flashings you can't see at the back of chimneys on roof slopes – are a common weak point.

Solution *Refix the flashing into existing joints with fresh mortar, or fix to a new position as follows:*

- Cut a new groove in the chimney about 150mm (6in) above the level of the roof covering, normally into a mortar joint.
- Turn the metal flashing at least 25mm (1in) into the groove.
- Fix it in place with metal wedges and seal with mortar.

Defect: Vertical cracks, damaged brickwork or render

SYMPTOMS
Visible cracks; severe weathering of masonry; damp to walls below.

Cause **Internal flue masonry suffering from expansion and cracking**

Solution *Install a flue liner.*
As noted above, condensation of gases on cold surfaces inside the flue eventually causes chemical erosion of the masonry and mortar. Thermal expansion in the old flue can then cause vertical cracks in the chimney. Installing a flue liner will prevent leaks and will improve thermal insulation. Selecting the right kind of liner is important and depends on the type of fire or appliance used. Lining is a specialist job. See Chapter 10.

In roof spaces, modern chimney breasts are rendered as a precaution to lessen the risk of fire. However, 1930s ones were seldom rendered, which is another good reason to have the flues lined.

Cause **External brickwork badly weathered**

Not solved by dodgy rendering

Solution *Defective areas of frost damaged spalled brick must be cut out and replaced.*
If the upper bricks are loose due to soft mortar, partial rebuilding may be required.
Make good old mortar joints as described right, (under 'Leaning stack') by raking out old joints and repointing with a sulphate resistant mortar, and point up cracks. Where cracking or erosion is extreme, the stack will need to be taken down and rebuilt using sulphate resistant mortar and low sulphate bricks.

Cause **Rendered surfaces cracked or loose, allowing damp penetration**

Solution *Patch defective areas of render.*

Rendered stacks have thin layers of protective mortar applied to the exterior, but over time small cracks may have allowed water to penetrate and loosen the render. This can be treated as follows:

- Hack off loose, cracked, or hollow areas with a bolster and club hammer (wear eye protectors). Cut back to a sound base, scoring any smooth surfaces to improve the bond.
- Coat the underlying masonry with a diluted 1:6 solution of PVA bonding.
- Using a suitable pre-mixed render (or a 1: 4 mix of cement / sand plus waterproofing agent), prepare a stiff mix – not too wet.
- Dampen the masonry then apply the mortar with a trowel, press onto the wall and smooth off. When completely dry apply a surface coat.

Defect: Leaning stack

SYMPTOMS

Blown mortar joints; distinct leaning, often away from wind direction.

Cause **Expansion of eroded mortar joints**

If a stack has a large exposed surface facing the prevailing wind constant wetting can lead to expansion of mortar joints, causing the stack to lean away from the wind. When bricks get consistently very wet, any sulphates in the masonry or mortar can react, causing horizontal expansion cracks along mortar joints as a result of 'sulphate attack'. The use of Portland cement in the 1930s (rather than traditional alkaline lime mortar) means that stacks are more prone to sulphate attack. Expansion of mortar joints on the windward side commonly results in leaning.

A small degree of lean is quite common in old stacks. Many have leaned considerably more than the 'official' limit of 1mm in 100mm (see technical data on page 49), but in most cases the stack can be stabilised. In severe cases, the chimney will need to be taken down. A structural engineer will need to confirm whether a lean is too extreme to be made safe. The remedy of last resort is to rebuild the stack. To comply with Building Regulations, a rebuilt section will need an internal diameter of 200mm (8in), or a minimum of 185mm (7.5in) with a relined flue.

Solution *Rake out and repoint the mortar joints with fresh mortar.*

Old mortar joints may have become loose, crumbling or cracking with age, so that repointing is necessary anyway. Rake out to a depth of between 20mm and 35mm (0.8–1.4in), taking care not to damage the edges of the brick or stone, and repoint with a sulphate resistant mortar.

Cause **Acid attack inside the flue**

Solution *Install a flue liner.*

Mortar joints may have also deteriorated internally. Again, the stack may be colder on its windward side and have suffered more erosion there from condensing acidic gases, causing uneven movement and leaning. See Chapter 10.

Cause **Structural alterations**

Solution *Check support from chimney breasts below.*

If a chimney breast has been removed but the remaining masonry above has not been properly supported, it can cause instability to the stack, which may then need to be taken down. See Chapter 10.

In severe cases, stacks may need to be taken down.

Unorthodox solution (right) – metal ties.

Defect: Damaged pots and flaunching

SYMPTOMS

Broken, missing or crooked pots, causing possible problems with downdraught to fire; cracked and loose mortar at base of pots; some pieces may have fallen off.

Cause **Excessive weathering**

Solution *Replace broken pots. Secure or replace unstable pots. Repair flaunching.*

Up close, chimney pots are surprisingly large and heavy, so if you have to remove one you will need a helping hand. Look for frost damage in the form of flaking/delamination of the pots. The only practical solution for broken pots is replacement, ideally with appropriate modern ones of a similar style.

'Flaunching', you'll remember, is the large blob of mortar that holds pots in place, as well as providing a capping to protect the brickwork below. Cracks are commonplace, as the flaunching tends to decay more quickly than the pots themselves due to frost action. But it is fairly simple to replace it. Take care not to damage the pots when cleaning off the old mortar. Also, cover the flue to prevent debris falling down and causing blockages.

If the flaunching is loose, it's best to remove it completely and replace it with a 1:3 cement/sand mortar mix, carefully formed to slope outwards to disperse rainwater.

Cause **Condensation at the head of the stack**

Solution *Line the flue.*

If the pots are sagging drunkenly into the chimney stack it may again be due to a severe case of damp flue gases eroding the internal masonry, causing the brickwork to expand. The solution is to line the flue. Some repointing or partial rebuilding of the stack masonry may also be necessary. The flashings are also likely to have suffered movement and may also need attention.

Defect: Damp chimneys

SYMPTOMS

Damp and staining to walls and fireplaces below.

The main causes of damp in chimneys (other than the common problem of leaks at flashings) are ingress of rain from outside, and condensation from inside.

Cause **Pots and flues exposed to rain**

Solution *Flues should be protected to exclude entry of rain by 'capping' the pot or fitting a cowl or hood.*

Rainwater down an open chimney pot will soak into the internal chimney brickwork, as well as reaching further down the flue where it mixes with old soot. The ensuing staining to chimney breasts appears the same as that caused by condensation. Even where a flue has been relined, the problem may appear to get worse, since rainwater that was previously soaked up by the old mortar parging may now dribble straight down the new flue liner, which acts like a downpipe, creating small puddles in the fireplace.

There are a whole range of caps, cowls, and hoods available to protect flues that are in use or to ventilate old redundant flues. Specialist advice may be useful here, as the wrong choice of cap can affect the way the fire draws, causing it to smoke excessively.

Cause **Thin and porous stack walls with no DPC. Eroded mortar joints**

Solution *Ensure the pointing is sound.*

Sometimes rain can get around an otherwise perfectly good flashing because there is no damp-proof course above roof level in older stacks. Some more expensive 1930s houses had DPCs here, but many did not. Modern stacks have a DPC through the chimney at approximately 150mm (6in) above the roof and another one below the cap or the brickwork head. Repointing the brickwork joints should normally solve the problem. Otherwise, unless the old stack is being rebuilt, this can be difficult to solve, although fitting flashings that extend higher up and deeper into the brickwork is an effective remedy.

Cause **Condensation inside the stack**

Solution *Fit a suitable flue liner.*

As described earlier, burning fuel produces water vapour which turns to moisture when it hits cold walls up the flue, especially if the flue is very tall, very wide, or faces a cold outer wall. Fuels such as freshly cut timber are particularly wet, and give off a lot of water vapour when burning. Even if fireplaces are sealed up and you don't want to use them, there should be a through flow of air both top and bottom to prevent condensation leeching through the brickwork and causing damp, sooty stains. This may be visible on chimney breasts in bedrooms as well as in the roof space. See Chapter 10.

PROJECT: Renewing a flashing

New flashings should be formed using Code 4 lead, or alternatively suitable modern lightweight GRP flashings, available from builders' merchants.

Stacks that are located centrally over the ridge of the roof have flashings called 'aprons' to the front and back, and a 'saddle piece' in the middle.

Stacks located lower down a roof slope have the same apron flashing at the front but a special rear flashing called a 'back gutter' at the rear. Both types of stack have flashings and/or soakers at the sides.

The strips of lead flashing are attached to the stack by folding over their upper edges into mortar joints in the brickwork and securing them with lead wedges and fresh mortar. Lead sheet is cut with special tools called tin snips and formed into shape with a bossing mallet.

1 First fit the front apron flashing along the base of the stack brickwork by cutting a groove in a mortar joint in the chimney about 150mm (6in) above the level of the roof covering. Fix the apron at least 25mm (1in) into the groove and secure with metal wedges, then seal with mortar. It must overlap the surface of the tiles below and be dressed around the sides of the stack by about 150mm (6in).

2 To the sides, there are separate lead soakers inserted underneath each tile. The soakers are folded up at the sides against the stack and then covered by a flashing cut into a stepped shape. For modern concrete interlocking tiles soakers aren't needed – instead they have a combined 'step and cover' flashing dressed over the top of the tiles.

3 For 'back gutters' (at the upper edge of the stack) two pieces of lead are needed. One forms a gutter along the back of the stack and the other a cover strip flashing attached to the stack itself. The back gutter fits over a timber base, part of the roof construction. For dimensions see the technical data box on page 49.

4 For stacks located centrally on the ridge, the 'ridge saddle' is the last section to be installed. The saddle piece should be dressed over the ridge tile, ensuring a generous overlap with the side flashing. It should be cut with a stepped edge and anchored in two courses of the stack's brickwork.

CHAPTER 4 1930s House Manual

RAINWATER FITTINGS

Does your house suffer from green slimy walls, damp patches, stains or splash marks? Have you noticed indoor damp smells, blown or mouldy plaster? Then it's probably time to overhaul or replace your gutters and downpipes. Here we investigate common problems such as blockages, leaks, splits, cracks, sagging and corrosion, and look at all the options when it comes to selecting the correct replacements. Then we go underground to show how to prevent serious damp problems by constructing a simple soakaway.

Although not the most glamorous part of your home, they're certainly one of the most important: if the gutters and downpipes don't work properly, sooner or later water will invade the very heart of the property. Rainwater allowed to drip or leak down walls will lead to damp problems and, in time, rot. Worse still, consistently wet ground by the main walls can eventually undermine those shallow foundations and lead to possible structural movement.

Take a rain check

To judge whether your system is running smoothly, or is grimly hanging on by its last rickety fixings, it is worth taking a few minutes to stand back and contemplate your property. Starting at the top, visually follow the route the rainwater takes. You may find that all the water from the main roof discharges down a complex series of hoppers and downpipes, before ultimately cascading off an old lean-to garage or porch roof with nothing much in the way of guttering, causing unhealthy ponding next to your walls.

A simple practical test of the rainwater system is to pour a few buckets of water into the gutters at the highest point (or carefully hose down the lower roof slopes) and check for leaks, ponding, or overflowing. Or invest in an umbrella and take a stroll outside on a rainy day.

Serious faults in rainwater fittings are surprisingly common – undersized or sagging gutters, missing fixings, downpipes that are needlessly complicated or badly positioned blocking windows, and pipes wrongly sited in relation to gullies. Such defects can all cause water to overflow and gush down the walls. The resulting dampness often appears at low level and is then wrongly diagnosed as rising damp.

Designer guttering

There is more to the world of guttering than you may think. To design a new system or to check your existing arrangements, you need to consider some key factors:

- First calculate the 'effective design area' (EDA) for each roof slope. This is roughly equivalent to its surface area in m^2 (see the technical data box).
- To convert this to a figure showing how much water each gutter has to deal with – ie the actual water run-off in litres per second – simply divide the EDA by the magic number 48.
- Work out the required size of the gutter and the number of downpipes needed. Standard 112mm (4.4in) 'half-round' gutters should be able to cope with a flow of up to one litre of water per second, assuming there's just one downpipe at the end. But the best place for a downpipe is actually in the middle of a gutter, as there it will double the amount of water the gutter can cope with. For even greater flows you will need to either use larger gutters or provide an additional downpipe.

TOP: The Rolls Royce of guttering – copper. Unknown on mainstream Housing.
RIGHT: Original cast iron.
FAR LEFT: Hmm? ... foul waste should be kept separate from rainwater pipes.
LEFT: Not ideal.

Fortunately, most roof slopes on 1930s semi-detached and terraced houses will have an EDA of less than $37m^2$, which means they should only need standard guttering with a 68mm (2.7in) wide downpipe. A very approximate rule of thumb is at least one downpipe for every 10m (30ft) of guttering, but the calculation is affected by any sharp bends in the guttering, which slow the rate at which rainwater is discharged.

FALLS

Nothing to do with Niagara – unless, of course, your stop-ends are missing. Guttering is supposed to slope or 'fall' slightly in the direction of the downpipe to help the water flow away. The fall should be between 10mm and 25mm per 3.5m run (up to 1in in 11ft). Too steep, and water will overflow at the downpipe outlet; too shallow, and a build-up of water and sediment may cause overflowing.

Equally crucial is the manner in which the water leaves the edge of the roof. Gutters should normally be positioned centrally under the roof edge, and no more than 50mm (2in) below it. If falls are too steep the lower end of the gutter may have to be positioned too far below the roof edge, causing water to overshoot, and the gutter may even block windows from opening fully.

MEET THE NEIGHBOURS

In semi-detached or terraced houses the rainwater fittings act as one system for the whole building, so you and your neighbour(s) are mutually dependent on each other. Which is fine, if everyone shares your good taste. But replacement guttering in all kinds of clashing styles and colours can cause connection problems at joints, as well as being visually challenging.

Also, your guttering may discharge via a neighbour's downpipe, which, on the plus side, saves you worrying about maintenance, but means that you are dependent on their DIY skills and enthusiasm for clearing blockages. So it's worth checking your legal rights in advance, in case any emergency problems need to be swiftly rectified whilst they're away on a world cruise. And should the onus fall on you to provide an additional downpipe that benefits other homeowners, there may well be a case for sharing the costs.

VALLEY GUTTERS

Guaranteed to send shivers up the spine of even hardened surveyors, valley gutters are often a case of 'out of sight, out of mind' and a common cause of leakage and damp. Fortunately open valleys are fairly rare on 1930s houses, usually being found on semi-detached properties with large front gabled roofs, where they nestle over the party wall between the two houses. They are normally lined with lead sheet pointed up with mortar to the sides. See Chapter 2.

Materials

CAST IRON

The original gutters and downpipes on 1930s houses were predominantly of cast iron, which is very durable provided it is properly looked after. The most common failings result

ABOVE: Plastic gutters connected to the original iron downpipe.
BELOW: Authentic modern replacements for original cast iron – new half-round gutter and circular, square and rectangular downpipes in aluminium. (Photo: Angel Plastics).
BOTTOM RIGHT: Weakest link: plastic, left meets aluminium, right.

from a lack of routine maintenance leading to corrosion, but this can be prevented by regular protection with paint (including the vulnerable back part by the wall). The 'half-round' shaped gutters are normally supported on brackets fixed to fascia boards. The old downpipes generally last much longer than the gutters, hence a mix of plastic guttering with original iron downpipes is quite common.

PLASTIC

Many houses will by now have had their original gutters and downpipes replaced in PVC of varying styles and ages. These don't suffer from corrosion but can be prone to leaks at joints due to expansion and contraction, and older fittings tend to become brittle with age, degrading in sunlight. Resting a ladder against guttering can damage it, so a special ladder fitting called a 'stand off' should be used.

Unlike iron gutters, the PVC variety are prone to sagging between brackets, which affects the alignment and causes discharge problems. The two main types are half-round and 'squareline', and they are available in colours such as black, white, grey, and brown. Imitation designs are now available in plastic or glass-reinforced polyester that look similar to the original cast iron fittings.

ALUMINIUM

Replacement aluminium gutters can provide an excellent lightweight modern alternative to cast iron. They are available either as durable cast aluminium or as the thinner 'extruded' type, roll-formed in continuous seamless lengths using a mobile profiling machine on site. They are normally screwed directly to the fascia or rafter ends. The benefits are low maintenance with no integral joints, and good corrosion resistance, although they can be vulnerable to acid attack from pigeon droppings. They are, however, relatively

expensive. A potential weak point can be the inadequacy of connectors to any remaining sections of old guttering (eg to next door).

ASBESTOS

Asbestos cement was sometimes used for rainwater fittings during the 1930s. It is a hard, thin, lightweight material that can be spotted by its 'natural' light grey-white colour or blotchy peeling paint – which has difficulty adhering to the surface. As long as it's in good general condition there should be no significant hazard, but never attempt to sand, scrape, wire brush, drill, or subject it to abrasion in any way. The problem is, fittings of this age will now be nearing the end of their useful life, and removal must be carried out by a licensed contractor, which can prove expensive.

OTHER MATERIALS

Some regions persevered with local traditions, such as Sheffield's famous timber guttering. Fittings in copper or lead are extremely rare on mainstream housing of this period.

NB The 'Defects' section overleaf makes specific reference to PVC and iron fittings, as these are by far the most common materials found on 1930s properties.

Above: Painted asbestos hopper

Technical data

For a flat roof, the effective design area (EDA) is the same as its surface area. For pitched roofs it is the plan area plus half the area of the roof height, or alternatively the plan area increased by a factor determined by its angle of pitch – x1.15 for 30° pitch, x1.4 for 45° pitch, or x2.0 for 60° pitch. See the Building Regulations for a full table of these factors (these can be found at www.ThirtiesHouse.co.uk). For a lean-to roof against a wall, calculate the area of the wall above and add half this figure.

To calculate the appropriate size for a soakaway, multiply the total EDA for all roof slopes by the average hourly rainfall (in mm per hour) and divide by 3.

Defect: Gutters overflowing

SYMPTOMS

Damp, stained, or slimy walls; splash marks to lower walls; internal damp smells; mould on walls, blown plaster etc. There are several possible causes:

Cause Blocked gutters

Solution *Clear out gutters.*
You may find small roof-gardens taking root and choking your gutters. To prevent leaves and silt getting into, and blocking, the downpipes, fit special wire or plastic balloons in the gutter outlets (leaves etc will then cause the gutter to overflow so you can clear it before it gets down the pipe). As a general maintenance point, you should clear out gutters, hoppers, downpipes, and gulleys each spring after the leaves have fallen in the autumn.

Cause Corroded iron gutters

Solution *Replace or overhaul.*
If the whole system has corroded, replacement with new aluminium, plastic, or cast iron fittings will be necessary. However, if it's only one section it should be possible to obtain a matching replacement, but it's important to carefully check the shape and diameter. Cast iron guttering is normally sold in 1.8m (6ft) lengths, so it may have to be cut to size. See 'Defective gutter joints' below.

Cause Sagging or damaged gutters

Solution *Improve support and replace any defective lengths of guttering.*
Plastic guttering can be prone to sagging or twisting due to either old age or to lack of support resulting from broken brackets or loose fixing screws. Damage is often caused by ladders being leant against it. First remove the defective section of gutter, then secure any loose brackets before replacing the guttering.

Usually one bracket per metre of guttering is necessary for good support, so you may need to provide some additional brackets. If there is no fascia to support them, the gutters may be held in place by 'rafter brackets' fixed to the rafter feet, sometimes hidden under the first few courses of slates or tiles. To save having to strip these to fit new brackets, an alternative solution is to use special brackets that screw onto rafter ends or directly into the wall.

Another cause of damage results from plastic gutters warping due to close proximity to hot boiler flues: a simple solution is to fit a protective metal deflector plate under the gutters.

Cause Blocked hopper

Solution *Clear out hopper or replace if corroded, split, or leaking.*
A hopper is an open box on top of a downpipe, which collects water from pipes or guttering and channels it down the pipe. Hoppers are fairly common on original rainwater systems, sometimes also taking waste pipes from bathrooms. But they are a maintenance issue, being prone to blockage from leaves, debris, hair etc, so need to be checked every few months.

Cause **Insufficient fall to gutter**

Solution *Realign the gutter.*
Some metal support brackets can be adjusted in situ to adjust the fall of the guttering, but unfortunately most can't, and have to be fitted right first time. If the brackets are fixed to a timber fascia board, the fascia may have rotted or may not be level, and will first need to be overhauled or replaced. Note the required fall described above.

Cause **Not enough downpipes to discharge rainwater**

Solution *Fit an additional downpipe.*
If a well maintained system overflows, the problem may be one of design. A typical pair of semi-detached houses is likely to require at least three downpipes. To be exact, you need to calculate the EDA as described earlier. If the downpipes are located at the front and rear, then the highest point of the guttering would be to the side walls in order to achieve the required fall.

To provide an additional pipe you need to first consider the best position. Check the likely visual impact on the house, and plan a straight run that avoids windows and doors. Above all, think how it will discharge: will it be by connection to a soakaway, to the street, or, if permissible, to the main system?

Cause **Defective underfelt**

Solution *Check that the felt laps fully into gutters.*
1930s roofs were often built without sarking felt, which was only introduced on new mainstream housing from the 1950s. But many older roofs have now been reclad and have felt laid underneath the tiles to form a secondary barrier. The felt should project down into the guttering about 50mm (2in) to minimise the risk of rainwater running down the wall – don't be tempted to cut off any felt which projects in this way.

Defect: Gutters leaking at joints

SYMPTOMS

Localised internal damp patches; white 'tide marks' or green mould stains at joints; staining to walls with puddles below.

Cause **Defective gutter joints or fittings**

Solution *Repair or replace the defective gutter, connectors, or stop ends.*
Plastic gutters: listen carefully – you may be able to hear your rainwater system creaking in the sun, as plastic is very prone to expansion in hot weather. Stresses occur at brackets, joints, and connectors, and in time the rubber seals can degrade or become silted and start to drip. Rubber seals can normally be replaced by undoing the union clip that surrounds the joint, cleaning the surfaces, fitting the new seal, and then replacing the clip. Or the faulty joints can be replaced with new connectors, taking care to leave expansion gaps (of approximately 7mm) when joining them. Alternatively, a flexible sealant may provide a temporary solution.

Cast iron gutters: inadequate paint on cast iron or galvanised iron guttering leads to premature rusting. Unless the inside surfaces of metal gutters are fully protected, water that does not drain away will cause corrosion inside. Gutters are often tarted up outside with a quick lick of paint when a house is sold, so check the insides for rust. See 'step-by-step' for advice on the maintenance of iron guttering.

The joints in some old cast iron gutters are held together with screw-headed nuts and bolts and sealed with red lead and putty to make them water tight. A leaking joint can often be cured by applying a bitumen-based mastic inside the joint; otherwise the old connecting bolt will need to be sawn off and the joint remade, sandwiching a new layer of mastic between the two sections and securing with a new galvanised steel bolt. The joint will then need to be protected with bituminous paint.

Connecting old with new: in semi-detached and terraced properties there are particular problems matching different type of guttering: joining up your shiny new system with next door's decrepit old stuff may prove to be a bit of a problem. Fortunately, adaptors for cast iron to PVC and from half-round to squareline PVC are available in standard sizes; otherwise it may be possible to fabricate a connection in situ with the help of a glass fibre repair kit (although different expansion rates of different materials may eventually cause leakage). The only effective solution may be to replace the entire system – but talk to the neighbours first!

A satisfactory join between new guttering and old downpipes is normally possible, with the new gutter outlet fitting inside the old pipe.

Defect: Leaking downpipes

SYMPTOMS

White 'tide marks' or green mould stains and rust on pipes; damp, stained, or slimy walls and puddles below; apparent rising damp or penetrating damp in rooms; mould on walls, blown plaster, damp smells etc.

Cause **Downpipe blocked and overflowing at a joint or rusted through**

Solution *Overhaul or replace downpipe.*
Before unblocking a downpipe, cover the gulley below the pipe to stop any debris entering the drainage system. Use a long pole or stiff wire to push down the pipe and dislodge the blockage.
Cast iron pipes: a blockage that is allowed to build up will accelerate corrosion. For maintenance of iron pipes see 'step-by-step'.
Plastic pipes: in modern replacement systems, downpipes are often connected directly to underground drains rather than discharging over gulley gratings, and access for clearing blockages can be restricted unless connected via a 'back inlet' gulley with an integral 'rodding eye'.

Cause **Downpipe hanging loose**

Solution *Replace defective brackets or broken section of pipe.*
Cast iron pipes: the pipe is held by metal brackets or by integral metal 'earlobes' attached to the wall with special pipe nails driven into metal or wooden plugs. Sometimes there are spacers behind to prevent the pipe contacting the wall. Starting at the base of the pipe, remove the brackets by levering out the nails with a claw hammer and remove the downpipe section. Sealed joints can be loosened with a blowlamp. Dig out old plugs in the wall and replace with new ones. Refit the downpipe with a new bracket. Ensure that any unsealed joints in iron downpipes are filled with a suitable mastic. See 'step-by-step'.
Plastic pipes: unscrew and remove old defective brackets and replace with matching new ones. Brackets are required at every joint, and no more than 1.8m (6ft) apart.

Cause **Downpipe split or cracked**

Solution *Replace defective section.*
Cast iron pipes: if water in a blocked iron downpipe freezes it is likely to expand and split the pipe, saturating the wall to which it is fixed. Pipes that have rusted right through will also discharge water straight onto the (porous brick) wall. Replacement cast iron rainwater materials in imperial sizes – even replica downpipes complete with old-style fixing 'earlobes' – are available from specialist suppliers.
Plastic pipes: a common problem with plastic downpipes is impact damage. Cracked and broken pipes should be replaced. A temporary remedy is to patch with bitumen-backed foil (sold in strips for flashings), but the surface must be dry and clean before applying.

Defect: Main walls damp at low level

SYMPTOMS

As for rising damp – damp walls, blown plaster, damp smell, rot etc.

Cause **Downpipe discharging on ground next to house (or defective gutters and pipes as described above)**

Solution *Connect downpipe to rainwater drainage system.* If the water from a downpipe is spraying everywhere except where it should go – into the gulley – the pipe can be extended at its base with a fitting known as a 'shoe', so that it discharges accurately. Connecting pipes to a water butt is not necessarily a good solution as these very often overflow, causing ponding and damp problems.

The ideal solution is to connect to the existing underground rainwater system, but this may not be practical, depending on available space and closeness of the downpipe to the existing drains.

To the front of the house, there may be a 'soakaway' buried under the lawn, or in some cases the traditional method of a horizontal pipe through the garden wall onto the street. To the rear it may be possible to connect to the main system (subject to Building Control approval) or to run a new pipe away from the house to a ditch or a soakaway (see Constructing a soakaway project below).

Cause **Blocked gulley**

Solution *Clear gulley and flush through.*
'Ponding' of water around the gulley indicates that the water is not running away properly, which can eventually cause dampness in the walls. This is often due to a build-up of grease and solid matter in the trap, or a blockage caused by cement and debris washed down during building works.

A simple blockage may be solved by just removing leaves and other matter from the gulley grating, or can be cleared with a solution of caustic soda (take care!) or flushed through with a high pressure hose. A basic protective kerb surround should be placed around the gulley and a cover fitted to restrict ingress of leaves and debris.

Ensure that the water from the downpipe discharges without overshooting and splashing the wall. Modern gulleys have a fitted 'back inlet' for this purpose, or a shoe can be fitted as noted above. See also Chapter 12.

Underground dispersal

The final stage of your rainwater dispersal system is underground. The pipework is likely to be run in original vitreous clay, or may have been extended or replaced in modern plastic pipe, typically of 75mm or 100mm (3in or 4in) diameter.

Rainwater (also known as 'surface water' or 'storm water') is normally kept separate from foul drainage such as bathroom and kitchen waste water, and instead often discharges into a soakaway or nearby stream. For new pipework, it is not normally permitted to connect rainwater to the main system for fear of flooding causing tidal waves of raw sewage during storm conditions. Not pleasant. But in older properties, and in some large urban areas, it may be permitted for rainwater to discharge into the same system that takes the sewage, known as a combined system. This can be verified with your Local Authority. One clue is where you can see that bathroom waste pipes discharge into the same hopper or gulley that takes the rainwater from the gutter, rather than into the soil pipe.

ABOVE: New shoe and downpipe – with traditional 'ears' bracket – but not much use without a gulley. (Photo: Angel Plastics)

BELOW: Modern rainwater gulley.

GULLEYS

A gulley is a water-sealed trap that leads to the underground drainage system but keeps smells at bay. The original gulleys were normally made of salt-glazed clay, but if defective they can be replaced with new ready-manufactured plastic ones. Rainwater downpipes may discharge either directly into an underground system, or over a gulley, as do some kitchen or bathroom waste pipes. Simple blockages can be cleared as described above. Modern 'back inlet gulleys' are covered with a grid and provide an additional drainage point for rainwater from the surrounding surface.

SOAKAWAYS

Rainwater needs to be taken well away from walls and foundations, otherwise it may eventually cause structural problems. If connecting to the main system is prohibited, and there is no handy ditch or nearby stream, then a simple solution is to construct a soakaway, assuming space and ground conditions allow.

Soakaways are the traditional 'hole in the ground' method of dispersing rainwater, and in recent years they have become more widely used in urban areas (when space allows) to help prevent overloading public sewers with water that does not need treatment. They take the form of either a conventional pit filled with rubble, or a ready-made concrete chamber with holes in the walls, and must be designed to store the immediate water run-off from roofs and hard surfaces, and to then disperse this stored water into the surrounding soil.

PROJECT: Constructing a soakaway

1 Excavate a hole of appropriate size for the total roof area and volume of water discharged (typically around 3m^3) at least 5m (17ft) from the foundations of the house and the boundaries, in accordance with advice from Building Control.

2 Link the hole to the foot of the downpipe next to the house by digging a shallower trench and laying 100mm (4in) underground pipes with a gentle fall of about 1:100 towards the soakaway.

3 Fill the soakaway hole up to the level of the trench with masonry, rock, or rubble, using large pieces around the sides to prevent them caving in. Leave large gaps between the pieces as, when complete, these will need to fill with water prior to its final dispersal into the surrounding ground through natural seepage.

4 Place the end of the pipe so it discharges roughly into the centre of the soakaway. Then add more rubble to cover the pipe, except at the end, which must be left clear so that any debris carried in the water will fall down into the pit rather than accumulating at the point of discharge and blocking the pipe.

5 Backfill the pipe trench, first with gravel around the pipe, then soil.

6 Place about 100mm (4in) of gravel around the top of the soakaway. Cover this with a heavy-gauge plastic sheet prior to covering with at least 100mm (4in) of concrete, ideally incorporating some form of inspection access. Finally, once the concrete has cured it can be hidden with topsoil for plants and grass.

If a soakaway is not built correctly there can be problems with overflowing or silting up, and the foundations of the house can be seriously affected if it is built too close. Maintenance can also be a problem – the main one being how to find it! Some form of access should be provided, but often isn't.

Soakaways work best in non-clay, low water table areas, otherwise ground water can fill the soakaway instead of the other way around. First, you need to arrange for Building Control to check the soil and advise on the required depth and distance from the house, and to make periodic inspections during construction. This may involve digging a trial pit to the same depth as proposed, and filling it with water three times in succession to monitor the rate of seepage. The site should avoid any risk of waterlogging to downhill areas. In most cases where the soil drains well, and the roof area is less than 100m^2, you should be able to construct a traditional type of soakaway.

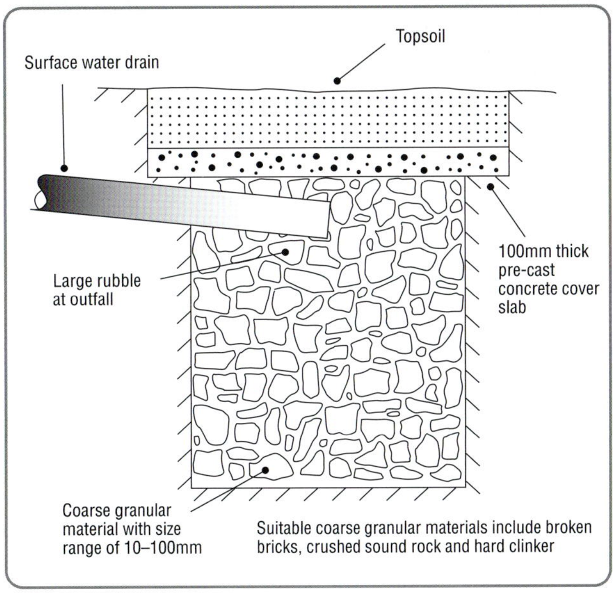

STEP BY STEP

Maintaining cast iron guttering and downpipes

Cast iron guttering and downpipes enhance the appeal of a 1930s house, but they do require periodic maintenance. Small leaks and loose pipes can be rectified fairly easily.

TOOLS REQUIRED

- **Ladder with a stand-off bracket (to protect guttering)**
- **Screwdriver**
- **Hammer**
- **Wire brush and sandpaper**
- **Drill**

MATERIALS

- **Wooden or plastic wall-plugs**
- **Pipe nails or screws**
- **Metal paint and primer**

GUTTERING

1 Clean out insides of guttering, ensuring that the outlets to downpipes are clear. Use a wire brush to remove all rust and flaking paint.

2 Wash insides of guttering. Treat corroded areas with a rust remover. Leave to penetrate, then remove. Rinse and dry.

3 Touch up any bare metal with metal primer (never leave bare metal exposed overnight). After 24 hours apply a coat of black bituminous paint inside guttering and allow to dry. After eight hours apply undercoat to outer areas, followed, when dry, with a topcoat. Use a cardboard strip to avoid smudging walls.

DOWNPIPES

If a section of cast iron downpipe is damaged, it can be replaced as follows:

1 This downpipe is fixed to the wall by pipe nails in wooden plugs which have come loose. Remove nails by levering with a claw hammer (protect wall with a piece of wood).

2 Loosen sealed joints (take care – these may contain lead). Then, having checked that the section above is fully supported, pull away the lower section.

3 Remove old wall-plugs, then extend both holes using a 12mm masonry bit (holes approx 65mm deep).

4 Hammer replacement plugs into both holes (cut round wooden plugs slightly larger than the holes). Take the opportunity to rub down and paint the back of the pipe with suitable metal paint.

5 Replace the section of pipe so that the bracket holes are level with the plugs and hammer in two new pipe-nails or secure with screws.

6 To prevent the downpipe cracking, force some fresh mastic (jointing compound) into the joint and seal with bitumen paint.

7 To maintain original cast iron downpipes, first thoroughly clean, and remove rust with a wire brush. Sandpaper rear of pipes.

8 Ensure any areas of bare metal are painted with primer. Apply topcoats as described for gutters.

THE WALLS

These were the early days of cavity wall construction – but old cavity wall ties can be notoriously prone to rust. Even if your house has traditional solid brick or rendered walls, it is surprising how vulnerable they can be. An unseen battle is constantly being waged with frost and sulphate attack, extreme damp and chemical erosion – and sometimes with stresses from incompetent structural alterations. The results of neglect can be plain to see – cracking, crumbling, bowing and leaning, porous render, rotten lintels, and the risk of injury from unstable masonry at height. As if that wasn't enough, foundations of this age are relatively shallow – making the possibility of damage from subsidence a real concern.

If there were award ceremonies for major advances in wall construction, the 1930s house would be right up there. You may not think of your home as having pioneered much in the way of technological breakthroughs, but in its day it was quite simply 'the dog's pride and joy'.

This was the first generation of mass-developed housing to employ modern cavity wall construction – although some persevered with traditional solid walls, perhaps 'sexed up' a little with cool bands of cement render or art deco motifs. Many builders hedged their bets, with cavity ground floor walls and rendered or tiled solid construction above. Both types were now built using modern Portland cement mortar (instead of the old lime variety) and a few even incorporated that very latest introduction: breeze blocks.

In truth, this brave new era of advanced cavity construction wasn't so totally new. Walls built in the form of two thin parallel 'leaves' with a gap in between had been experimented with since Victorian times, albeit in fairly limited numbers. They were known to have superior structural qualities and improved damp resistance and so were sometimes used for houses in exposed locations. But by the 1930s previously radical techniques and materials were being introduced for the first time into high-volume mainstream housing.

Modern cavity walls with their exclusive use of 'stretcher bond' (with all the bricks laid lengthways), typically about 250–280mm (10–11in) thick, contrasted with traditional solid walls with their 230mm (9in) thick brickwork laid in one of the two main styles of bonding, English or Flemish. English bond consisted of layers of bricks laid lengthways to show their sides (stretchers) alternating with courses laid crossways to show their heads (headers). But the most common solid wall style was Flemish bond, in which the stretchers were alternately punctuated with headers.

Inevitably, with the introduction of new materials came the demise of old ones. Even in regions where stone had been the traditional, universal house-building material it was

1

2

3

4

1 London Brick Co (LBC) reds, popular on front walls.
2 Solid brickwork, traditional Flemish bond.
3 Red semi-engineering bricks, Grimsby.
4 Popular Fletton 'rustics'.

BELOW: Cheaper common bricks to side wall.

now rarely used. Stone had become relatively expensive compared to mass-produced brick, and was too bulky for easy adaptation to new cavity wall construction methods. It was also not particularly 'in vogue' in an era of streamlined white render and jazzy Hollywood moderne styles, so its use was often restricted to decorative 'infill' panels. And the elaborate, coloured local brickwork much beloved of Victorian builders was now considered rather passé (so *last century!*), and was duly consigned to history.

The main front walls were now usually built of the best locally manufactured plain facing bricks, or perhaps from widely available Fletton 'rustics' with their distinctive reddish colour and wire-pressed wavy texture, or from such bricks as the popular 'LBC reds'. Cheaper, mass-produced Fletton commons were used for areas of masonry to be rendered, and very often for the less visible rear and side walls.

Many types of 1930s brick can still be obtained today. In Scotland and the North, cheap mass-produced commons made from shale clays were frequently used. There was also a regional difference in size – northern bricks were typically about 0.25in (13mm) thicker than in the south (so four courses gauged 13in/330mm, not 12in/305mm).

Brick killers

It is not always appreciated that bricks are actually quite absorbent. If you take a bucket of water and place an average house brick in it, you will see the water level reduce as the brick sucks in the water. Similarly, brickwork will temporarily absorb rainwater and then release it by evaporation in dry weather. This is why sealant fluids should only be used sparingly, as they can trap moisture and inhibit natural evaporation if used extensively.

There are two main killers of brickwork:

FROST DAMAGE: water expands by about ten per cent when frozen, so if bricks are unduly porous and wet freezing will exert great pressure and cause them to 'burst' (de-laminate). The exposed soft clay core will then quickly deteriorate.

SULPHATE ATTACK: bricks that are continually saturated are also at risk from sulphate attack. This occurs when sulphates in the bricks and mortar start to react and steadily expand, causing cracks along mortar joints (sometimes also evident on the inside of the walls) as well as spalled faces to bricks. It is particularly common to brickwork in exposed positions such as chimney stacks or parapet walls, or under defective sills.

However, good building design should ensure that walls are protected from the persistent passage of rainwater, by the construction of overhangs like projecting roofs, sills on windows, and coping stones.

Crumbling and spalling

Brickwork can become excessively weathered and increasingly porous with age, but some parts of the walls will absorb more rain than others. Decorative features such as projecting band courses can allow water to settle and penetrate, so their top surfaces should slope down and away to disperse rainwater.

As noted above, when moisture penetrates behind the hard outer surface and then freezes it will expand, causing some bricks to crumble, dislodging the outer face. With other types of brick the face can start to fall away in layers, exposing the soft interior, which has little resistance. Spalling is more likely where the pointing has been neglected. It can also be caused by damp penetrating from inside, which is why you sometimes see bricks that have been eaten away following the line of a chimney flue up a wall.

Where a brick has crumbled badly one answer is to cut it away and replace it, using a sharp cold chisel, which can accurately remove smaller fragments. Matching replacements may be found elsewhere around the house (eg old outbuildings), or reclaimed bricks may be available from local salvage yards. To locate specific types of brick, check out brick libraries, e.g. at the Building Centre in London. Otherwise there are companies that can make replicas, at a price.

But if only the surface of a brick is damaged, an approved remedy is to cut away a shallow recess about 30mm (1.25in) deep, which can be filled with a small matching section of brick called a 'slip', fixed in place with mortar. If the damage is extreme the wall could be rendered or clad for protection, subject to aesthetic considerations.

Bowing and leaning

A common weak point is the tendency for main walls to bow or lean if not restrained, particularly by the floor and ceiling joists. In houses where the joists run in a front to back direction, they are helping hold the main front and rear walls in but not the side wall(s). The problem is made worse if the stairs run parallel to the side wall, since all the open space around the stairwell means that there is less floor structure holding it to the house. Conversely, in designs where the joists run from side to side, it is the front and rear walls that may have little to tie them in.

Such a wall may develop a vertical lean in either direction with its maximum at the top, or sometimes a distinct outward bowing at first floor or roof level. This is why tie bars can often be seen on the end walls of terraces. But a bulge just below the point where the floor joists rest in the wall could also be due to movement in an overloaded floor.

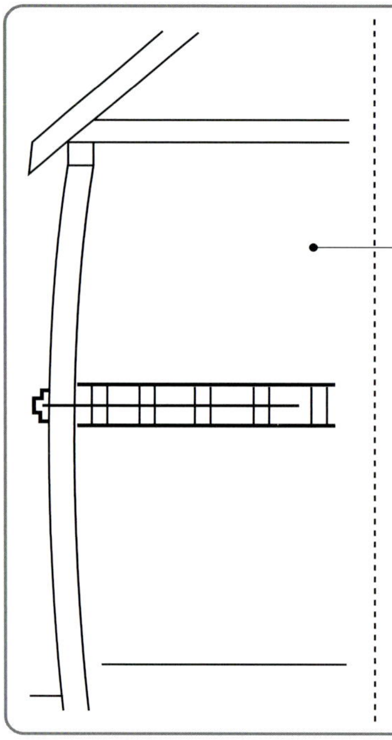

This side wall has bulged half-way up because the first floor joists are parallel to it and do not provide any support (or 'lateral restraint'). Ties can be built in at first floor level, fixed to the floor joists, if the wall is still reasonably stable.

The other main cause of leaning is 'roof spread', where the rafter feet push the top of a wall out because the rafters aren't securely tied in by ceiling joists or collars. This can sometimes be spotted upstairs where gaps to window reveals are wider at the top than at the bottom.

As noted earlier (in Chapter 3), roof spread may be particularly evident in 1930s houses where a side wall (under an unrestrained hipped roof) leans outwards at the top, while in sharp contrast the tall side stack above it is sadly wilting inwards.

Visible signs of movement inside the house are vertical

cracks to the plaster where internal partition walls meet the main walls; cracks between ceilings and the main walls; and gaps between the floor and skirting. But don't panic: a wall which is out of plumb by up to 25mm (1in), or bulges by up to 12mm (0.5in) over a single storey, is considered within acceptable tolerances and should not normally require structural repairs.

Foundations and subsidence

Until the mid-1970s, foundation depths were not a major issue for either builders or District Surveyors. Although it was generally appreciated that foundations needed to be deep enough to avoid unstable topsoil and frost penetration of the earth, as well as seasonal moisture changes (which can all cause the ground to move), many were, in fact, not built to a sufficient depth to tolerate climate change and the growth of nearby trees.

If the 1930s builder was reasonably competent he would start by digging a trench about 600mm (2ft) deep and about 450mm (18in) wide. This would then be filled with poured concrete and the wall structure was then built up on top, in a similar way to modern foundations (except that these are usually more than 1.2m deep and 600mm wide). This was an improvement on the old Victorian footings of stepped brickwork and was just about adequate on suitable ground. But some properties built in areas of soft ground have since had to be underpinned. Hot dry summers such as those of 1975–6, 1995–6, and 2003 caused the clay sub-stratum to dry out and shrink, leaving many shallow foundations unsupported.

The words 'subsidence' and 'settlement' are sometimes used rather willy-nilly to denote the movement of a building. More specifically, 'settlement' tends to imply an acceptable, limited movement of a new or altered structure as it settles down, whereas 'subsidence' has an air of menace about it, denoting dangerous, unforeseen sinking that can lead to structural collapse.

The ground has subsided and the concrete foundation has followed it down. But the main wall hasn't sunk so much (yet), leaving a gap at the bottom of the brickwork (trowel inserted). (Photo: Neil Curling, Halifax General Insurance)

All buildings settle after construction, as the ground adjusts to the new weight imposed upon it. Where the ground is clay, peat, or silt, settlement can take many years, whereas for new buildings on rock, gravel, or sand, initial settlement may be complete soon after completion of the build. But anything that later disturbs the balance between a building and the ground – such as growing trees, leaking drains, droughts, and structural alterations – can promote new movement.

Underpinning is one well-known solution. This involves digging under the shallow footings down to a stable ground level, then pouring in concrete. But it is a costly, complex, and disruptive task that is not always necessary and can actually lead to future problems. If a structure has been only partially underpinned (eg just one house in a terrace), future damage may occur if that part of the building which is not underpinned continues to settle. And properties that have been underpinned never seem to quite recover from the stigma – insurers will often decline such properties.

Fortunately, underpinning is not normally necessary where movement has ceased and is unlikely to recur, or where the rate of movement is manageable and doesn't threaten the stability of the structure: just expect the need for occasional redecoration and adjustment to doors and

windows. This was the traditional way of dealing with movement prior to the hot summers of the 1970s, when insurance policies began to include subsidence as a 'claimable' defect. So underpinning should be avoided if at all possible. Sensible precautions taken in the first instance, such as pollarding (severe pruning) or removing nearby trees and repairing leaking drains, may solve the problem.

Foundation problems are more likely on clay subsoils (ie much of central and southern Britain), on sloping sites, or where there are trees nearby. Any tree or shrub that grows fast, like eucalyptus or the notorious leylandii, or thirsty broadleaf trees like poplars, oaks, and willows, will extract a lot of moisture from the soil and can upset ground conditions, causing subsidence to shallow foundations. One method of treatment is to dig out the affected ground near vulnerable buildings or drains and crop the roots in that area.

There are no foolproof rules for distinguishing the causes of movement, but when parts of a building sink or subside, any ensuing vertical cracking often appears wider at the top – a tapered 'V' shape. Conversely, if wet saturated clay soil freezes it expands, pushing the shallow foundations upwards. Or say you cut down a large, thirsty tree nearby: the ground can then swell with moisture (which is no longer being absorbed by the tree) and expand. Known as 'heave', this is the opposite of subsidence, and the resulting vertical cracking is often narrower at the top. This is why care should be taken when deciding whether to prune, pollard, or remove a tree, especially when the tree is older than the building. Be aware, too, that cutting down a tree protected by a Tree Preservation Order can lead to prosecution. If you suspect subsidence, notify your insurer, who will appoint a specialist to initiate the appropriate stabilisation action and repairs.

Most older buildings have settled to some extent over time, and there are plenty of houses with inadequate foundations by today's standards which remain perfectly upright thanks to the walls being reasonably thick, with adequate restraint from floors and internal walls. It's only when such walls or floors are disturbed – such as when new openings are cut in the walls, or internal walls are removed – that new stresses are caused and trouble can really begin.

Foundations should be the same depth for all walls taking similar loadings. So where the old house adjoins a modern extension built with deeper foundations, cracking often occurs due to different rates of settlement between the two. See 'Defects' below.

Cracking

Diagnosing the causes of cracking is a very specialist area and a structural engineer's advice should be sought. Investigation can initially involve digging bore-holes, trial pits, and testing drains for leaks. Engineers often need to monitor crack damage for six months or more using calibrated glass 'telltales' fixed over cracks. This helps tell if the movement is seasonal (not usually serious) or progressive (serious). All buildings move and most crack and very often the cracks are longstanding and of little significance. But not always.

COMMON CAUSES OF CRACKING INCLUDE:

- Shallow foundations: problems with the foundations generally show themselves by fractures through the brickwork, often via window openings (the weakest point).

- Structural alterations: if there's a recent opening cut in a wall, like an enlarged window, or a wall has been taken out, this may have been done without taking any account of the loads carried above. So all of the old load may now be thrown down through the remaining brickwork, causing parts of the foundations to adjust to the new unequal loadings and settle. A common area of cracking is over window lintels where the window has been replaced and the masonry above has settled.

- Expansion cracks: vertical cracking due to thermal movement on a long wall (such as a row of terraced houses) is quite common due to modern cement being so rigid. Walls that are south-facing get maximum sun and are subject to greater forces of expansion.

Other possible causes include cavity wall tie failure (see below) or ground movement brought about by old mines, coastal erosion, or nearby excavations.

When diagnosing cracking, it is important to note its direction, its depth, and whether it tapers – ie is it wider at the top or the bottom? If a crack extends right through a cavity wall to the inside, it is far more likely to be serious. The Building Research Establishment (BRE) defines cracks up to 5mm wide as 'slight', while cracks of less than 3mm (the width of a one pound coin) are often not considered serious. In some cases the cause of settlement may lie below the highest point of a diagonal crack (eg a leaking drain). But these are only rules of thumb and should not be relied on exclusively – the cause and appropriate solution will depend on many factors. One thing that is generally agreed is that cracks should be repaired to prevent water entering and causing further damage.

Pointing

'Pointing' is the visible edge of the mortar joints between bricks. 'Bucket handle' and 'flush' joints were common styles of pointing, being about 10mm (3/8in) wide and respectively slightly recessed in a curved shape and level with the brick surface.

For re-pointing, 'bucket handle' joints are generally considered best for durability and weather resistance. Modern slanted 'weatherstruck' pointing was originally rarely used, but today it is technically preferable for some less visible areas of exposed masonry, such as chimney stacks, although it may be visually inappropriate elsewhere.

TYPES OF POINTING

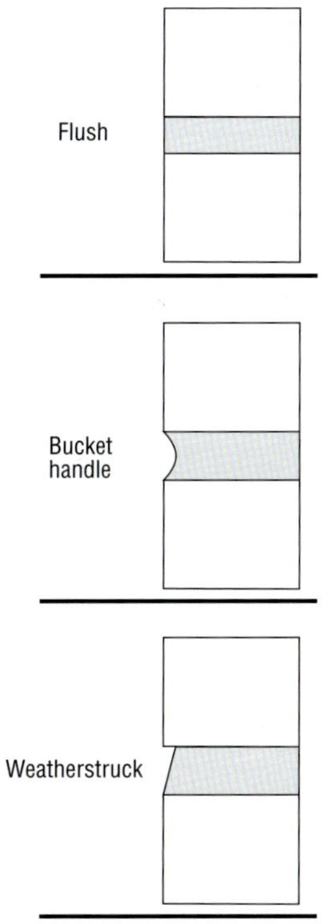

Pointing not only enhances the appearance of brickwork but is also important in protecting the bricks from damage by damp and frost. Like masonry, mortar is prone to frost and sulphate attack when damp, so if mortar joints become soft and porous they need to be raked out and re-pointed. Some parts of the walls are exposed to more severe weather than others, so it is unlikely that all the mortar will fail simultaneously. Re-pointing is therefore usually carried out in small areas at a time.

It is a mistake to think that re-pointing with a strong, hard cement mortar will last forever. If the mix is too strong the re-pointing repairs can trap water, and the bricks decay as a result. The mortar used for re-pointing should therefore not be appreciably stronger either than the original mortar or the masonry.

The art of re-pointing is that it should resemble the original as closely as possible. The emphasis is supposed to be on the brickwork and nothing mucks up the character of a building like bad re-pointing. If your house suffers from this, great care will be needed when cutting out the mortar, to ensure that the bricks don't get damaged in the process.

The old mortar should be raked out to a depth of at least 20mm (0.8in) and the joints brushed and moistened before pressing in the new mortar, otherwise the key will be poor and it will drop out.

Wall tie failure

Most 1930s houses, and just about all homes built since, have main walls of cavity construction. For strength, they rely on the two leaves being secured to each other. Some early cavity walls were tied with bricks across the cavity, others with iron ties, but wall ties in the 1930s commonly came in the form of a twisted

Distinctive wall tie repair holes, since filled.

All in the mix

Traditionally mortar was made from lime mixed with sand, but during the 1930s Portland cement (so called because of its grey Portland stone colour) had largely replaced or at least supplemented the lime. Cement is stronger and more durable and sets far quicker than lime. However, it is also very brittle and on older buildings it can pay to add some lime to the mix to produce a less rigid mortar that is less likely to develop cracks due to thermal movement. Opinions on what mix to use vary widely, but a typical mix for medium strength bricks would be 1:1:6 cement/lime/sand. The sand used for re-pointing mortar should be builders' sand as opposed to sharp sand, which is coarser and more suitable for render and concrete.

strip of steel ('vertical twist ties') which either had a protective coating of black bitumen or were galvanised with zinc.

As a general guide, ties are fixed in the wall (sloping slightly down and outwards) about 900mm (3ft) apart horizontally and about 450mm (1.5ft) vertically, staggered in a 'domino five' pattern. Around door and window openings the density is normally increased, and they should be positioned no more than 225mm (9in) from the edge.

The required maintenance for a cavity wall is pretty much as for traditional solid brickwork. But the big worry is that the metal ties may have rusted and failed, expanding and blowing the mortar joints. As mortar ages, it can become more acidic due to absorption of carbon dioxide in the atmosphere. This, together with the presence of chlorides or sulphates in the mortar mix, can eat away at the protective coatings on the metal ties, resulting in extreme expansion of the steel tie up to six times its original thickness. The risk is greater in properties located near the coast because of salt corrosion.

Wall tie failure tends to manifest itself in the form of horizontal cracking along mortar joints at regular points corresponding to the position of the wall ties. This may be accompanied by expansion and possible bulging to the outer wall, usually at the more exposed higher levels. (NB: cracked mortar joints resulting from sulphate attack look similar but are not restricted just to wall tie positions at about every sixth course.) Where the ties corrode within the inner leaf, expect to see a similar pattern of cracking on the plaster inside, sometimes with localised lifting of floors and accompanying cracks where partition walls meet the outer walls.

In the 1980s the problem of cavity wall tie corrosion started to become evident. Some steel wall ties were discovered deteriorating prematurely, so in 1981 the British Standard for the protection of metal wall ties was swiftly upgraded, with a tripling in thickness of the recommended zinc protection plus the use of new plastic coatings. Not surprisingly, the problem is more serious in walls in exposed areas, but also in walls built with particular types of mortar, like the infamous 'black ash mortar' which is unduly acidic and eats away at the metal. Fortunately, wall tie failure is still rare and major remedial structural work may only be necessary in extreme cases, since modern techniques now make it possible to insert new ties without demolishing and rebuilding as was previously required. Usually the first step is to remove a few bricks and examine the condition of the ties. Evidence of old filled drill holes may be indicative of past remedial work (often to the most exposed wall only).

Concrete blocks

'Breeze blocks' were made from cement mixed with sand and pulverised and aerated fuel ash – clinker, coking breeze, and slag, the noxious waste products of burned coal and coke from industrial furnaces, gasworks, and metal smelters.

Modern houses use manufactured concrete blocks for the inner leaf – for economy as well as for their superior insulation properties – whereas 1930s inner leaves tended to be of common brick, some incorporating a course of blockwork at skirting level so that the skirting boards could be nailed into place.

There are a few exceptions to the rule, such as houses built with experimental structures comprising blockwork with a reinforced concrete ring-beam surrounding the whole building under the first floor. To strengthen the walls, every other block was laid across the cavity (resulting in 'cold bridging'). But because inner leaves are load-bearing, there was generally a lack of confidence that these early, cheaply made blocks would be of adequate strength.

With hindsight, it may be that in some cases waste materials were used which, like asbestos, may not be particularly safe when disturbed or drilled. It is now virtually impossible to tell, but facemasks should be worn when drilling as a precaution, particularly when dealing with internal walls where breeze blocks were used extensively (see Chapter 8). What we do know is that many early blocks had a high carbon content in the form of ash that, in the rare cases where they were used in main walls, can potentially hasten the corrosion of metal wall ties.

Mundic block

Despite sounding rather like an embarrassing holiday complaint, the menace of mundic block has been known to blight whole estates. Peculiar to parts of Cornwall and the South-West, it mainly affects houses built between the 1920s and the 1950s. Because local clay for bricks was scarce or non-existent, main walls of rendered concrete blockwork were introduced long before their appearance throughout the rest of the country. The problem is that the concrete was produced with local aggregate materials such as rock waste from mines and quarries, and from free supplies of beach gravel and sand. 'Mundic decay' refers to the deterioration of such materials, which, in damp conditions, for example, can oxidise and form sulphuric acid that then attacks the cement, causing expansion and structural weakness. Fortunately only about 5 per cent of the houses tested overall have been classified as 'clearly unsound', but others that appear sound actually contain sufficient 'problem aggregate' to cause potential problems if poorly maintained. And in some areas the risk is far higher. Local councils should have records, and you should check before you buy.

Cavity wall insulation

Many houses will have cavity wall insulation that has been injected into the walls, either as expanded plastic foam or mineral fibre 'loose fill'. It can sometimes be detected where foam may have oozed through gaps at openings or at the top of walls in the roof space, and where there are small injection holes in the walls for the pump nozzle, since filled.

Insulating cavity walls is a fairly straightforward job which can be done in a day. Professional firms of installers will drill small holes in the outside wall and use specialist equipment to inject insulating material into the cavity. Along with loft insulation, this is considered one of the more cost-effective and worthwhile improvements. It should cause little disruption, and you should recover the cost within four or five years, depending on the size of house and number of outside walls. Many firms give minimum 20-year guarantees and Local Authority grants may be available. Note that in some very exposed locations, filling cavities with insulation may not be desirable if it allows damp to bridge across the cavity.

Rendered walls

Render is a thin layer of mortar applied to exterior walls to prevent rain penetration through porous brickwork. It was fashionable in the 1930s in the form of pebbledash or roughcast, but especially when applied with a smooth white finish, either in streamlined 'moderne' style or 'mock-Tudor' (featuring decorative black timber strips). Another favourite nod to tradition at the corners was to sometimes contrast render with brick quoins (corner stones).

Traditionally, it comprised a 1:1:6 cement/lime/sand mix, applied in two coats, but this was gradually superseded by modern sand and cement render. Unlike today's houses, where it is usually applied over blockwork, in 1930s houses the render was normally applied direct to brickwork, or sometimes over a base of timber lathing (eg to gables and bays). It also presented a tempting opportunity for builders to disguise cheap brickwork.

Both pebbledash and roughcast are better at shedding water away from the face than plain render, and they do not tend to crack excessively even with a rich mix. Render will normally absorb some rainwater but should not readily transmit it into the wall, instead allowing it to dry out during the next

fine spell. It should be mixed so it is strong enough to resist damage but flexible enough to cope with slight movement and sufficiently porous to allow the masonry behind to breathe, so that no water becomes trapped behind. Problems occur with cement-rendered walls when small cracks allow water to penetrate and soak into the wall, eventually causing the render surface to deteriorate.

Horizontal cracking to render along the lines of expanding mortar joints is likely to indicate sulphate attack, as opposed to fine cracks due only to shrinkage. Excessive wetting of the walls combined with sulphate in the materials causes this, but can be avoided by minimising exposure to damp through good design (overhanging eaves and verges, flashings, DPCs etc) and the use of sulphate resistant render. In houses with 'mock-Tudor' decorative timber strips, cracks caused by shrinkage of the timber where their edges meet the render are a weak point, allowing damp to penetrate. These should be filled.

Areas of cracked or loose render must be hacked off and renewed once any trapped moisture has thoroughly dried out from underlying brickwork. Completely removing cement-based renders from walls may not be possible because it adheres so firmly to the adjoining surfaces that removal can damage the original fabric. Where render is poor or unsightly a good solution is to clad the wall with traditional tiling, which also improves insulation – always ensuring that window and door sills still project adequately to disperse rainwater away from the walls.

Tile-hung walls

Tile-hung bays and gables were very popular on privately built houses. As with roof construction, tiles were traditionally hung from wooden battens (and nailed), which unless well treated with preservative can be prone to decay. But being vertical the overlap could be much less than on a roof, typically only about 38mm (1.5in). Ideally there should be some underfelt and insulation to reduce heat loss. If none exists, this is a very worthwhile improvement. Otherwise, expect the same defects as for roof tiles, like corroded nails and decayed timbers. One particularly vulnerable area is beneath window sills, so a metal flashing or 'apron' was normally provided for weathertightness.

Lintels

Openings in external walls would normally be spanned by lintels to support the weight of the masonry above. Large brick arches were another popular way to span openings, often seen as a big architectural statement over the front door porch.

New reinforced concrete lintels were starting to be widely used in mass-produced cavity wall construction, often hidden behind brick soldier courses.

Meanwhile, some 'old school' builders had steered clear of the newfangled cavity wall revolution and stayed loyal to walls of solid brick employing traditional timber lintels, also hidden behind brick soldier courses or brick arches. But as in Victorian houses, these are only one brick width away from the wind and rain, so if the mortar pointing is soft or eroded damp can penetrate, causing rot and sagging to the timber which eventually allows the brickwork above to drop.

Particularly at risk are large hidden timber lintels found above openings to single storey bays (they can rot if the roofs leak). Lintels were also sometimes omitted altogether, relying instead on the window frame to hold up the wall above. Both such situations are fortunately fairly rare.

Large Tudor-style hardwood beams were sometimes used as 'in your face' pseudo-period features, also seen adorning entrance porches; but despite their exposed locations the quality of the timber employed has resulted in them being usually relatively resistant to decay.

Parapet walls

These are sometimes seen as curved rendered 'balcony' walls on top of 'moderne' bays, or above garage doors, craftily concealing flat roofs behind. Parapet masonry is always at risk, being exposed to driving wind and rain at high level. So it helps if the parapet was built with good quality bricks and with decent coping stones on top to disperse water.

But in the 1930s large overhanging coping stones were considered architecturally rather uncool, so instead they

Technical data

Building Research Establishment give the maximum permitted height for a single brick freestanding wall in Wind Zone 1 (South-East England) as 1.6m (5.25ft).

Some useful websites for discovering more about period bricks are www.brick.org.uk (The Brick Development Association) and www.buildingcentre.co.uk (The Building Centre). For information on Building Regulations, planning, and specialist firms, see www.ThirtiesHouse.co.uk.

ABOVE: Stylish balcony topped with protective coping.

BELOW: New copings (right).

were sometimes just 'rounded off' on top with render. Defects are pretty much as described for rendered walls above, multiplied by the exposed location and the additional risk of damp from flat roofs or gutters hidden behind parapets. The risk of unstable masonry at a great height has to be a serious concern and, as with leaning chimney stacks, some rebuilding to parapets may be needed once the cause of any instability has been rectified.

Thin brick walls

A word of warning: brickwork in 'stretcher bond' isn't always superior cavity wall construction – it may actually be a cheap, thin, single leaf wall, only 115mm (4.5in) thick. These are sometimes found in rear additions and can be structurally weak. Kitchens or bathrooms in rear additions of this type will be particularly prone to condensation and damp when steam hits the thin, cold walls. All you can really do, short of rebuilding, is dry-line and insulate the walls and make sure the outer face is sound. If there's any sign of cracking or movement you will need to get a structural engineer's report, not least because this could otherwise prove to be a significant issue when you come to sell.

Artificial stone cladding

This is possibly the worst ever DIY project, guaranteed to knock thousands off the value of your house at a stroke! A bit of a joke, until you consider the damage it can do. Made from coloured fuel ash, the tiles are glued on with mortar dabs. The trouble is they are often badly applied, leaving windows unopenable, airbricks covered, and DPCs bridged. Any cracks can trap damp, which soaks into the brickwork, being unable to evaporate externally; or it can freeze,

expand, and blow off individual pieces. Try hacking it off, but be warned: strong cement may well leave the brickwork damaged and pock-marked, requiring subsequent rendering or tile cladding. Spray-on textured finishes such as 'Tyrolean' render can also cause damage and are best avoided.

Stains

To remove grime from the face of masonry, high pressure hosing (at 300–600psi) is preferable to sandblasting or abrasive tools, as it is less likely to damage the surface of the brick, although the absorption of large amounts of water can cause temporary white salty efflorescence marks. Powerful water jets should be used with care, since in the wrong hands they can erode pointing, loosen tiles, and smash glass. Alternatively, chemical brick cleaners are available, but these can be very acidic so protective clothing must be worn. Try a small test area first.

Defect: Cracking to brick walls

SYMPTOMS

External cracking in masonry, internal cracks in plaster; damp penetration.

There are two main kinds of crack: those that run straight down vertically through the bricks, and stepped cracks that follow the mortar joints in a zigzag. It is easier to make good stepped cracks by pointing with mortar or using a clear flexible mastic, whereas vertical cracks normally require damaged bricks to be cut out and replaced.

However, cutting out all the cracked bricks and replacing them with new ones can be problematic if no matching bricks are available. Another remedial technique for areas of substantial cracking is to drill a series of holes along the crack and inject them with a special thixotropic resin grout. The face of the brick is then repaired with colour-matched mortar and should be undetectable.

Diagnosing the causes of cracking can be difficult; sometimes even the experts are flummoxed and need to monitor cracking for up to a year. Most houses show some signs of movement, the big question being, is it historic movement or is it 'progressive' and likely to move still more? Before the masonry can be repaired, the cause of the movement must first be dealt with. The most likely causes are:

Cause Expansion and contraction due to changes in temperature

Solution *Thermal movement is likely to occur between different materials (eg old brick walls joined to modern blockwork walls), resulting in cracking. An expansion joint can be formed with a flexible mastic sealant to keep the structure weathertight. Hairline cracks are common where different building materials have expanded and contracted, or dried out, at different rates.*

Cause Subsidence or heave of shallow foundations

Solution *Eliminate likely causes such as nearby trees, leaking drains, etc.*
Cracking due to subsidence may require the foundations to be underpinned. Your insurance company may want to monitor the cracking to diagnose the risk of future movement. Subsidence or heave is more likely in older properties with shallow foundations on clay subsoil, on slopes, and with trees nearby. Drains should be checked for hidden leaks affecting the ground.
**See also 'differential movement' under the heading 'defective render'.*

Cause Structural alterations, physical damage or poor quality original materials

Solution *Movement due to structural alterations may require additional localised strengthening, whereas physical damage – such as from vehicle impact – normally only requires making good to the area affected (unless structural damage was caused).*

Cause Corrosion of cavity wall ties

Failure in cavity walls can be down to insufficient numbers of ties or badly installed ties, but is more likely to result from corrosion. Once corrosion takes hold, deterioration can be rapid. Rust can expand the original steel by up to 600 per cent, so it is well within the power of corroded ties to lift up several metres of brickwork. Such upward movement can result in the walls pushing up the roof – particularly at gable ends (known as the 'pagoda effect') – or else bulging out if the weight of the roof resists the upward thrust.

It is typically evident as horizontal cracking along mortar joints (or render), sometimes causing loose masonry at higher levels. Other signs are cracking around windows or doors and at internal wall/ceiling junctions, as floor joists are pushed up by expansion in the walls.

(Photo: www.timberwise.co.uk)

Solution *The solution starts with a survey to analyse whether the old ties need be removed or isolated.*
First locate the wall ties using a metal detector. Next remove a brick below cracked joints and inspect a sample of the existing ties; alternatively a boroscope inserted through 12mm drill holes can examine the ties. Defective corroded ties can then be cut out if likely to cause further damage. New holes are drilled into the internal leaf externally – through the brickwork – one course below the ties, and new stainless steel ties are installed into the drilled holes and permanently fixed in place with epoxy resin.

Defect: Bulging brick walls

SYMPTOMS
Walls bow outwards; cracks internally to plaster at main walls.

Cause **The walls were not fully tied in when built**

Solution *Eliminate the cause of the bulging, then repair or rebuild the affected wall sections.*
Inadequate restraint is common in side walls (eg to end terraces) and may require building-in metal ties from the outer wall to the floor or ceiling joist structure.

Cause **Roof spread**

Solution *The rafters lean against the top of the main walls and can push them out if not held back by ceiling joists.*
The timbers here may be poorly nailed together or may have rotted. Roof spread is more common in lean-to roofs, where the top of the wall can be seen to bow out and the roof above sags where the rafters have sunk. The solution is to provide additional restraint such as new ceiling joists or collars, and, in serious cases, to rebuild the upper wall.

Cause **Corrosion of cavity wall ties embedded in walls**

Solution *As described above under 'Cracking to brick walls'.*

Cause **Overloaded walls**
Walls built too thin, or alterations to building have added to loading.

Solution *Excessive loading of the structure (eg due to botched structural alterations) means the specific cause must be identified and additional support provided – a structural engineer will need to advise.*

Cause **Rotting timbers built into walls**

Solution *Rotten timbers (eg floor joist ends) must be cut out, the masonry in the immediate area treated, and the timber replaced with new, protected with a DPC. This can require temporary structural support to floors.*

Cause **Extreme damp or chemical attack**

Solution *Damp can result from several possible causes. Rising and penetrating damp can soak into the masonry, which then expands and bulges when frozen or suffers sulphate attack (see Chapter 6).*

Defect: Flaking or eroded brickwork

SYMPTOMS
Spalling of brickwork; blown or soft masonry; eroded mortar joints. Moisture can also leave salts appearing as 'blooms' on the surface, or causing pitting, powdering, and flaking.

More likely in exposed areas like parapet walls at roof level. Common causes are:

Cause **Frost in the brickwork**
Water getting into porous masonry will expand on freezing, causing the masonry to disintegrate, or will result in sulphate attack.

Solution *Cut out and renew badly affected brick.*
At worst, walls may have to be partially rebuilt using sulphate resistant mortar and low sulphate bricks.

Cause **Previous repointing with too strong cement mortar**

Solution *Repoint porous mortar joints with suitable mortar mix to prevent moisture getting in.*

Cause **Excessive weathering, old age, or poor quality masonry**

Solution *Check damp-proof course is effective. See comments above under 'Crumbling and spalling'.*

Defect: Defective render

SYMPTOMS

Cracking or bulging of rendering.

Cause **Differential movement to the wall**

Solution Cracking is commonly found where render runs across vertical joints, often between the main house and a later extension. Different foundation depths and loadings mean these will move at a different rate, causing seasonal cracking. The render should be carried across the joint on metal lathing. If the cause is due to the wall itself being unsound, see the sections on 'Cracking to brick walls' and 'Bulging brick walls' above.

Cause **Physical damage**

Solution *Rendering a large area is a skilled job but patching is less difficult – see 'step-by-step'. Alternatively, the wall could be reclad with appropriate tiles over the old render.*

Cause **Frost action on moisture trapped between the rendering and the wall**

If the render is loose but the wall is intact, it is likely to be due to water penetrating through small cracks, then freezing and expanding.

Solution *Defective areas of render should be hacked off. The wall surface then needs to be prepared by repairing any damaged masonry or painting with a stabilising solution and the render replaced.*

Cause **Incorrect mix of cement render**

Solution *A common problem is too strong a mix of cement render, leading to shrinkage, cracking, and moisture penetration. Hack it off and start again.*

Cause **Corrosion of cavity wall ties embedded in walls**

Solution *As described above under 'Cracking to brick walls'.*

Defect: Defective tiling

SYMPTOMS

Broken or slipped tiles; internal damp patches.
Tile-hung bays and gables are a common architectural feature, but tend to require periodic maintenance.

Cause **Water penetration due to poor sills and aprons/flashings above. Fixing nails may have rusted and timber battens may have rotted, or tiles themselves may be defective. See Chapter 2**

Solution *Replace slipped or missing tiles. In severe cases, strip and renew the tiles, fixing nails, or battens, and overhaul sills and aprons.*

STEP BY STEP

TOOLS REQUIRED
- Hammer and bolster/cold chisel
- Mixing board/hawk
- Buckets and shovel
- Plasterer's trowel
- Throwing shovel
- Paintbrush and sponge
- Safety goggles and gloves

MATERIALS
- Portland cement
- Sharp sand
- Hydrated lime
- PVA bonding
- 10mm shingle (or match existing)

Repairing roughcast and pebbledash

Many 1930s houses are at least partially rendered, often with a pebbledash or roughcast finish. Pebbledash is created by throwing a layer of dry pea shingle against the final render coat so that the 'pebbles' stick to it. It is very often left unpainted. With roughcast, the shingle is actually mixed into the final render coat, which is then thrown on and left rough. It is then normally painted. The type of shingle must be chosen to match the existing finish. Both types were usually applied to bare brickwork, but sometimes also to timber stud framework covered with timber or metal lathing, commonly found on bays and gables.

Where larger cracks have appeared or render has come loose, the damaged areas need to be cut away and made good. To repair typical vertical cracking in roughcast render finish:

LARGE CRACKS

1 Hack off the old render to expose an area about 100–150mm (4–6in) wide around the crack. If the roughcast sounds hollow when tapped with a hammer, or there is more than one crack, it may be necessary to expose a wider area.

2 Inspect the exposed crack to determine the likely cause of the problem. Here, differential movement between the main house (right) and the extension has been aggravated by water overflowing from the poorly maintained parapet wall. Make good any such defects before attending to the render. Rake out the exposed brick mortar joints and brush off loose particles.

3 In older buildings it is advisable to use some hydrated lime mixed with the usual sand and cement. This helps improve the render's flexibility so that it can move with slight changes to the building's structure over time without cracking. It also allows it to 'breathe', so that any trapped moisture can evaporate, and reduces shrinkage when dry.

4 First, add some hydrated lime to water and mix to the consistency of thick cream. Goggles and gloves should be worn since lime is a caustic material. Then make up the base coat by mixing this 'slaked' lime with Portand cement and sharp sand to a ratio of about 1:1:6 cement/lime/sand.

5 Wet the exposed brickwork with a brush, especially around the edges.

6 Trowel on the base coat using a small plasterer's trowel. Apply the render in small trowel-fulls until the area is filled, and then smooth it over.

7 Once it has started to stiffen, but before it has gone hard (about one hour), cut back the base coat to the thickness of the shingle in the roughcast coat (10mm).

8 Key the base coat to accept the roughcast finish by scratching it with a sharp object. The base coat should then be left to harden for at least 24 hours.

9 Mix the roughcast topcoat: 1:1:2 lime/cement/pea shingle. For pebbledash use a finish coat mix (try 1:1:1 cement/lime/sand mix), onto which the dry pea shingle is later thrown.

10 For roughcast, take a thin layer of the topcoat on the throwing shovel. Use only the tip of the shovel, and make sure the amount on the shovel is never more than one stone thick (10mm).

11 Throw the roughcast onto the wall with a flick of the wrist.

12 Smooth off the edges of the repair with a soft brush.

13 Clean off surrounding splashes with a damp sponge.

FINE CRACKS

Even fine cracks in render must be repaired at the earliest opportunity, since if neglected they will soon cause more extensive damage. But just filling them doesn't solve the problem – they must first be opened out so that new mortar can be pressed under the edges of the old render.

1 Chisel along cracks and cut underneath edges with a scraper.
2 Brush out loose material.
3 Brush undiluted PVA bonding into cracks and work in fresh mortar with a scraper.
4 Remove excess with a wet brush and leave to dry.
5 Dampen the surface and smooth with a scraper.

DAMP, ROT AND WOODWORM

Most 1930s houses had timber floors – so any adjacent dampness can potentially pose serious risks.

But just how real is this threat? We explain the true causes of damp and its unsavoury bedfellows, rot and woodworm, and show how to tell whether your house is really at risk, or not. Plus how to make your home warmer and free from condensation and toxic mould.

It's the stuff of nightmares: rising damp, dry rot, toxic mould, death-watch beetle. These are words you simply do not want to see in your survey report. Along with the word subsidence, they have passed into modern property folklore.

The reason for so much consternation about damp is that it can eventually lead to timber decay and beetle infestation, the two major threats to structural timbers, ultimately causing them to collapse.

By modern standards, 1930s house design is quite vulnerable to problems of this type, although features such as cavity walls (in many houses) and decent damp-proof courses made them generally superior to their Victorian counterparts.

There are two basic sources of damp: water outside trying to get in, and water inside trying to get out. In fact, it's water from internal sources – such as leaks, condensation, and building works – that accounts for the vast majority (70 per cent) of moisture in houses. So to keep your house free from damp problems, there are essentially two things you need to do: minimise water reaching the walls and getting in, and maximise evaporation to allow it to get out.

More specifically, dampness in buildings is often the result of a combination of causes, such as earth banked up against walls, condensation running down steamy windows, and rain seeping through small cracks.

This is one of the most serious defects in buildings as it can quickly lead to deterioration as well as affecting the health of occupants. But it's not always obvious – rot to your structural timbers may be quietly taking place long before any wet patches are visible, so a damp-meter can be a useful detection tool.

Rising damp

Musty smells. Clammy plaster. Rotten skirting. Spongy floors. That's the rising damp experience. Moisture from the ground can rise up about 750mm (30in) through the walls if there's a problem with the damp-proof course (DPC) that was designed to prevent this.

Be warned: true rising damp is very rare, particularly in properties with cavity walls. There are many instances of specialist firms merrily injecting DPCs where none were needed. Wetness in walls may look like rising damp, but it is often due to other causes such as condensation, plaster contaminated with salts, or water seeping back under window sills. So an injected DPC should really be a last resort. Just to make it more difficult to diagnose, there are a number of fiendish imposters. For example, a wall that is already saturated – say from a leaking gutter – will be colder than a dry wall and will attract condensation on the inside due to 'cold bridging'. Then there's the case of warm steamy air inside the house that condenses back to water when it hits a cold wall surface and runs down the wall, accumulating at the bottom, only to then rise up in the form of rising damp. Moist air can easily get through normal plasterboard on dry-lined walls, so all this can take place completely unseen.

You may be able to remedy the problem by first carrying out some common-sense improvements:

- Ensure that earth is not banked up against outside walls.
- Check that the external ground levels are at least 150mm (6in) below the DPC level, to reduce the risk of rain splashing off the ground and saturating the wall. Reduce the height of paving outside and fit drainage channels to paving near the house.
- Repair any leaking drains or rainwater fittings.
- Insulate and ventilate inside the house to reduce condensation.
- Install a gravel-filled shallow ditch known as a 'French drain' around the main walls so that rainwater drains away from the wall. Damp in the wall can then evaporate by making contact with the ventilating air within the gravel instead of migrating upwards.
- If the walls are rendered externally the rendering should stop just above the DPC, ideally curving out in a 'bellmouth drip' at the base so that rainwater clears the wall below.
- Remove old salt-contaminated plaster inside and let the wall dry before replastering with a new salt-resistant waterproof render or plaster.

LEFT: Nice bit of rising damp (complete with salts in plaster).

RIGHT: Rendered over DPC to the ground – not good.

LEFT: DPC of dark engineering bricks. RIGHT: DPC at correct height above ground. BELOW: DPC injected (but still damp inside).

DAMP-PROOF COURSES

Damp-proof courses were a well-established building practice by the 1930s, having first been required by the Building Acts of 1875. The traditional method was to provide two layers of slates bedded in mortar – usually evident as a wide mortar joint about two brick courses above the outside ground level – or, alternatively, courses of hard engineering bricks. But bituminised felt (or hot-laid molten bitumen) had increasingly become the norm, continuing in use as the material of choice up to the 1980s, when it was superseded by modern strips of plastic.

But damp-proof courses are sometimes hidden, typically where the walls are rendered down to ground level or if there is a plinth (a thick rendered base typically about 600mm/24in high). It is also common for the DPC to have been pointed over with mortar. You can check if there is a DPC in the wall from the inside, by raising a floorboard and raking out a little of the mortar from the joint.

After so many years, DPCs may have worn out or broken as a result of physical movement in the walls. Damp can also get round, or 'bridge', an otherwise sound DPC when something has linked the ground below to the wall above – typically where earth in flower beds is piled up against the wall or paving stones have raised the ground level. In such cases, the ground should be lowered to 150mm (6in) below the DPC and paving should slope away to prevent rainwater 'ponding' against the walls.

Cement rendered plinths can also cause bridging. Although unfashionable by the 1930s, and thus fairly rare,

LEFT: Render plinths can let damp get past the DPC by 'bridging'.

they were traditionally applied to external walls as decoration to conceal ugly DPCs and to emulate more expensive brick plinths. If plinths are cracked or loose they will let water in but won't allow the brickwork to dry out, so it is important that they are well maintained. If you try to hack the cement render off completely it may look very unsightly, as it can take lumps of brick with it, but removal of the portion around the DPC is normally advisable.

Damp-proof membranes (DPMs) are basically DPCs for solid floors, traditionally in the form of a layer of waterproof bitumen or, in modern floors, a thick polythene sheet. There should be a connection between the DPM and the DPC in the walls, otherwise bridging can occur from inside.

REMEDIES

In the vast majority of cases, what appears to be rising damp is in fact penetrating damp resulting from high ground levels and persistent leakage of water from defective sills, gutters and pipes etc. Moisture generated inside the house can also be a major contributor in the form of condensation soaking into the walls. This is commonly misdiagnosed as rising damp for which the usual remedy is to inject a new chemical DPC. Water repellent silicone or resin is pressure-injected through closely spaced horizontal holes drilled into the mortar or masonry just below floor level. The silicone-based liquid soaks into the wall and prevents water rising through the pores in the brick.

If such work is genuinely required, it is best carried out in late summer, when walls are at their driest. Normally this is done by a BWPDA-registered specialist firm, which can provide a 20-year guarantee (BWPDA stands for The British Wood Preservation and Damp-proofing Association). But with some contractors such guarantees may prove of limited value due to extensive exemption clauses and the fact that small firms tend to come and go. And no injected DPC can ever be 100 per cent efficient.

Hacking off the plaster – it is easy to underestimate the mess caused by DPC work.

One common condition of warranties is that the internal plaster must be renewed, as it will be contaminated by salts, and this work is disruptive and expensive. Nor do all firms do a good job – if the walls aren't dry when the DPC is injected the chemical may form an incomplete barrier; and DPCs are often injected at the wrong level, or left incomplete, with insufficient fluid injected and holes not sealed.

Nowadays you can hire the necessary equipment, so if you're not bothered about a warranty it is a job that should be within the capabilities of many homeowners. But precautions must be taken. See 'step-by-step'.

There are other methods of installing a replacement DPC. One alternative is to insert a plastic strip of the type used in new construction: a small section of the mortar joint in a solid wall is cut open just below the level of the timber floor (or at screed level on a solid floor) and the strip inserted. This procedure is then repeated on the next section of wall, and so on.

But, before celebrating the elimination of your damp problem, wait a while. It can take months for the drying out of a saturated standard 230mm (9in) thick wall. And damp can be elusive. When a house is left empty for a while signs of damp may disappear, but when rooms are heated moisture reappears on the surface of the plaster. It is also seasonal. It can disappear in the summer months only to reappear in the winter.

PLASTERING

Even when you've fixed the cause of the damp, a strange thing can happen to the old plaster on the inside. You would imagine that after the damp in the wall had gone away and the plaster had all dried out, that would be the end of it. But no. The water that rose up the wall wasn't pure: it would have been contaminated with nitrate and chloride salts picked up from the earth and the masonry, and these hygroscopic salts will have found their way into the surface plaster. This is a different kind of damp altogether – each time the air in the house becomes a little humid the salts in the plaster absorb the moisture and liquefy, so patches of dampness on the plaster occasionally return. But when the atmosphere is dry, the damp mysteriously disappears again.

When plaster has been contaminated by salts, the only remedy is to hack off all the affected plaster, wash down and seal the exposed brickwork (which contains further salts), and replaster with a 1:3 cement/sand base coat and a 'Multifinish' type plaster topcoat to at least 300mm (12in) beyond the edge of the old damp problem. It is best to mix in some waterproofer with the cement, and always ensure that the sand used is washed sharp sand – never soft builders' sand, which can contain impurities. Rising damp normally affects the walls up to 750mm (2.5ft) above the floor, and your repairs may therefore have to extend a metre or more (3.5ft) above the floor in order to blend in neatly with the old plaster, so do not underestimate the mess and disruption!

Some experts say that most damp problems are actually a result of these salts having leached through from damp walls and taken up residence in the plaster, and that replastering to the right formulation is the key.

Penetrating damp

Damp coming through the walls, rather than up them, can occur at any level but is more likely higher up, though 1930s cavity walls are far more resistant than solid walls. Where they are exposed to wind and driving rain, or where the pointing is a bit iffy, damp can penetrate, leaving brown patchy stains on the plaster or wallpaper. If neglected, rot can take hold inside. In much of Britain winter rain usually comes from the south-west, so the effects of driving rain are most noticeable on the walls, doors, and windows facing that direction.

DAMP PATCH PLACES

It is because brickwork is porous that extreme driving rain can penetrate solid walls. And a surprisingly large amount of water can enter a building even through tiny cracks. In very exposed locations, rendering or cladding the outer wall with tiles may be the best solution. Tiles have the advantage of allowing any damp already in the wall to disperse, as they don't seal in moisture.

Brickwork is sometimes coated with masonry paint to improve its appearance, hide graffiti or blemishes, or reduce rain penetration. But masonry was not really designed to be painted, and moisture in the walls may actually increase if modern vinyl paints seal it in. If rain has entered through joints and cracks, the paint can restrict the drying out process. It may be better to use special micro-porous masonry paint so that damp can escape by evaporation.

There are some specific areas where penetrating damp commonly enters the house:

Miracle solutions

The advertisements that promise maintenance-free wall coverings guaranteed to last a lifetime are very appealing. They claim that by spraying your walls with a tough yet flexible coating you can rejoice in the knowledge that you'll never need to lift a paintbrush again. But what the salesmen don't point out is that water enters your house not only from rain but also from other sources, including rising up from the ground, soaking down from the roof, and condensation from water vapour produced inside the house, so that the coating can actually have the effect of trapping moisture inside the walls. Also, the new surface will only be as good as the condition of the wall behind it. Preparing and drying out the wall first is essential, and the temptation to contractors is to rush this.

Similarly, liquid silicone damp sealants are advertised with claims of preventing water getting into walls, but if the surface of the wall is sealed damp may, again, be unable to escape, which can store problems for the future.

- The sills of windows were usually made of timber such as oak, but some also have traditional 'sub sills' of tiles, concrete, or brick that can crack due to slight settlement over the years. The cracks allow dampness to penetrate the wall below, showing internally as damp patches or soft and loose plaster and an attack of rot in the skirting. Sills must project sufficiently away from the wall and have a drip-groove or 'throating' underneath, otherwise rain will run back under the sill and soak into the wall.

- Windows and doors: rain quickly runs down and seeks out the numerous joints between the frames and the walls, or the glass and the putty. On tile-hung bays, lead 'aprons' are needed under the bedroom window sills to protect the tiles below from damp. Then above the living room window the tiles should splay out to help disperse water away from the house.
- Overflowing gutters or downpipes that are too short are another common cause of damp through the walls, as are leaking overflow pipes from WCs and water tanks.
- Decorative band courses of brickwork, or any protruding ledges on walls present an invitation to water. Unless sloped away from the wall, rain will pond and soak into them.
- Roofs and stacks are another major area of damp penetration, commonly at flashings and down chimney breasts, not forgetting damp coming through from inside the flues. See Chapter 3.

Other common sources of dampness include condensation, faulty plumbing, flooding, damp rising through floors, and from creeping plants on walls. As noted above, even once the sources of dampness have been eradicated, it can take a while for the fabric to dry out. And dampness drying out can look identical to a continuing problem, especially if plasters and finishes have absorbed salts. Like an unexploded 'damp-bomb', they can come back to haunt you with their strange ability to 'self-dampen' long after the source of the problem has been rectified, unless correctly replastered.

BELOW GROUND

Some 1930s houses built on steeply sloping sites utilise the resulting extra space (below the downhill part of the ground floor) as an 'undercroft'. These are usually accessed from an external side or rear door. Whilst not strictly an underground basement or cellar, they can suffer from similar problems and tend to have a 'dank and festering' ambience.

The causes of damp in basements include water pressure from waterlogged ground as well as from penetrating damp and condensation. 'Tanking' is one solution for walls below-ground. This may involve dry-lining the walls with insulated plasterboard with a polythene vapour-barrier, using non-corrodible plastic fixings or special bituminous lathing. Alternatively applying waterproof rendering internally to a sound wall can be effective. The floors may have only a thin covering of concrete and may need to be replaced with a new insulated concrete slab, but this takes away precious space by reducing available height. Finally, effective ventilation must be provided with extractor fans.

But the expense of all this can be considerable and the results are not always too successful. Better to console yourself with the thought that damp cellars are said to be better for storing wine!

It's lucky that you had no intention of using that musty old undercroft anyway. It does, however, provide a useful opportunity to check the floor timbers above, to ensure that they aren't built into damp walls, as this will cause rot in the ends of the joists that hold the floors up. Left to its own devices the rot will spread, until ultimately, in true horror movie style (albeit in slow motion), the foul fungus and spores of dry rot will come searching for further nourishment...

See sections on 'Wet rot' and 'Dry rot' below.

Single-glazed window timbers need regular painting, to protect against condensation.

Condensation

Americans call it 'toxic mould'. Steamed up windows, damp walls, and moist ceilings will eventually attract black speckled fungal mould. Even clothes and carpets can acquire the unpleasant smell of damp when there is excessive humidity. Patches of mould growth resulting from moist air condensing commonly occur where there is little air movement, eg behind bulky furniture and unventilated cupboards. In extreme cases the same black mould can even grow in the lungs, exacerbating bronchial or asthmatic conditions.

When steam or moist warm air in your house hits a cold surface it will cool and condense back to water. And the source of this water vapour? You and the family, just doing normal everyday things. The biggest living emitters of moisture are actually dogs and children. This is how many litres of water vapour are typically produced in a day:

A bath or shower	**1**
Tumble drier	**4**
Cooking	**2**
Two adults breathing and sleeping	**2**

Add to this pets, washing machines, kettles, gas heaters, and houseplants and you'll have well over 10 litres (up to 3 gallons) of water vapour a day, and it has to go somewhere.

The solution is to do exactly what you do in the car when it steams up: wind down the windows and turn up the blower, ie improve the ventilation. If you also improve the insulation and reduce emissions of vapour in the first place, the problem should be solved.

VENTILATION

1930s houses were built with open fireplaces, which together with additional vents in walls to ventilate bedrooms (required by the 1936 Public Health Act) ensured

ABOVE: The effects of damp and condensation on a cold solid floor.

RIGHT: Passive ventilation may not be enough (extractor fans are needed in bathrooms and kitchens).

a steady flow of air through the house, dispersing damp air and steam before it could condense into water.

But the modern obsession with eliminating draughts encourages condensation. Hidden areas like lofts and under timber floors also need cross-ventilation to keep them dry. If you do nothing else, fit extractor fans (with humidistats) in kitchens and bathrooms to expel all that humidity and cut the air moisture content.

INSULATION

This was not a strong point of original inter-war houses, which were generally built with zero loft insulation. Fortunately, many lofts will have been insulated since then; and cavity walls (which are considerably warmer than traditional solid walls) will in many cases have been injected with insulation. Making the walls and other cold surfaces in the house warmer means humid air won't condense back into water on impact. A good solution is to dry-line the inside of the main walls with insulated plasterboard, and to fit secondary or double glazing with trickle vents.

Warm moist air rises, so ceilings especially need to be insulated (eg with mineral wool in the loft to 270mm (11in) depth, allowing a path for ventilation above that. Constructing a new suspended ceiling below the original one using foil-backed plasterboard is an excellent alternative if there's space (vapour can pass through normal plasterboard).

Increasing room temperatures near cold surfaces like windows, say by locating radiators nearby, also helps reduce the amount of water vapour condensing, as warm air can retain more water, although a certain amount of condensation on single-glazed windows in wintertime is normal.

If you live in a semi or terrace, at least the party wall(s) are insulated – at next door's expense!

WEAK POINTS

Condensation weak points are found anywhere with a cold surface that humid air can reach. Major offenders are dormer windows (the ceilings and side 'cheeks' often have no insulation), cold walls behind kitchen units (the damp can cause hidden rot), and uninsulated pipes in concrete floors. The resulting pools of water are often mistaken for leaks or rising damp. Cavity walls can be at risk from 'cold-bridging', typically around window and door openings, or where cold metal wall ties sometimes attract condensation, as described earlier.

Wet rot

When the water content of wood rises above about 20 per cent (ideally over 30 per cent) it becomes attractive for rot. Wet rot is often found externally in woodwork such as window and door frames where water can settle. It also attacks window and door frames on the inside as condensation drips down the glass. Wet rot thrives best in damp, dark, and poorly ventilated

places: timber lintels and the ends of floor joists embedded in damp walls are areas typically at risk.

ERADICATION

It can be hard to tell wet rot and dry rot apart in the early stages, but all rots thrive in damp conditions. They are fungi, like mushrooms, so if you cut off their water supply by eliminating the source of the damp, they die.

Bad ventilation is often a big part of the problem, and must be improved so that damp can evaporate away. Most ground floors are made of timber boards over joists, which are particularly vulnerable to damp and attacks of rot. Airbricks are essential to ventilate and dry out damp under floors, but they're often blocked. To see if they're working, hold a lighted match against the grate – the flame should be drawn towards the opening. If not, rake out and clear them. You should have at least two or three airbricks on opposite walls, depending on the size of the house, for a through flow of air.

Very minor damage (eg to window frames) can sometimes be repaired by drying the affected wood and then using a wood hardener, a resin that soaks in. More serious damage requires the wood to be replaced; damaged joists, for instance, can be cut back to good wood, treated with preservative, and have an extension bolted on, not forgetting that any wood meeting a wall must be protected with a plastic DPC.

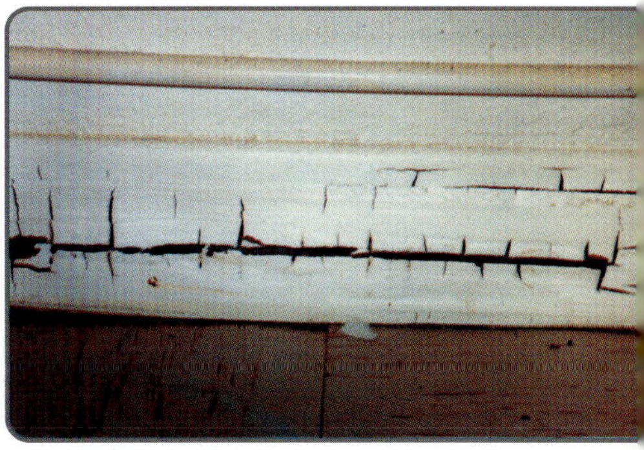

ABOVE: Wet rot in your skirting. (Photo: dampbuster.com)

RIGHT: Wet rot is often found at the base of door and window frames.

Dry rot

Breathe in that fresh air – and the chances are you will have just inhaled some spores of dry rot fungus. These are present in the air of most towns and cities, and older houses frequently provide a welcome invitation to the fungal spores to feed and breed. Those damp, badly ventilated spaces under timber floors are most suitable. Otherwise old window and door frames, timber panelling, or beams in contact with damp walls will do nicely.

Given time, the fungus will consume its wooden host, all the while emitting a decaying dank aroma. What is so insidious is that it can lie undetected, in roofs or behind skirting or under floors, before spreading throughout the house. Dry rot is extremely infectious and can be difficult to isolate once it gets a hold.

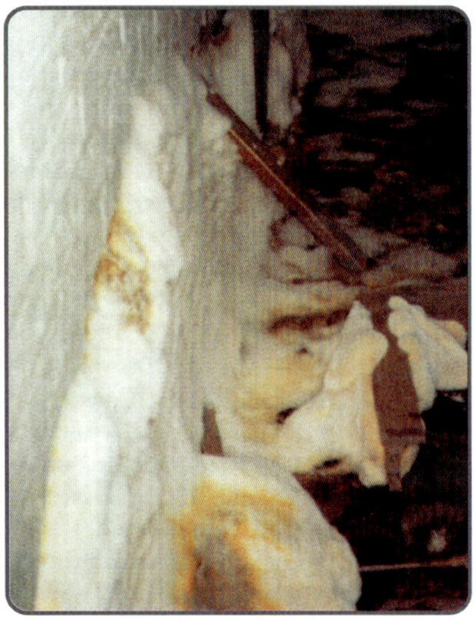

(Photo: EG Books)

When the airborne spores settle on damp timber, they send out thin grey web-like root strands that spread across the surface of the wood. The fungus feeds by sucking the moisture from the wood, making the timber dry, brittle, and structurally useless. These fungal root strands (hyphae) quickly multiply in moist conditions and rapidly become matted, completely engulfing the wood. They then adopt the appearance of cotton wool, becoming grey with lilac tinges and yellow patches, until finally morphing into a mature, pancake-shaped, rust coloured fruiting body, which emits millions of spores that float off into the air.

But the really creepy thing about dry rot is its rate of spread. The web-like strands can extend behind plaster or even penetrate through mortar and porous brickwork in search of more timber to consume. In severe cases, whole houses have become infected throughout in as little as three months, although a rate of 1m (3.3ft) a year is more typical.

ERADICATION

Damp wood + poor ventilation = rot. Some claim to be able to detect dry rot by smell (it is variously described as smelling like urine or mushrooms), and it is true that detector dogs have been successfully used to locate it. As with woodworm and wet rot, treatment first requires eliminating the source of the moisture and improving ventilation, as described above.

The standard treatment has for a long time been to cut away all timber for a metre beyond the evident signs of decay and burn it, replacing with new pre-treated timber and applying two coats of fungicide, soaking it well into sawn ends. Where fungal strands are in or near plaster, mortar, or masonry, it should be hacked off, cleaned up, and the surrounding area thoroughly sprayed with fungicide. Allow to dry out fully before replastering. NB: fungicides are toxic – see advice under 'Treatment' subheading below.

However, modern thinking takes a greener, less aggressive approach. It is now understood that the dry rot fungus, *(serpula lacrymans)*, needs about 25 per cent moisture to survive. So after the badly affected decayed areas are cut out and replaced, and the immediate area treated, the moisture levels should be reduced below 20 per cent using dehumidifiers, ventilation, and improved heating, so that the fungi cannot re-establish itself.

Beetle infestation

'Woodworm' is the generic name for wood-boring beetles and insects that eat away the wooden components of your house. When the moisture in wood gets above 18 per cent it can become attractive to insects. Furniture beetle is by far the most common type of woodworm; longhorn beetle and woodboring weevil are less common, and the infamous death-watch beetle is rarely encountered in British homes – but climate change may yet see termites dining out on your skirting boards.

As they munch their way through the nutritious cellulose, their boreholes eventually destabilise wood by hollowing out its insides, causing collapse. It is not unknown for people to fall through floors riddled with beetle.

And yet, you may have infestation in your house and not even know it. The grubs may be happily tunnelling around unseen inside the wood, often for several years. Eventually small holes appear on the surface (like dart holes) when the grubs gnaw and excrete their way out to emerge as adult beetles.

Some common places where you might find woodworm include:

- Floorboards, particularly where antique furniture might have stood, or near floor vents and around WCs (the grubs like the proteins in urine-soaked floorboards).

- Under the stairs, or in old cupboards, especially in plywood panelling.
- Behind skirting boards.
- The roof space, often around loft hatches (where it is warmer – they like to be cosy), or at eaves, where they may have flown in.

But moist timbers anywhere are at risk. Look for the signs of telltale 'flight-holes', about 1mm in diameter (or 3mm for death-watch). The big question is, is it an active colony? You may be looking at 20-year-old holes whose occupants have long since departed. If you see very fine timber dust near the holes from around April/May onwards, it is active. Fresh holes show clean, white wood inside. One simple test is to spread wax polish into the holes and monitor to see if they are reused.

Death-watch beetles prefer old hardwood, more often found on period buildings like churches; you may hear their trademark 'tapping' noise (like a fingernail tapped on wood a few times in quick succession).

Furniture beetles are matt brown and about 3mm long. Death-watch beetles look similar but are bigger, up to 9mm long. And take care not to kill those other shiny blue-black house-beetles as they are allies, being predators on larvae.

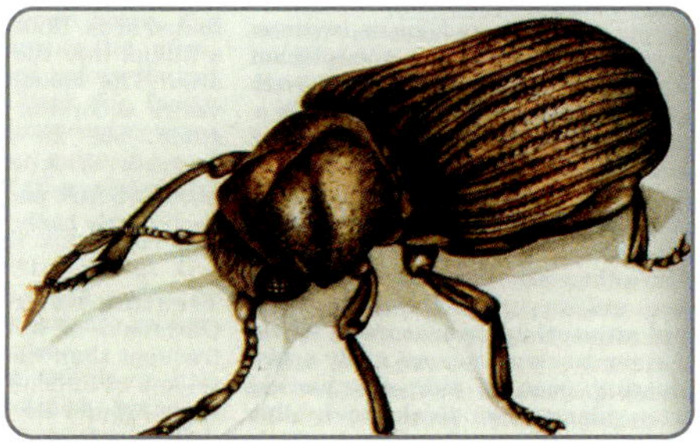

Common furniture beetle. (Photo: Liz & Tony Bomford/ ardea.com)

TREATMENT

A mild, localised attack can be treated by painting the damaged area with woodworm fluid (insecticide). However, grubs may be tunnelling unseen beyond the flight holes, so methods of treatment like low-pressure spraying may be necessary, but protective clothing, gloves, masks, and eye protectors must be worn. To treat floors, every fourth board should be taken up so a spray-lance can reach underneath and between the joists. Severely damaged timbers have to be cut out and replaced with pre-treated timber.

Timber treatment fluids often contain toxic chemicals and must not be inhaled. Water tanks and electric cables must first be protected and loft insulation removed. And because these fluids can be flammable, electricity should be turned off in the area for 24 hours.

But treatment need only really be carried out if infestation is active – most infestations seen today are old and may have already been treated several times. For more extensive infestation, specialist BWPDA-registered contractors can spray or pump quantities of insecticides into the house to poison insects living in the damp timber. On completion, professional installers will issue 20-year timber treatment guarantees. However, although insecticides might kill insect pests they also kill friendly natural predators like spiders.

An alternative 'green' solution is simply to take away the attractive damp environment so that insects and fungi slowly diminish. Timbers can be dried out using dehumidifiers and background heating, but not so quickly as to cause cracking. Pressure impregnating new timbers with chemicals has implications in terms of pollution and toxicity to wildlife and humans, and some Housing Associations specifically ban this method. Bats, a protected species, can be harmed by sprays.

Defect: Rising damp

SYMPTOMS

Damp plaster at ground floor main walls, musty smells, rotten skirting or floors; white 'tide marks' on walls.

Cause **Dampness from the ground rising up the wall by capillary action through porous brick due to a defective or bridged DPC**

Dampness is usually restricted to within about 750mm (2.5ft) above the ground floor level.

N.B. damp to internal walls is often caused by leakage from nearby pipework run below or within the floor.

Solution *Ensure that the outside ground level is at least 150mm (6in) below the DPC.*

- Reduce ground levels and clear away earth or debris. Ensure that surface water in the garden runs away from the house.
- Dig a shallow trench around damp walls to make a 'French drain', about 300mm deep x 300mm wide. The trench base should slope away from the house. Place a permeable liner at the base then fill with gravel (20–40mm size). Leave it loose – do not compress the gravel. This also helps prevent the risk of water entering the airbricks.
- If the DPC is defective or missing inject a new one, and replaster (see 'step-by-step'). If the property already has a modern injected DPC check the guarantee, as the work may be defective, or the affected plaster inside may not have been replaced. Or the problem may not be rising damp at all.

Defect: Damp patches on main walls

SYMPTOMS

Damp and stained plaster, often at higher levels.

Cause **'Cold bridging', often due to mortar dropped onto the wall ties during construction, allowing moisture to travel across the cavity**

Also, moist air in the cavity can condense on the cold metal ties. Often seen in the form of regularly spaced patches corresponding to locations of ties, or general dampness to cold spots around windows.

Solution

- Dry-line walls with vapour-check board – see 'step-by-step', Chapter 8.
- Cut down on steam and moist air produced indoors.
- Fill cavities with special loose mineral fill insulation to increase thermal insulation (but this may also restrict ventilation).

Modern cavity walls are ventilated with small weep holes in some of the vertical mortar joints to the brickwork. They also have 'cavity trays' over cold lintels to help condensation moisture evaporate or drain harmlessly away.

Cause **Porous or cracked masonry. Eroded mortar joints. Cracked render**

Solution *Overhaul brickwork and pointing to mortar joints. Make good defective render. Fill any gaps to walls, eg around pipes. Check any tile cladding for gaps.*

Cause **Leaking gutters or downpipes**

Solution *Overhaul or replace as necessary. See Chapter 4.*

Cause **Roof leaks. Defective flashings or stack brickwork, often showing as damp and stains around chimney breasts**

Solution *Repair stack/roof defects – see Chapters 2 and 3.*

Defect: Mould staining

SYMPTOMS

Recurrent black mould growth; general smell of dampness in the house; peeling paint and wallpaper.

Cause **Condensation due to humid or steamy air. Poor ventilation and insulation**

Solution This is a common problem, particularly evident to the ceilings, walls, and windows in bathrooms and kitchens (where most steam is produced). The steamy water vapour hits a cold surface and condenses back to water. Mould staining occurs particularly often in thin-walled rear extensions. The solution is:

- Insulate cold surfaces like walls and ceilings.
- Get steam out of the house: open windows and close bathroom doors.
- Improve ventilation. Fit extractor fans with a built-in humidistat to kitchens and bathrooms. Open up fireplaces. Fit windows with trickle vents.
- Reduce emissions of humid, moist air at source by ensuring tumble driers are ventilated to outside, and if possible minimise indoor clothes drying. And it can help to put the dog in the garage and cut down on boiling food!
- Use a heavy-duty dehumidifier.
- To get rid of the mould, clean off with water and a suitable fungicide. Finish with a coat of mould-resistant paint.

Defect: Damp patches to ground floor walls

SYMPTOMS
Damp and stained plaster, typically to side walls.

Cause **Penetrating damp** (see also rising damp)
Dampness penetrating through walls at ground level need not be rising damp. It can penetrate from adjoining garden walls etc.

Solution *Inject a vertical DPC to form a waterproof barrier between your house and any adjoining structures that might remain damp, such as garden or neighbouring walls.*

Defect: Damp decaying timber

SYMPTOMS
Wet wood is spongy and appears cracked and wrinkled along the grain.

Cause **Timber becoming wet over time, often below ground level, due to rising damp or plumbing or drainage leaks, etc**

Solution *Eliminate the cause of the damp. Cut out and replace affected timber. Treat adjacent wood with rot fluid. Wet rot will only persist while timber is moist.*

Defect: Soft, dry decaying timber

SYMPTOMS
Small cube-shaped cracking pattern; fungus growth; mushroom smell; grey strands extending out; wood is light brown colour and feels dry and brittle.

Cause **Timber infected by fungal spores**
Timber becoming moist (but not wet) in a cool, poorly ventilated area allows the spores of the dry rot fungus to thrive.

Solution *Eliminate the cause of the damp and treat timber. Improve ventilation. Badly affected timber cannot be treated and must be taken out and burned.*

Defect: Wood beetle infested timbers

SYMPTOMS
Fine wood-dust around flight holes (like dart holes); possible structural instability to timbers.

Cause **Insect larvae in wood**

Solution Insects fly in and lay eggs in wood; larvae hatch inside wood and eventually bore out. Old furniture stored in lofts can contain beetle, which then spreads.

Rectify causes of damp by controlled drying out of timbers and improved ventilation, and carry out chemical spraying of affected timber.

STEP BY STEP

TOOLS REQUIRED
- Drill and masonry bits (+ eye and ear protectors)
- Hammer and chisel
- Hand applicator gun
- Tools for re-plastering

MATERIALS
- Damp-proofing cream
- Render and plaster

Technical data

For suppliers of damp-proofing cream, damp meters, and information on specialists in treating 1930s houses, see www.ThirtiesHouse.co.uk.

Injecting a damp-proof course

Photos and text: Ian MacMillan and Freeman Dawson Ltd.

True rising damp is extremely rare, so injecting a new one should be a last resort. But although many 1930s houses have modern cavity walls they can still suffer from damp problems. If mortar or rubble was dropped down the cavity during construction the walls may in effect be solid, at least near ground level and bays were often built of solid 230mm (9in) thick brickwork regardless of the type of main wall construction (photo 1 below).

If your house has a row of little holes in the main walls just above ground level, it is probably where a chemical damp-proof course (DPC) has already been injected.

The main reason for providing a new DPC is to protect floor timbers and internal plasterwork from damp and rot. However, you may notice that the injection holes are actually above the level of any timberwork – in which case they will not be doing the intended job, as it is essential that they are positioned accurately. Fortunately injecting a DPC is a fairly easy job for a competent DIYer – if you're not bothered about guarantees.

Traditionally, this has involved drilling holes externally and then pumping in a chemical DPC silicone fluid from a 25-litre drum, using a pressure pump. But modern damp-proofing creams are a new development which make the job quicker, cleaner, and easier. They are safer (BBA-approved, less toxic, non-caustic, non-flammable) and are OK for tricky areas like party walls. Once installed, the cream diffuses into the wall before curing and forming a water-repellent resin that prevents the damp from rising up the wall. They only require a hand applicator gun instead of heavy duty electric pumps, hoses, and drums. For information on suppliers of damp-proofing cream, see www.ThirtiesHouse.co.uk.

For solid walls, modern best practice is to work from inside the house, although for cavity walls it is best to inject each leaf separately (accessing the outer wall from outside).

1 First check your floor levels to determine the lowest level of any floor joists and timberwork. Make sure that any external ground levels are at least 150mm below this level.

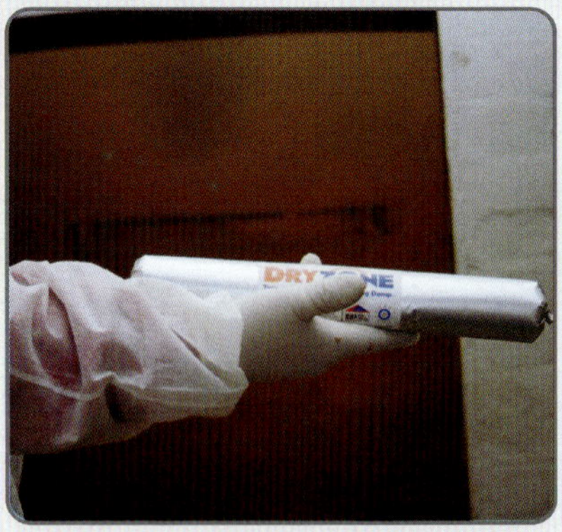

2 Insert DPC cream cartridge...

3 ...into applicator gun.

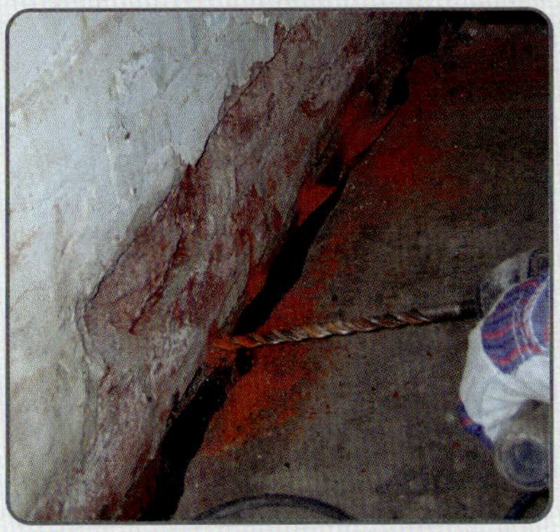

4 To give the walls time to start drying out, remove old plaster a week in advance of doing the work. Hack it off up to about 1m (40in) above floor level or about 450mm (18in) beyond the obvious edge of the damp, using a hammer and bolster chisel. Carefully lever the skirting boards from the walls being treated and remove any adjacent radiators etc. Lift floorboards next to the wall.

In this picture all the plaster was removed, since much of it had already lost its key to the brickwork. The original timber floor had been replaced some years ago with a new concrete floor, which has yet to be screeded. The new damp-proof membrane under the floor is visible at the edges and will need to line up with the injected DPC.

5 Using a 13mm (0.5in) masonry bit, drill holes at intervals of about 100mm (4in) along or very near a mortar course. For timber floors this should be below the level of the lowest timber beams, and for solid floors as close to the floor as possible.

6 Angle the hole downward slightly with the entry point as low as possible. For solid walls the holes should be about 150mm (6in) deep, and only about 50mm (2in) for each leaf of a cavity wall. Do not drill right through the wall (225mm), as this would weaken it.

As a result of the rising damp, internal plasterwork may have become saturated with hygroscopic salts, which will absorb any moisture in the atmosphere and if left will continue to give you problems with dampness. Replastering may be beyond the capability of many DIYers, in which case you will need to ensure that the plasterer is aware of your DPC work, as it is very important that the correct plaster is used – ordinary finishing plaster from your local DIY store is not appropriate.

Before replacing skirtings and timbers, treat the backs with preservative. Replace floorboards. Redecorate using a light wash of a breathable paint, with final decoration being left for at least six months.

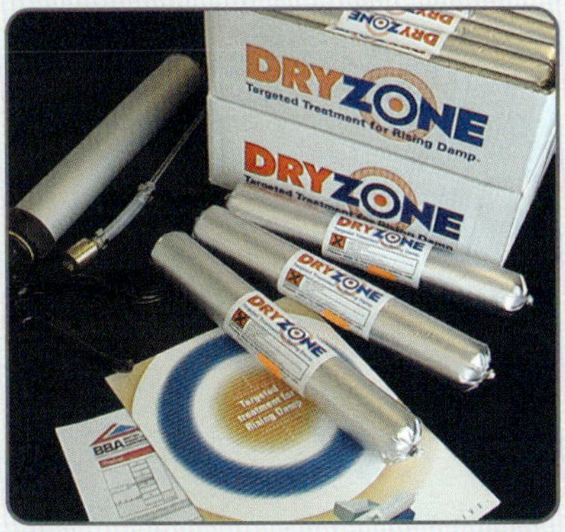

7 Cut open the nozzle of the cartridge containing the cream (like a mastic cartridge) and load into the applicator gun. It is advisable to wear protective gloves and clothing.

8 Slowly inject the cream into the first hole but stop when you see the cream dribbling back out – it expands slightly.

9 Repeat this process until all the holes have been filled and the wall saturated. Leave overnight, then clean off any excess. Leave walls to dry for a month or more (depending on the extent of dampness).

WINDOWS, DOORS & EXTERNAL JOINERY

Probably the single most important architectural feature of 1930s houses. Yet more money has been wasted fitting the wrong replacement windows and doors than on just about anything else. An inappropriate choice means, in effect, paying good money to knock thousands off a property's value.

In this chapter we investigate the key high-risk areas – from corroding steel windows to quietly rotting timber lintels that threaten ultimate collapse – as well as exploring such common problems as warping, splitting, loose joints, poor security and ingress of damp.

Nothing you can do to a house seems to cause more outrage than messing with the windows and doors. This is particularly true with 1930s houses, as the window design was fundamental to the architectural flavour of the whole building.

But the curse of the double-glazing salesman has cast a long shadow over many a road of 1930s semis – all manner of clashing styles in varying shades are there to behold. One person's dream aluminium bay is another's aesthetic nightmare. But, hey, let's get real here. Waking each day to puddles of water from rusting old windows and sticking doors isn't everybody's idea of fun. We may like the look of the originals, and estate agents advise that 'period' features should be retained, but in reality a well-insulated, quiet home, with secure modern replacement windows, is a very seductive proposition.

LEFT AND BELOW: Curved glass 'suntrap' windows.

The originals, left, and unsympathetic replacements next door.

The trick is to try and achieve the best of both worlds, ideally by overhauling and upgrading the original units. Otherwise it should now be possible to replace the original units with similar new equivalents. However, whilst there are numerous firms selling superb replica replacements for rattling old Georgian and Victorian sashes, it has not always been so easy to find anything matching 1930s styles, particularly curved 'suntrap' windows. Consequently many owners have been sold unsympathetic new units as the only option.

Talk to the guys whose job it is to rip out the old frames and they'll tell you that the quality of naturally-seasoned 1930s timber was generally far superior to much of the fast-grown, kiln-dried stuff used in a lot of modern housing. Whereas today's fascia boards will often have started decaying by their mid teens, many timbers on inter-war properties are still going strong. Problems are mostly associated with excessive weathering due to lack of protection as all external timbers require periodic decoration to survive.

Windows

The eyes and soul of a 1930s home originally came in a choice of two main styles: timber or metal framed casements. These modern hinged windows had almost completely superseded the ubiquitous sashes of the previous century.

Timber casements were normally designed with a 'cottagey' look, perhaps augmented with 'pretend' period features such as leaded lights and quaint coloured glass panes, some even featuring fake repairs for extra antique realism. Smart two-tone paintwork, in colours such as green and cream or black and white, is still evident today on many surviving originals.

Metal framed windows, on the other hand, spoke the language of the cool 'moderne' style, with their wide 'H' shape and advanced technology allowing impossibly thin glazing bars. Unfortunately many have since been replaced, losing their distinctive curved glass corners.

Meanwhile, the side walls on many houses were adorned with another 1930s design classic, the tall ladder-shaped staircase window spanning between two stories, or perhaps a splendid porthole. If fenestration is your thing, this is your kind of house.

photos can be an important clue. Substituting stylish new replicas of the original windows for inappropriate first-generation replacements is likely to pay off handsomely in terms of 'kerb appeal', ultimately adding to the property's value.

BAYS AND ORIELS

The archetypal 1930s house has a massively imposing front bay window, considered the 'must-have' fashion accessory of the time. Developers knew this was a good way to make a house look more expensive than it really was, and projecting bays attracted sunlight and fresh air as well as affording a good view of the street. A highly fashionable variation of the bay was the small, projecting oriel window upstairs, often found to the small bedroom above the front door.

Bay windows serving the living room and front bedroom were pretty much universal on privately-built housing. Gone were cumbersome Victorian stone mullions and ornate piers with narrow sash windows and fancy plasterwork. In came robust wooden frames with easy-to-open casements. To add a bit of style, panes of coloured glass would be incorporated in the top lights of bay windows or maybe traditional leaded lights.

And if one bay was not enough, an additional one at the

ORIGINAL AND GENUINE?

The chances are that the original windows will by now have been replaced. To discover what kind of windows your house was built with look in the back and side rooms, where there may still be one or two old ones; or some of the neighbouring houses may still have their original windows, which can be copied. Even old street

back would be an agreeable way to enhance the light in the dining room. Even many cheaper dwellings could boast a single-storey bay window, although most Council designs dispensed with such luxuries altogether.

There were three main styles of bay: the earlier square design with its Edwardian origins, the popular 'splayed' type with angled sides, and the more fashionable curved version. These were usually two-storey, with a choice of hipped or gabled roofs. Some had flat roofs finished in metal sheet, which, on houses of more cutting-edge design, might be surrounded by a rendered balcony parapet. Bays were often of solid masonry construction, sometimes part-tiled or rendered.

Unfortunately, bay windows can pose some serious structural problems. Like their Victorian predecessors, 1930s builders were sometimes tempted to skimp on foundations to bays, and as a result they can be prone to cracking and settlement. The thinking was that because the bay was a fairly light structure compared to the main house, the foundations didn't need to be too deep. But this thinking was mistaken. Even a dwarf garden wall needs foundations 450–750mm (1.5–2.5ft) deep to be clear of seasonal movement in the ground surface (topsoil). But dry summers, clay soil, sloping sites, and large trees growing nearby, combined with the lack of foundation depth, has caused some bays to go 'walkabout'. (See Chapter 5.)

But there's another, much more common problem, which isn't down to poor construction but rather to poor replacement work. When bay windows are renewed, it is critical not to permanently remove any vertical timber or steel supports to the roof or floor structure above. Many bays are topped with a large, heavy gable or hipped roof, and it is crucial to ensure that the new window frames can adequately transfer the load of the gable pediment and rafter feet down through the structure to foundation level. Those that have bowed out from being overloaded may, in severe cases, require partial rebuilding.

GLAZING

Glass was bedded into the rebate of the frame with linseed oil putty and secured with small metal pins called sprigs. Today, it is common to use small strips of beading to retain the glass, except in the case of modern aluminium or plastic windows, which employ special rubber or plastic seals. Older windows were often divided into smaller panes with timber or metal glazing bars (known as 'mullions and transoms'). Whereas modern sheet glass is available in thicknesses between 3mm (0.125in) and 6mm (0.254in), 1930s glass was typically about 3mm thick (24oz). This is usually adequate, but if necessary can be replaced with panes up to 6mm thick (48oz) depending on the rebate.

Elsewhere, more progressive 'moderne' builders were fitting curved 'suntrap' windows, so called because they were designed to receive as much sun as possible. New, supposedly health-giving 'Vitalite' glass, specially designed to admit ultra-violet light, was sold with the slogan 'Let health flood into your home'.

PROJECT: Reglazing a window

Replacing a damaged pane should be fairly simple (unless windows are leaded or have stained glass). Always wear thick gloves and eye protectors, and proceed as follows:

1. Very carefully chip out the old glass with a chisel, keeping your legs well clear of any falling shards. Old hard putty can be softened with paint stripper then chipped out. Clear and rub down the old frame rebate and remove the small metal sprig nails that retain the glass, using pliers.

2. Measure the opening, deducting 3mm (0.125in) from the height and width. Get a new pane of glass cut to size – modern 4 or 5mm thick glass should normally be suitable.

3. Roll some fresh putty into a line between your hands and press into the rebate in the frame. Carefully place the new glass into the puttied frame. To secure the pane, gently tap in some new sprigs, protecting the glass from the hammer with a sheet of thick card.

4. Make another line of putty to press over the edges of the glass, using a putty knife dipped in water to smooth into a bevel shape and cut off any waste. Wait at least two weeks for the putty to harden before painting.

LEADED AND COLOURED GLASS

Windows to the front and side often featured traditional leaded lights – panes formed from thin strips of lead in small diamond or lattice shapes. These were supplied from builders' merchants ready for fitting. One common problem is rain leaking in where the glass fits into the grooved lead strips (known as 'cames') but this can normally be rectified – see 'step-by-step'.

The Edwardian taste for expensive coloured glass had spread to mainstream housing by the 1930s as costs had reduced, and it now appeared in many hallways, porches, and bay fanlights, where it could be fully appreciated by visitors as well as helping to maintain privacy. To the side there might be octagonal or diamond-shaped windows, sometimes set into inglenook fireplaces. Because these faced next door, stained or obscured glazing here also

(Sheila Dixon Glass Designs)

avoided the risk of social embarrassment from the prying eyes of nosy neighbours.

The small windows to the upper sections of bays and to landings often featured frosted and coloured glass with the popular rising sun motif or images of flowers, sailing ships, lighthouses, seagulls, windmills, etc. It wasn't just 'Olde Worlde' houses that featured coloured glass: 'moderne' windows also adopted it, with modish chevrons or sunray patterns.

TIMBER CASEMENTS

At Number One in the window charts was the hugely popular 'neo-Tudor' casement with painted timber frames. These modern outward-opening windows are hinged from the frame at the side, with an iron 'hook and eye' stay at the bottom to allow graduated opening, and a 'cockspur' fastener at the side. Above the main casements there were usually top-hung opening lights.

Although generally robust, timber windows of all kinds are vulnerable to rot from damp – either externally from lack of painting or internally from condensation. Typical problems with casements include windows that are hard to close, cracked glass, and worn fittings, but they are usually quite easy to refurbish, as described below.

METAL WINDOWS

Although not the only manufacturer in town, there is one name that is synonymous with steel windows – Crittall. Their mass-produced, stylish yet inexpensive steel windows caught the 'moderne' mood of the moment perfectly, and literally millions were supplied and fitted.

People had tired of draughty old Victorian sashes that jammed and rotted and were hard to paint, redolent of Dickensian smog and the workhouse. The new fashion was for light, airy, and well-ventilated buildings, and these new large windows with their wide horizontal emphasis and strong metal frames fitted the bill. They were often painted white (or fashionable black), with side-hung main casements and top-hung opening lights, often wrapping

around curved corners (technically referred to as 'curved on-plan H type').

But these revolutionary new steel windows had a serious flaw: they relied for protection only on a thin coating of painted zinc or toxic red lead. So within as little as 30 years of their installation problems had started to appear. Sometimes they became distorted, causing gaps around the frame, but more commonly rust took hold, cracking the glass as the metal expanded. Hence they were the first to be targeted by double-glazing salesmen – which is a shame, since they can normally be refurbished (see below) and exact replicas can now be made, even down to the curved glass. In listed buildings, many of the corroded original steel casement windows have been replaced with double-glazed steel windows (with aluminium sills) that closely match the original profiles.

PROJECT: Restoring metal windows

Metal windows are routinely criticised for being prone to condensation. But that's no reason to just hoick them out and chuck them into the nearest skip. Even ones that appear to be well beyond repair can often be restored in situ.

Steel windows made after the mid-1950s were normally 'hot-galvanised', with a tough silvery finish evident beneath the paint. Original 1930s ungalvanised metal windows are more likely to suffer from corrosion, but the surface rust usually looks much worse than it really is.

Common problems include distortion, rust, excessive build up of paint, and failed hinges and fittings, but a well-restored metal window will last as long as many new replacements yet will cost far less and be more pleasing in appearance, being an original part of the building. Planning consent shouldn't be an issue, even if the house is listed or in a conservation area.

Windows can be overhauled in situ as follows:

1 Remove the glazing and old putty from the metal frames. Strip old paint from the surface of the metal. Wire brushes or grinders can then be used to remove surface rust. Of the primers originally used, red lead was the most effective, but it is highly toxic and waste removed during cleaning should be treated accordingly.

2 After cleaning, any remaining corroded sections of metal can be identified. It is the bottom rail or sill that is most likely to deteriorate though prolonged contact with moisture, and is more vulnerable than the side jambs or heads. Although rarely found, should there be any sections that are too badly corroded to provide adequate structural support, the frame will need to be removed and professionally overhauled. See below.

3 Light surface rust will appear as soon as cleaning is finished, so a protective coating of sprayed zinc primer or similar pre-paint treatment for ferrous metals should be applied as soon as possible.

4 It is important to use the correct materials when refitting the glass: putty is traditional and normally preferable to mastic.

Where damaged windows have to be removed for restoration, the frames and glazing should be protected with heavy gauge plastic sheeting, and the openings temporarily boarded for security. Ideally every item should be photographed before work commences, to ensure everything is later returned to its original location. Severe cases of rust may require specialist 'acid-pickling' or blasting with fine grit 'air abrasives'. Defective steel may be repaired by cutting out the corroded section and welding in place a replacement piece, made from a similar material to the same profile. When reinstalling the refurbished window, the metal or timber surrounds are bedded to the masonry with mortar incorporating a suitable DPC surround and are pointed up, with any gaps to the reveals sealed.

SASH WINDOWS

In private housing, casement windows had completely superseded Victorian sashes. Paradoxically, some large Council developments persisted with sashes, as had some 1920s neo-Georgian grand houses architect-designed for the wealthy few.

The most common problems encountered are that the sash cords become clogged with paint or become frayed and break. But sashes that have become loose and rattle can often be fixed by fitting a new fastener catch and refitting the timber beading which holds the sashes in place. You can upgrade your existing windows with DIY sash window kits. See www.ThirtiesHouse.co.uk.

DOUBLE AND SECONDARY GLAZING

Although today we don't necessarily share the 1930s passion for fresh air, good ventilation in the house is now recognised as important in preventing condensation problems. But even in well-ventilated houses a certain amount of condensation on single-glazed windows in cold weather is hard to avoid.

To comply with Building Regulations, replacement windows now have to be double-glazed, even though this actually ranks fairly low in the league-table of cost-effective energy conservation measures. Double-glazing consists of two vacuum-sealed panes of glass with a gap typically of at least 20mm between them. The panes are sealed at the edges into a single unit that is fitted into the window frame. Yet it is surprisingly common to find units that have 'misted' after only a few years, defective seals having allowed in moisture that looks like condensation but is actually trapped inside the cavity. The bad news is that there's nothing you can do except replace misted units – and when one unit goes, the others are sure to follow. Hence the importance of warranties.

Secondary glazing is an independent system of windows fitted to the inner window frame that can also cut down noise, prevent draughts, and help heat insulation. The gap between the outer and inner windows is consequently much wider than in sealed double-glazed units. The secondary frames should be aligned with the main window frames to cause the least possible visual disruption. The advantages are that it is cheaper than replacing the original windows and should not interfere with their appearance. Also, the bigger the gap between the exterior and interior panes the better the sound and thermal insulation should be; but in practice this tends to be a less efficient alternative.

REPLACEMENT WINDOWS

The difficulty in making single-glazed windows condensation-proof or combining them with double-glazed sealed units has encouraged many owners to replace them. The trouble is, some new windows can look

Inappropriate anodised aluminium replacements.

hugely inappropriate, ruining the character of the building (to the extent that it can be hard to differentiate them from plainer 1950s houses). This is particularly evident where a pair of semis have windows of wildly different styles.

To be fair, it has not always been easy to find specialist firms that are able to match original 1930s styles, but today replacements are available that precisely imitate the original window architecture and yet incorporate double-glazing.

It's advisable to think twice before fitting new 'off-the-peg' windows yourself. The money saved may be small compared to the value you can add to the house by having good quality 'new originals' fitted. Also, ready-manufactured DIY windows come in strict factory-made sizes which may not match the old openings, particularly since houses often settle over time and movement to the walls may have caused openings to distort and windows to stick – some still bear the scars of wartime bomb damage.

Building Regulations (Part F) now require new windows to meet certain thermal standards, which can affect their appearance. However, if your house is listed or in a conservation area you will need to talk to the planners first, as the requirements of Building Control may be overridden by those of the Conservation Officer. Get them to clarify any such issues before you order new windows.

Modern replacements come in a variety of styles and materials:

- Replacement timber casements: if chosen carefully these can look very similar to the originals, and it may be possible to retain some of the old timber framework. Because old buildings tend to move with the seasons, timber is a good choice, being relatively conducive to 'easing and adjusting' – ie it can be planed to fit. But poorly chosen timber replacements have the double drawback of not only often looking out of place, but also of needing periodic maintenance.

Authentic replicas in UPVC.

- UPVC double-glazed (plastic) windows: although much derided, they are easy to live with and provide good insulation. The trouble is they can also ruin the look of an old building, and many are poorly manufactured or carelessly fitted. Some, however, can be made to achieve a good imitation of the original casements, complete with reinstated coloured glass panels and curved panes.
- White aluminium windows: these look similar to UPVC and are often set within tough hardwood surrounds, but because metal tends to be cold they can attract condensation unless insulated internally. Older, silver-coloured anodised aluminium windows invariably appear strikingly incompatible and are best ripped out and replaced.
- Galvanised steel: ideally it is best to replace like with like. Original Crittall-type steel windows were not 'hot-galvanised', hence their problems with rust. Modern replacements are a different animal altogether. Made from rolled steel, long-term corrosion resistance is achieved by 'hot-dipped galvanising', where the frames are immersed in a bath of molten lead and zinc at temperatures reaching 450°C and then polyester powder coated. These replica 'moderne' windows are dearer than UPVC but should look just right, and incorporate the modern benefits of double-glazing, safety glass, and good security. They can be manufactured using exact matching sections, even incorporating some salvaged original fittings and glass. They are available in a range of colours and finishes, often with a 15-year warranty.

Sometimes after the installation of new unvented sealed double-glazing serious condensation problems can arise elsewhere in the house. If you've read Chapter 6 you'll know that 'trickle vents' are important in helping to alleviate condensation, and these can sometimes be fitted retrospectively (eg in hardwood frames).

Another problem occasionally encountered when windows are replaced is the awful discovery that the brickwork over the lintel has dropped, or even that the lintel is missing, necessitating expensive structural improvements and emergency temporary support. One early warning of this may be when the old frames have become bowed or casements have jammed – see 'Defects' below. Before commencing replacement works, it is worth also bearing in mind that in any one room the openable area of any window must be at least one-twentieth of the floor area of that room.

SILLS AND REVEALS

In a change from tradition, the huge stone sills favoured by Victorian builders had largely been superseded by neat modern timber sills integral to the frames, although tiled sills were occasionally also used (a few Council designs persisted with stone sills). Softwood timber frames often had sills of durable oak, this being an area highly vulnerable to rot.

The important thing with sills is to check that there's a clear groove underneath (under the front edge, set back about 8mm). This allows water to drip harmlessly off the sill instead of tracking back underneath to the wall, where it can penetrate and cause rot. If the groove is clogged with paint, or doesn't exist, cut a new groove with a router or chisel. Also, rainwater should run swiftly off the tops of sills to prevent rot, so they must be sloped away from the window. If they are flat, or you can see small puddles on the surface, wooden sills will need to be planed into shape while stone sills will need to be resurfaced with mortar.

No sill here means greater risk of damp problems.

Windows were traditionally rebated – set back at least 25mm (1in) from the outer wall in order to provide some protection from driving rain. Gaps at the junctions of window or door frames with the surrounding masonry 'reveals' are a common maintenance issue, normally due to erosion or slight settlement in the house over time, or as a result of poor replacement window workmanship.

The solution for gaps less than 10mm (0.4in) is to seal with a suitable mastic. Larger, irregular gaps require pointing up with mortar. But if the gap to upstairs window reveals is obviously wider at the top, this may be indicative of 'roof spread', where the roof has pushed the upper walls out – see Chapter 2.

ROOF WINDOWS

The days of households employing gangs of servants living in pokey attic rooms had gone for ever, so 1930s roofs were rarely built with integral windows – with the exception of those glamorous new house types, chalet bungalows. Today, the generously proportioned roofs of this era are much appreciated for their conversion potential, and most windows found at roof level will therefore have been added in relatively recent times.

New dormers and rooflights should not jar with the existing architecture and planning consent may well be needed, at least for the front elevation. In order that new openings in a roof do not weaken its structure, the adjoining rafters should be doubled-up for strength, and, as for all structural work, Building Control must be notified in advance. The aim should be to use the smallest number and size of windows possible, and to respect the general architectural theme. Instead of a dormer, less intrusive replicas of traditional rooflights are available; alternatively double-glazed 'Velux' type windows, supplied complete with flashings, may be suitable.

Defect: Rot to timbers or gaps at corner joints

SYMPTOMS

Soft decayed wood; flaking paint; sticking windows.

Cause **Water penetration causing deterioration of timber**

Solution *To test for rot, check to see if the wood is soft and spongy and can be dug away with a screwdriver.*
See Chapter 6. Sills and lower frames are especially vulnerable. If parts of the timber are in bad condition, it may be possible to cut away the damaged area, treat the remaining sound wood with preservative fluid (take care!), and graft new sections of replacement timber into place. In severe cases complete replacement may be necessary, but localised damage from rot can be dealt with as follows:

- Cut out areas of rotten wood and remove any loose material.
- Using a two-part wood repair system, first use the brush-applied chemical hardener to strengthen the wood by reinforcing any remaining decayed wood (it also adds a moisture-repellent seal).
- Then apply the filler paste that sets to a solid material that can later be sanded and planed. Preservative tablets can be inserted in holes drilled in the sill or frame, which release a preservative into the timber.
- Finally, the timber should be primed and an undercoat and two topcoats of exterior paint applied.

Cause **Corner joints worked loose**

Solution *Flat, galvanised L-shaped steel brackets can bridge the damaged area after cutting out any decayed timber.*
The brackets can be countersunk and the joint treated and repaired with epoxy filler. Alternatively, secure with three glued dowel pegs: two through the side of the stiles and one from the front. Timber casements that stick may simply require routine maintenance – planing, sanding, and then painting to protect them from damp.

Cracks and gaps at joints can be treated by cleaning off flaking paint, cutting out any rotten wood, and then treating, priming, and filling. Cracked or loose putty must be renewed. Finally, paint with undercoat and one or two topcoats.

Defect: Movement to bay

SYMPTOMS

Distortion; internal cracking; bowing out, usually at central and higher levels.

Cause **Replacement windows have insufficient vertical strength to support loadings from roof or floors above. Or shallow foundations have allowed differential movement to the main house**

Solution *Ensure that the new window frames can adequately transfer the loads through the bay structure to foundation level.*
Specialist advice will be needed, and temporary structural support whilst windows are removed and new supports installed. Some degree of movement is normally acceptable, but in severe cases rebuilding or underpinning may be necessary. See Chapter 5.

Defect: Cracking over windows and doors

SYMPTOMS

Jammed casements; broken glass; cracked masonry above; bowed frames.

Cause **Missing or defective lintels**

Solution Some cavity walls were built without lintels to the outer leafs, instead relying on the window or door frame to support the masonry above. This commonly becomes evident when windows are replaced and stresses on the masonry above cause it to crack and drop. If the new window frames have sufficient strength and casements operate satisfactorily, the brickwork may just need to be pointed up. At worst, new lintels will need to be provided, with localised rebuilding to masonry. More rarely, old timber lintels in solid walls may have rotted and need to be replaced. See Chapter 5.

Doors

The front door and its porch surround was a major architectural opportunity to broadcast the glories of modern design. Inspired Odeon-like entrances can be seen vying for attention with glorious baronial arches complete with heraldic motifs, while the more 'Jacobethan' house would boast a sturdy oak front door studded with nail heads and strap hinges.

Most houses had a painted front door, typically with vertical lower panels under stained or patterned glazed panes, in popular oval or rectangular shapes. It was usual for halls to gain more light from

additional windows to the sides of the door frame, with small coloured panes, and perhaps a fanlight above. Porches were never fully enclosed, so front doors were usually visible, together with a prominent quarry-tiled or brick front step, brightly coated in Cardinal red paint polished to perfection.

Good quality front doors would typically be of oak, or more commonly of pine Douglas fir, about 44mm (1.5in) thick with moulded panels, set within a spruce frame. To the kitchen, there may have been a part-glazed, panelled garden door and a pair of fairly narrow 'French doors' (a.k.a. 'French windows') leading from the dining room into the back garden.

COMMON DEFECTS

Being constantly exposed to the weather, an external door may become damaged beyond repair if neglected. It is quite time consuming and costly to fit a replacement door, so it is worth repairing original doors where possible. Joinery near ground level is always at risk, particularly the bases of door

frames, which can become saturated with moisture from the ground. Small areas of rot in an original door may be repaired using special filler, as described above for windows. However, if the existing door is only a cheap modern one, replacement is likely to be preferable.

Choosing a replacement door for older houses isn't always easy. Sizes can be non-standard, frames may be distorted, and styles can't always be matched, although specialist firms will make replicas – at a price. Doors manufactured in UPVC come as a complete unit including the frame – they're maintenance-free but are visually inappropriate. Timber is still the most popular material for replacement doors, but avoid the temptation to buy a significantly over-large door in the hope of cutting it to fit, as anything more than minor cutting can structurally weaken doors by slicing through joints.

If you're planning on altering an existing door or forming a new opening, it is important to ensure that there is an effective DPC below the frame, aligned with the main DPC in the walls to reduce the risk of damp.

A common defect with old doors is where the bottom rail has rotted to the extent that the door needs to be partially rebuilt with new wood. The rail can be replaced by removing the door from its hinges and sawing through each joint between the rail and the vertical stiles to the sides. The plywood panels can be slid out and replaced if necessary. Depending on the size of the door, a new rail can be made from three pieces of planed 100 x 50mm (4 x 2in) treated softwood, cut to shape and positioned between the two stiles to form a new bottom rail 300mm (12in) high. It is secured by drilling through the stiles from the outer sides and driving hardwood dowelling pegs through into the new timber, having first applied exterior PVA glue, then clamping the structure until dry. Finally a new weatherboard and water bar should be fitted (see 'Defects' below) and the door re-hung.

Older doors are often heavier than modern ones and need to be hung with three 100mm (4in) brass butt hinges. Hinges should be fitted about 150mm (6in) from the top and 200mm (8in) from the bottom, and always fitted to the door first, not the frame.

If original doors or windows need to be stripped, it is best to use a paint stripper rather than sending them away for 'hot dipping' in tanks of caustic solution, which can dissolve old animal glues, making joints widen and warp.

Common door problems include:

- Warping: it is not normally cost-effective to try to fix a warped door, although a good carpenter can usually adjust or repair light warping.
- Split panels: repair should be straightforward. The mouldings that retain the panel can usually be prized off and the panel replaced with plywood.
- Loose joints: if the top or bottom rails have come loose at the join with the stiles, the door will have to be dismantled and the joints glued and clamped.
- Sticking doors: if the door sticks in wet weather, it is likely the door itself has distorted. If it sticks in dry weather, this usually indicates that the frame has changed shape. Frames should have a DPC around them to prevent damp from the adjoining masonry causing decay. Loadings over frames need to be supported by suitable lintels or the frame will deflect – cracking in the wall above may confirm the problem. A distorted door needs to be removed and trimmed with a plane. If the paint is poor the door may be damp and must be allowed to dry out first.
- Door hinges, knobs, and fittings may be broken or worn, requiring replacement.

Defect: Rain blowing under door

SYMPTOMS

Damp floors, sticking door.

Cause **Rain runs down the face of the door and back underneath instead of dripping off the front**

Solution *Fit a weather board (with a grooved drip underneath, as for sills) to the bottom front of the door, and fit a water bar (a projecting strip of metal or plastic) into the threshold underneath the door.*

This requires the door to first be taken off its hinges so a rebate can be cut along the bottom edge.

The door sill should also be significantly higher than the ground level outside – at least 150mm (6in).

Security

Your local police Crime Prevention Officer will give free advice on home security. Surface-mounted locks should be fairly easy to fit to casements following the manufacturer's instructions: they are locked by a push-button action and unlocked with a key, and those for metal windows come with self-tapping screws. Consider also fitting blocking bolts for cockspur handles and staybolts for the stay fasteners. Neater looking but trickier to install are door-style mortise bolts bedded within the casement frame.

Window restrictors limit the amount of opening to a window, particularly useful with young children around. Modern replacement windows should have integral security locks, but it is worth checking that the beading is fitted internally so that it can't be prised off and the panes removed. Doors should have a separate five-lever mortise lock and a deadlocking cylinder Yale lock so that if a burglar breaks the glass he can't reach in and turn the latch. Additional rack bolts or conventional sliding bolts are also advisable on external doors.

NB Always remember that an emergency escape may be necessary in the event of fire, so keys must be readily accessible. Consider fitting 'thumb turn' rack bolts, or cylinder locks that can be opened without a key from inside.

Original sliding security grilles.

External timbers

Fascias are the horizontal timber boards that run along the eaves at the base of the roof slopes, to which the gutters are often fixed. They usually cover the rafter ends, with a soffit board infill underneath to make 'boxed' eaves, but may sometimes instead be attached direct to the brickwork.

Soffits may be of timber boarding or, on cheaper houses, of lath and plaster or perhaps asbestos cement. They can be

a useful place to fit grilles for loft ventilation (unless they're of asbestos, which mustn't be cut or drilled). Bargeboards are similar timber facings that run along the verges at gables (originally called 'vergeboards').

The 1930s craze for 'mock-Tudor' meant a profusion of black-painted half-timbering with 50mm (2in) thick softwood planks set in render, or pseudo-rustic weatherboarded gables painted with creosote. All terribly stimulating visually, but also something of a maintenance issue.

Timberwork ardorning mock-Tudor gables is not always purely decorative. Lintel beams over windows, together with their columns either side may support roof and wall loadings. Decay here can require (expensive) structural replacement work.

Naturally, being so exposed to the weather makes external timberwork particularly vulnerable, although much of it has proved surprisingly durable where regularly decorated due to the original skilled joinery and relatively good quality of the timber. Where decay is found, there is often a contributing factor such as leaking guttering causing rot to fascias.

The solution for decorative timberwork is pretty much as described for rot to windows and doors. Small, localised areas of decay can be cut out and the remaining timber treated and filled. Areas of more extensive rot will need replacement with pre-treated timber.

Owning an old house is rather like running a vintage car: the history and character can justify a premium in the value, but it comes at a price. To prevent deterioration, external timbers demand regular repainting. Recommended intervals between paint cycles vary from three years to five, depending on how aggressive the weather and exposed the location is. If your paint is crazed, flaking or peeling, the timbers will obviously need a good going over. But first check the advice given in Chapter 11 about wise precautions to be taken when dealing with lead paint, as original linseed oil based exterior paints of this age could contain white lead.

The other option, neglect, is always dearer in the long run, as replacing original timbers is not cheap, and potential buyers will knock large sums off the sale price at the first sight of rot. Exterior painting is best carried out between May and September, when the moisture content of the wood is lower. Compared to paint, wood stain is typically less durable, while varnish can become brittle from UV rays quite swiftly, and both require more frequent redecoration. With luck, thorough preparation may reveal a sound initial paint base only requiring spot priming and a finishing coat. Otherwise, the correct approach is to strip the timbers to bare wood with a blowlamp, cut out and replace any decayed wood, and treat end grains with preservative. After sanding and rubbing down, follow the five stages as for new wood: knotting, priming, stopping, undercoat, and finish coat(s). Finally, stage six: sit back and admire your gleaming, freshly-painted timbers – and the visibly enhanced value of your home.

STEP BY STEP

Repairing a leaded window

Leaded windows, or 'leadlights', were widely used as a decorative feature on 1930s houses. Many houses have simple leadlights in the top sashes of the front bay windows. Some also have elaborate designs in front porches, garage doors, and internal room dividers, with decorative patterns made from coloured glass.

The basic techniques for making leadlight windows have remained largely unchanged for centuries (although some mass produced 1930s windows comprised a single sheet of glass decorated with lead strips rather than traditional small panes joined together). The pattern is formed using H-section strips of lead or copper known as 'cames', which are soldered together where they join.

Although there are limits to the repairs that can safely be tackled at home, small repairs and general maintenance should be fairly straightforward. However, stained glass tends to be a specialist area. Professional repairs are usually carried out by removing the entire leadlight panel and laying it flat on a bench.

CLEANING

Glass can be cleaned with a mixture of distilled water and methylated spirits, applied with a soft clean cloth, allowed to dry, and then polished off with a chamois leather. Modern detergents should not be used on lead or glass and commercial window cleaning materials will leave a discoloration on both surfaces. However, neutral soap can be used to remove organic growth.

TOOLS REQUIRED

- Glass cutter
- Putty knife
- Pliers
- Soft cloth
- Gloves. (Lead can be poisonous and glass is sharp!)

Leadlight repairers also use the following special tools:

- Oyster knife
- Larrikin

MATERIALS

- Matching glass
- Black putty

REMOVAL

Before dismantling a complete frame glazed with leaded lights, a useful recommendation is to cover both sides of the glass with clingfilm, which sticks to the glass and helps prevent the individual panes from falling apart. Even so, just taking the glazing out in one large piece may weaken the joints enough to cause them to leak. In most instances the lead cement that holds the glass in the cames will also need overhauling and the lead around the edges of the glazing may need to be replaced.

RE-LEADING

This tends to be a specialist job. If a leaded light needs to be dismantled, a useful tip is to first photograph it or take a 'rubbing' to exactly record the diamond or rectangular pattern of the glass panes and lead cames. All the original glass should be kept for reuse and labelled.

LEADLIGHT REPAIRS

Small leaks can often be rectified by prising the came open slightly with a chisel and working in putty mixed with gold-size (from builders' merchants). The came can then be pressed back into place, working from the outside. Individual pieces of broken glass can be repaired in situ as described below.

1 Here a damaged single pane in a leaded light window needs to be replaced.

2 Suitable new replacement glass that will provide a near match to the original should be available from specialist suppliers. It is best to take a small sample of the original glass (or at least a photo) to the glaziers. The dappled clear glass used in this window is called 'small flemish'. If matching new glass is not available, specialist suppliers normally keep a stock of suitable second-hand glass types, such as crown glass and muff glass.

3 An 'oyster knife' is a specialist tool with its end bent into a slight curve. Use it to scrape the old cement out from between the glass and the came.

4 Starting on one side of the broken pane, use the oyster knife to gently prise up the 'leaf ' of the came and raise it away from the glass. Work in short sections, and try to lift the leaf cleanly, without leaving a jagged edge to it. The leaf should be bent up so that it is at about 90 degrees to the glass.

5 Next repeat the procedure, using the oyster knife to raise the leaf of the came on each of the next two sides. Note that the soldered joints will be harder and tougher than the lead of the came, and will require extra care to raise without damaging them.

6 Smash out the broken glass from the centre of the pane, collecting the pieces on a sheet or in a bucket.

7 Remove broken pieces from the sides. (Always wear gloves!)

8 Scrape out excess cement from the cames using the oyster knife.

9 Cut the new glass to shape by holding it up against the opening and running the glass cutter along the line of the exposed came. Repeat several times until the glass is well scored. Unlike glass which is to be fitted to an ordinary window with putty, leadlight glass should be cut to the exact size of the opening making no allowance for bedding.

10 Having scored the glass to the correct shape, very carefully snap off the surplus glass from the new pane. If you are not experienced at glass cutting, it can help to place the body of the glass pane over a hard flat surface with the surplus part projecting over the edge, prior to snapping.

11 Then carefully 'nibble' the corners of the new glass pane with a pair of pliers to allow for the space taken up by the soldered joints.

12 Fit the new pane into the old opening. It should fit snugly between the open cames.

13 Gently fold the leaf of each came back into place using a tool with a curved edge, to avoid the surface of the lead from being damaged. We have used a 'larrikin' (a specialist tool made from hard timber like mahogany). Any remaining undulations in the leafs of the cames can be straightened out by running the oyster knife along the edge.

14 Seal the joints between the glass and the came by pushing black putty into the gap.

15 Remove excess putty with the putty knife. The appearance can be improved by brushing Plumbers Black or Zebrite grate polish onto the lead.

CEILINGS AND INTERNAL WALLS

Cracks and bulges appearing in old ceilings can be a worry – are they merely superficial, or evidence of structural failure elsewhere in the building? Here we investigate common problems with original 1930s lath & plaster ceilings, as well as examining the materials that were starting to supersede them – fibreboard, plasterboard and asbestos cement. Also, the crucial difference between 'loadbearing' and partition walls is explained, plus how to minimise noise transmission, construct a suspended ceiling and create warmer rooms with basic dry lining.

Ceilings

The old joke about the lining paper being the only thing holding the ceiling plaster in place has some truth in it. Ceilings of this age may conceal a number of potential dangers, including that of asbestos panels, so for peace of mind's sake it's important to know that your ceilings are sound.

Impatient with tradition, builders of 1930s houses dispensed with the old space-wasting Victorian high-ceilinged rooms that were so draughty and expensive to heat. Gone, too, were the unnecessarily ornate plaster cornices and decorative roses (although discreet cornices were sometimes applied). Instead, rooms were now functionally designed to efficient modern dimensions – a typical ceiling height of around 2.3m (7.5ft) – as well as being brighter, with electric lighting and large airy windows. Modern materials were also beginning to change the way homes were built.

PLASTERBOARD

Manufactured sheets of plasterboard were starting to become popular in mainstream housing, having been made in the UK since 1916. Yet despite its increasing use by more progressive contractors in both private and public housing, many builders still persevered with traditional labour-intensive lath and plaster. Even architects initially tended to regard plasterboard with suspicion as a rather inferior material, opting instead for ceilings either of lath and plaster or of radical new reinforced concrete.

Essentially, plasterboard comprises sheets of compressed rigid gypsum plaster sandwiched between heavy duty lining paper. Today, boards are available in thicknesses of 9.5 and 12.5mm (0.375 and 0.5in) traditionally fixed to the ceiling joists with, respectively, 30 or 40mm (1.2 or 1.6in) clout nails, driven just below the surface without breaking the paper. Today screws are used instead of nails, due to their relative ease of fitting with cordless screwdrivers and the lack of vibration from hammering (which can loosen old plaster). The joints are then filled and scrimmed with tape and the surface skimmed with a thin plaster coat or a painted/textured finish. Faults tend to manifest themselves as hairline cracks along joints – see 'Defects' below.

LATH AND PLASTER

Some things hadn't changed. Lath and plaster was the traditional method of plastering, dating back to the dawn of time, and although still fairly widely used, the 1930s witnessed its death throes as it was steadily superseded by modern plasterboard. It comprised thin strips of wooden lath (about 25mm/1in wide) nailed under the ceiling joists, spaced about 5mm (0.2in) apart. Plaster, traditionally made from lime mixed with sand, was normally applied in two or three layers of increasingly fine finish. First a render base coat (mixed with horse hair for strength) was spread on the underside of the laths to create a key by being

squeezed through the gaps while still soft. This was followed by a floating coat, and it was finally skimmed with a setting coat of pure lime or plaster of Paris to give a smooth finish.

Lath and plaster ceilings are thicker and have better insulating properties than the skimmed plasterboard variety, but are not so able to cope with vibration and slight movement: slam a door in anger, and you risk clumps of thick ceiling plaster raining down. They look chunkier and generally not as even as modern ceilings, and they are more likely to be finished with lining paper. But in many older houses, some areas of plaster will have become 'live' and will sound hollow when you tap them. The first coat may have lost its key to the lath, or the coats themselves may have separated.

To see whether you have this type of ceiling, take a look under the loft insulation or lift a bedroom floorboard and check for lots of small timber laths with creamy blobs of plaster between them.

ABOVE: Fibreboard.

FIBREBOARD

You've doubtless heard of MDF (medium density fibreboard), the wonder material beloved of TV makeover shows. Well, the granddaddy of MDF was plain old fibreboard (lower density, but not known as 'LDF'). This comprised sheets formed from wood separated into its fibrous elements and reconstituted under pressure. The natural fibres produced resins that acted as an adhesive, but often additional adhesives were added to help bind it together. It has a natural light tan colour (unless painted), with an indented surface pattern similar to that seen on the back of hardboard and a fairly soft spongy feel if you poke it with your finger. It doesn't possess the inert fire-resistant quality of plasterboard but should prove adequate unless subjected to damp, which will cause it to lose strength and disintegrate.

Fibreboard sheets appeared as an alternative to plasterboard during the inter-war period. They were often used as compressed ceiling panels, supported by a timber framework at the board joints.

BELOW: Looks like asbestos, but actually fibreboard.

ASBESTOS CEMENT SHEETING

Asbestos cement sheeting (sometimes known as 'asbestolux') is a hard, thin, lightweight material that makes a hollow sound when tapped and, unlike other ceiling materials, you can't easily stick a drawing pin or sharp point into it. Its use for ceilings was fairly rare. It is more likely to be found in outbuildings or the ceilings of rear lean-

RIGHT: Asbestos cement ceiling panel.

tos or old boiler cupboards as fire-resistant 'insulation board'. But it was sometimes also used in living areas, with the panels set in an exposed timber framework similarly to fibreboard.

The heyday of asbestos cement sheeting was from the 1930s through to the 1970s, during which time it was also used for flues, eaves, gutters, and garage roofs etc. If it's in good general condition and not damaged there should be no significant hazard, and is normally best left undisturbed. It is essential not to drill, sand, or subject it to abrasion in any way, as the release of fibres constitutes a serious health threat. So check your survey report – if your house has asbestos ceilings it should have been flagged up, as its presence in large amounts can deter purchasers and detract from the value of a property. Specialist advice should first be obtained and the decision will need to be made whether to have it removed (expensive) or contained behind new suspended ceilings.

TOP LEFT: Asbestos cement board.
TOP RIGHT: Timber beam hides steal joist.
BELOW: Reinforced concrete store ceiling (to rear store).
RIGHT: Polystyrene foam tiles.

REINFORCED CONCRETE

Concrete ceilings are sometimes found in blocks of flats or as the flip side of flat concrete roofs, typically to rear addition stores (see Chapter 2). Being cold they are very prone to condensation, and can be improved by lining with insulated plasterboard.

Ceiling finishes

'Functional' and 'streamlined' may have been the architectural buzzwords of the day, but the British love of 'Olde Worlde' wasn't so easily dismissed. Along with leaded light windows, some more expensive houses sprouted false 'mock-Tudor' beams. These black-painted ceiling timbers are worth preserving as an original feature. (NB: some are actually structural, and some larger beams may conceal steel joists.)

Lining paper or wallpaper were the most widely used traditional finish on plastered ceilings, sometimes with an embossed decorative pattern. But a word of warning – stripping the paper from one area of lath and plaster can swiftly grow into a 'strip the whole ceiling' job, which in turn can cause old plaster to lose its key and come loose! What started as a small DIY job can somehow turn into a major building project.

Polystyrene foam tiles and linings have been a common DIY 'improvement' in recent years, in a bid to insulate ceilings or disguise poor surfaces. However, they are now considered to be a fire hazard, as well as being unsightly and of little practical use, and should be removed. The underlying surfaces need to be made good, which may require skim plastering. Polystyrene coving should also be treated with suspicion. Modern replacement plaster coving has a 'manufactured' look with crisp, straight, simple patterns, and is a definite 'no-no' for 1930s purists.

Tongued-and-grooved timber cladding was another popular DIY project some years ago. As with foam tiles, its installation actually downgrades the fire resistance of the ceiling and is especially hazardous in kitchens. The ability of flames to track across surfaces and cause ignition at some distance from the source of a fire is well known, so any potentially flammable coverings aren't a good idea.

Suspended ceilings

Depending on available headroom and ceiling heights, there is usually the option of hiding a poor original ceiling by constructing a new ceiling underneath. This is one way that converted flats are insulated for sound and fire. But the resulting ceiling heights should not normally be much lower than about 2.2m (7.2ft).

Suspended ceilings are relatively lightweight because they carry no loading from the floor above. They are normally built with a framework of 100 x 50mm (4 x 2in) joists spaced at 450mm (18in) centres, leaving a small space below the old ceiling. Additional support can be provided from hangers secured centrally from the main ceiling joists, though this will detract from its sound insulating qualities. Plasterboard sheets are screwed to the new joists, the joints are then scrimmed, and a thin skim plaster finish applied. Using foil-backed plasterboard will help resist condensation, essential in kitchens and bathrooms. Provision of mineral wool insulation in the void should significantly reduce heat-loss and improve sound insulation. Also, the void can be useful for running new electric cables and concealed lighting – but not for pipework, as access for maintenance is restricted.

Suspended ceiling kits of the metal frame type used in offices are also available, but these may have an exposed framework and use lightweight composite panels which – from aesthetic and insulation viewpoints – are a poor alternative.

Decoration

Ceilings were traditionally painted with distemper or whitewash (a mix of water and chalk or lime). These had a powdery finish, so modern plastic emulsion doesn't adhere to them very well. It should be possible to remove them using a brush and hot soapy water. In most cases they will have been painted over with modern paints that if necessary can be stripped with a solvent-based solution. Stains from tobacco smoke can be eliminated with sugar soap prior to decoration. Small areas of loose plaster can often be ignored as long as the cracks are filled and the plaster lined with heavy gauge plain paper before painting.

WARNING: REMOVING ARTEX

Between the1960s and the 1980s textured decorative paints were particularly popular, and were often used to hide defective surfaces. However, these may contain asbestos fibres that would become a health hazard if breathed in, so removal needs to be done with care. Licensed asbestos removal companies may need to be used, or if you do it yourself precautions must be taken (ie masks and protective clothing need to be worn). Artex can be quite difficult to remove without damaging the surface below, but you should be able to steam it off with a steam stripper so that the Artex splits from the plaster and can be scraped and peeled away. One thing you must not do is try to remove it with any kind of abrasive tool. If in doubt leave it in place. A better alternative is for a skim plaster coating to be applied directly on top, or a suspended ceiling could be installed to conceal it. If all else fails the whole ceiling can be taken down and replaced with new plasterboard.

Common causes of ceiling damage

Movement: Cracked or loose plaster is often the obvious initial symptom of most ceiling defects. Where a ceiling crack is more than about 2mm wide (0.1in), and where the plaster on either side is not level, it may indicate that a more serious problem has occurred in the structure. Localised cracking or bowing may be due to movement caused by structural alterations, particularly where old chimney breasts have been removed, and can be the first sign of a structural problem. See Chapter 10.

However, fine hairline cracks at plasterboard joints are extremely common and are often due to no more than shrinkage (drying out) or slight expansion and contraction of the boards. Cracks at the joints between walls and ceilings due to differential movement or expansion are also common. They can be filled, but may reappear as the house adjusts to seasonal ground and temperature changes. The provision of coving around the perimeter of the ceiling can be effective at disguising small cracks of this type.

Overloading: Cracks in ceilings of all kinds will result if the floors above are defective or the ceiling joists themselves are inadequate for the loading, eg when the roof space is used for storage of heavy items.

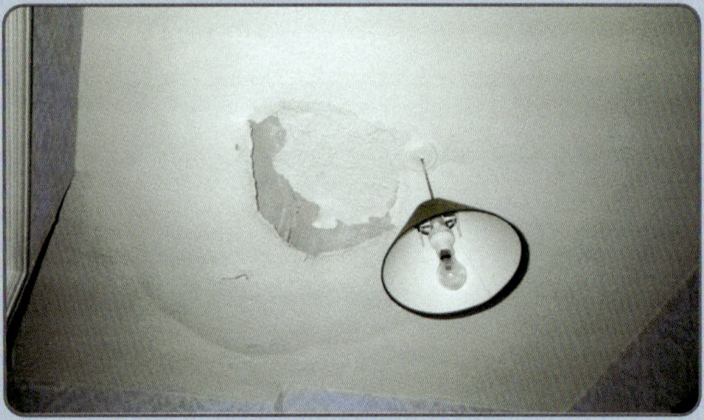

Vibration: Wild parties upstairs? 40-tonne trucks driving past your front room? With original lath and plaster, vibration will eventually cause cracking and loosen the plaster. Plasterboard is far more resistant.

Damp: Where ceilings have become saturated with water, lath and plaster is very prone to softening and can lose its key. The source of the damp must first be repaired, then if the plaster is still sound it must be allowed to dry out fully, which can take up to a couple of months.

Anyone seen my damp meter? – flat bay roofs can be very prone to damp.

Leaks can leave a legacy of decay in concealed timbers. However, because they're involved in different trades, roofers or plumbers repairing leaks rarely get round to advising homeowners on the hidden 'time-bomb' consequences of damp.

Damp plasterboard can warp and bow and needs to be cut out and replaced. Brown stains are typical of old water leaks, whereas black specks indicate mould (usually due to condensation) and should be treated with a fungicide (see below). Any staining should be sealed prior to decoration. Plastering is a hard skill to master, but small areas of less than a square metre should be within most DIYers capabilities. See 'Patch repairs' section below.

Defect: Cracks in plasterboard ceilings

SYMPTOMS

Thin straight cracks.

Cause **Poorly fixed panels or expansion and contraction at board joints**

Solution *Cracking between board panels is not normally a serious problem. Joints can be raked out and filled using a covering strip of paper or fabric across the joint before applying the plaster. Consider lining with a heavy gauge lining paper to conceal the joints.*

Another common defect is a line of small, round craters (about 10mm/0.33in wide) or lumps, due to plasterboard clout nails being nailed in either too far or not far enough. The solution is normally to apply a sufficiently thick skim plaster finish, having first inserted some additional screws for improved support to any loose boards.

Defect: Cracks in lath and plaster ceilings

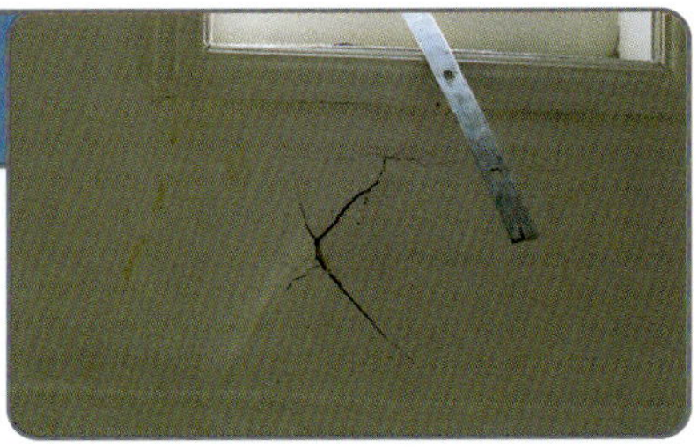

SYMPTOMS

Small irregular shaped cracks and unevenness.

Cause **Timber laths have come loose, or the plaster has lost its 'key' with the laths**

Solution *Carefully check the cracked area for lumps of loose plaster (eg by pushing very gently with a broom handle).*

Once one part has lost its key or the laths have slipped, other loose areas may fall down (or even the whole ceiling). If the problem area is fairly small, cut out the loose part and then screw the laths back to the joists and fix a suitable piece of plasterboard to the joists. Replaster to a flush finish.

Defect: Mouldy ceilings

SYMPTOMS

Recurrent black mould growth.

Cause **Condensation due to poor insulation and ventilation**

Solution *This is a common problem resulting from poor insulation and a lack of ventilation, usually more evident to ceilings, walls, and windows in bathrooms and kitchens, where steam is produced. The steamy water vapour hits a cold ceiling and condenses back to water. You may find this particularly in cold rear extensions or flat-roofed areas.*

The solution is to insulate above the ceiling with mineral wool to a depth of 270mm (11in), and allow a path for ventilation above that. A new suspended ceiling with foil backed plasterboard is an excellent alternative if space permits. Improving ventilation is important, eg with extractor fans, open fireplaces, and trickle vents in windows. Make sure tumble driers are ventilated to the outside, and if possible minimise indoor clothes drying and cut down on boiling food.

To get rid of the mould, clean off with water and apply diluted bleach (1:4 bleach/water) or a suitable fungicide. Finish with a coat of mould-resistant paint.

See also Chapter 6.

Defect: Sagging and bulging

SYMPTOMS

Ceilings uneven; cracked finishes and bowed surfaces.

Cause **Incorrect support**

Solution Plasterboard sheets may not be fully supported, particularly at the ends and edges. Boards should have been fixed to the joists in a staggered pattern with their sides butted up and 3mm gaps left at cut ends and nailed every 150mm (6in). Additional nailing or securing with screws will be needed to improve support.

Cause **Insufficient noggings, defective floor above, insufficient or wrong type of nails**

Solution *Timber noggings should be fitted between floor joists for stability. If they were omitted and the floor has excessive 'spring' the ceilings below can be affected and the floor must first be strengthened. See Chapter 9.*

Joists are normally spaced at either 450mm or 600mm centres (18in or 24in). With 600mm centres, plasterboard should be of the thicker 12.5mm (0.5in) variety.

If the defect is minor, additional nailing or securing with screws will be needed. Otherwise it may be better to fit a new or suspended ceiling.

Cause **Unsupported load above**

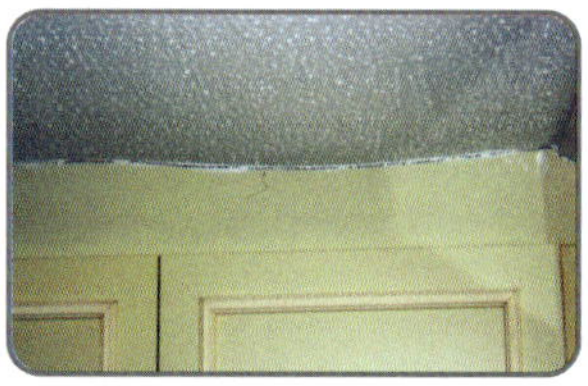

Solution *Provide new support, eg to water tanks in loft, and repair ceiling (see below).*

Cause **Wet plasterboard or loose plaster**

Solution *Plasterboard tends to warp when very wet. Once the cause of dampness has been eradicated, the area affected can be cut out and replaced with an infill piece of board and plastered to match.*

Cause **Loose laths. Plaster has fallen away**

Original ceilings can fail because the old plaster was mixed with insufficient hair reinforcement, or the laths were fixed too close together leaving too narrow a gap for the plaster to squeeze through and form adequate nibs. The plaster then loses its key and falls away from its backing. The laths themselves can also fail due to damp, decay, or beetle – see Chapter 6.

Solution *From below, prop the area of sagged plaster with a sheet of plywood and a length of timber to push it back into position. Then, from above, clean the ceiling, removing all broken nibs, and lightly spray with water to prevent the old material sucking water out of the new plaster. Pour rapid-setting plaster along the line of the gaps between the laths, to form new nibs. When dry, remove prop.*

Alternatively, if laths are loose or parts of the ceiling or cornices are sagging they can be screwed back into the joists using long stainless steel screws with large washers at frequent intervals along the joist. Screw heads are countersunk and filled.

If the laths are sound but the plaster has fallen away you can fill the damaged area using modern plasters (which are compatible with older plasters and will adhere to laths). First, all the old damaged plaster must be removed and raked from between the laths. Then an undercoat of browning plaster should be applied and pressed well into the laths. After two or three hours, when it has started to harden, the surface should be scratched to improve bonding. Twenty-four hours later it should have hardened completely and a thin coat of finishing plaster can be applied, using a steel trowel to achieve a smooth, level surface.

When skimming over an old ceiling, if the plaster surface looks crumbly the surface may first need to be stabilised by painting with PVA bonding fluid using a wide brush. When dry, a thin layer of finishing plaster can be applied.

Alternatively, construct a new suspended ceiling below the original. In severe cases, take down the old ceiling and replace with new plasterboard.

Deco oak veneer. (Minchinhampton Architectural Salvage Co)

Internal walls

If walls could talk, doubtless they would have some riveting tales to tell of decadent goings-on in 1930s suburbia. But if you know how to read the signs, internal walls can reveal a lot about the health of your house. The first signs of structural movement are likely to be evident here, and if any of the original walls have been removed, it is worth taking a few minutes to work out which other parts of the house they supported before they disappeared.

Private builders aimed to sell houses by giving the public what they wanted, and for 1930s homebuyers an important indicator of a property's status was to have a clear division between the reception rooms and the entrance hall. The modern concept of 'open-plan living' would have been considered something of a crazed architectural fantasy, and it was not until after the Second World War that

(Adrienne Chinn Design Company Ltd)

conventional layouts came to be reconsidered. So to our eyes it may appear that original houses do not make the best use of the available space. The solution, of course, was to open up and knock through, but so badly has much of this inspired 'home improvement' work been executed that some structures became seriously unsafe as a result.

THE GOLDEN AGE

In one important way, this was something of a golden age for internal walls. Even today there is a strong preference amongst homeowners for 'good solid walls', as opposed to the hollow sounding, lightweight timber stud partitions in modern houses. You can drill into them, hang things from them, and they aren't too bad at sound insulation. 1930s internal walls were strongly built with solid masonry, even for simple partition walls between rooms – unlike some of their Victorian timber studwork predecessors clad with lath and plaster. But they are usually not much more than 75–100mm (3–4in) thick – less than half the thickness of the main walls.

Construction was commonly of recently introduced dark grey breeze blocks (made from cement mixed with sand and waste 'fuel ash') or else of soft, uneven place bricks (of cheaper quality since they were to be plastered over). More rarely found are partition walls made from thin lightweight blocks of 'aerated plaster' with a consistency similar to that of an Aero chocolate bar, or lined with fibreboard (which was more commonly fitted to ceilings). You can normally identify the materials used by taking a quick peek under the loft insulation above an internal wall.

A view from the loft – partition walls of breeze blocks.

But this 'golden age' was tarnished somewhat by the fact that load-bearing internal walls providing essential structural support for the floor joists and roof were commonly built with only very rudimentary foundations. As a result, such walls are likely to have settled over time, in severe cases causing the support struts in the roof to follow and the roof to sag. Also, floors resting on these walls may consequently show signs of slight sloping.

It is no great surprise, therefore, to find that partition walls which merely divide one room from another were frequently just built off the floors, without any foundations at all, making them very susceptible to movement with the floor. See Chapter 9.

WALL COVERINGS

Internal walls were normally 'rendered, floated and set' with plaster made of cement mixed with lime and sand. This was a labour-saving advance on the old Victorian method of facing walls with lime plaster (a mix of lime and sand, bulked up with all kinds of cheap materials like dung, chalk, earth, etc), which had to be applied in several layers. To help bind the mix together, lime plaster also frequently contained thick black tufts of horse or ox hair, and although rare, some traditional builders were still practising these old methods in the 1930s. Wallpaper was the usual finish to plastered walls, often with 'half-tiling' to kitchens and bathrooms. See Chapter 11.

Another traditional technique was to apply a 'dry lining' of lath and plaster to the insides of solid main walls. This was designed to boost energy ratings with better insulation, but if the main walls became damp it was an open invitation to all manner of horrors, such as wet rot, dry rot, and woodworm, for which see Chapter 6.

For the more discerning client with a larger budget, the thing to have on the walls was 'faux-Jacobean' oak panelling, matching the period timber theme elsewhere. But such wainscoting is also prone to decay in the event of dampness.

At the other extreme, the more progressive techno-

conscious architect or builder would readily employ new materials, such as walls featuring exotic glass blocks in some 'international style' villas and apartments. But a more sinister new material was 'asbestolux' insulation board, used internally not only for ceilings but also for wall panels, boxing in pipework, and even for door panels. Thankfully it is extremely rare, but if found should be treated as described earlier for asbestos ceilings. If it is in good condition it normally presents no immediate risk, but if damaged dangerous fibres can be released and it will need to be given a high priority for removal or containment. Removal of insulation board containing asbestos must only be done by licensed contractors.

STRIPPING AND STEAMING

You may encounter walls covered with the dreaded woodchip wallpaper, or even with combed Artex for that authentic textured 1980s wine-bar look. To remove woodchip, you need to use a steamer. First scrape the surface using a toothed scraper or flat cheese-grater, which will help the steam and water to soak in. Then apply the steamer, but do not hold it in one place for too long as it can damage the plaster. Fortunately, modern plasters are compatible with the original materials and can be used to repair old surfaces. For walls covered with Artex, see the advice under 'Ceilings' above. For damp to internal walls, see page 95.

Party walls

It is important to be aware that if you plan to carry out any work on a party wall, under the terms of the Party Wall Act 1996 you are legally obliged to first get the written consent of the person on the other side, who is the joint owner. For full details see www.ThirtiesHouse.co.uk.

The solid structural walls that separate you from your neighbours should be of a similar thickness to traditional solid main walls, typically about 230mm (9in), made of bricks or sometimes of breeze blocks, but the temptation to save on materials and labour meant that some party walls

were skimped and built thinner. Even if they are of a decent width, they may still be very thin at loft level.

A common problem with these separating walls between houses is the lack of sound insulation. Inadequate construction, with thin walls of only single brick width or with gaps and holes in them, means that there is often a need for improvement. See 'Defects' below.

Is it structural?

As a general rule, it is best to leave walls alone: houses are often worth more with them intact, as buyers generally like original features. But the Achilles heel of many 1930s houses was the small size of the kitchen, making some form of extension or opening up almost inevitable.

To discover if a wall is load-bearing, you really need to inspect it from above. Starting in the roof space, see how the struts and ceiling joists are supported: they often rest on at least one cross wall or spine wall to the bedrooms below, which is in turn supported by the reception room walls.

It is crucial to check the direction of the floor joists, in order to ascertain whether the walls below are supporting the floors. Floor joists normally run the other way from the direction of the boards (so if your boards run from side to side, it means the joists are running from front to back), as can be seen from the visible lines of nailing. To be absolutely certain, lift a few upstairs floorboards over the wall below to confirm whether any joists are resting on it. But even walls with no joists resting on them, and whose only purpose seems to be that of dividing the rooms downstairs, can actually be structural, because they support an upstairs wall directly above, or they may be helping to support other adjoining walls.

It is therefore safer to assume that all walls are load-bearing until proved otherwise, and it's not a bad idea to first visit your local authority Building Control officer for a friendly chat before starting any work.

KNOCKING THROUGH

The internal walls most commonly demolished in 1930s houses are the ones dividing the front and rear receptions,

PROJECT: Making an opening

1 The wall above must be supported temporarily while a slot is cut for the new lintel. This is done by first cutting holes just above the position of the proposed new lintel about every 600mm (2ft).

2 Sturdy timber 'needles' of about 150 x 50mm (6 x 2in) are then placed through these holes in the wall, and are supported each side by adjustable steel 'acro' props, in turn resting on a scaffold plank to spread the load. (On suspended timber floors the joists must be checked first to ensure they can provide adequate support.)

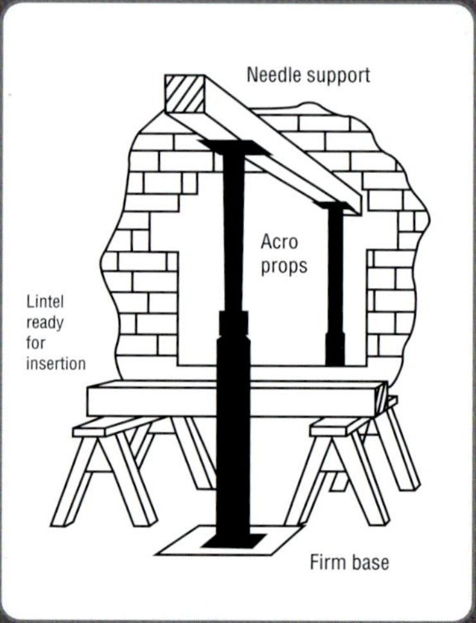

3 The new lintel is inserted in the wall and must extend either side of the proposed new opening by at least 150mm (6in) 'bearing'. A hard engineering brick or stone pad is normally needed under the lintel ends to improve support.

4 The lintel is bedded in mortar and the masonry above built up. After 24 hours or more, when the mortar is dry, the props can be removed.

5 The new opening below the lintel is first marked out on the wall and the plaster chopped out vertically with a bolster. An angle grinder can be carefully used to cut the masonry, dismantling small stages at a time. The resulting reveal can later be made good with plaster. Alternatively a timber frame liner can be screwed to the reveal, or installed with metal frame ties bedded into small pockets cut in the reveal wall, and pointed up once the frame is square. Finally, the surrounding masonry and gaps to the floor are filled and levelled.

and those between kitchens and dining rooms. Depending on which way the joists run, in a typical semi-detached house the reception room dividing wall may well be a major structural component, supporting the floor above as well as taking some loading from the roof. But if the joists run from side to side they are more likely to rest on that other popular target for removal, the kitchen/dining room wall.

Taking out load-bearing walls is a major job requiring professional advice, and structural alterations must always be carried out with Building Control approval. The removal, if done badly, can transfer loadings unevenly, thereby affecting foundations or causing deflection elsewhere in the structure, even to the extent of the main walls coming away from the house. And before wielding the sledge hammer in anger, be sure to check that your building is not listed and that the wall in question does not affect your neighbours.

Even partition walls that do not support any of the building's structure should not be bashed down any old way. An avalanche of heavy masonry could ruin your chances of playing in the Premiership. So caution is the watchword. Take it one step at a time. Shut down all adjacent water and electricity and start at the top, working in small sections.

OPENING UP

Door openings were usually spanned by timber or concrete lintels, with the masonry for the wall above built off the top. Where a new opening is required in a load-bearing wall, the weight of the structure above needs to be supported by a suitable new lintel, usually of steel or concrete. Again, as this is a structural job, Building Control must be notified in advance and may require engineers' calculations to specify the appropriate lintel type.

Cracking

Fine cracks may be caused by shrinkage or may be evidence of localised loose plasterwork. Shrinkage cracks can normally be filled by first scratching along their length to widen them, then removing any loose plaster, and finally filling with a fine surface filler. Quite often small cracks (up to about 1.5mm width) will open and close over the course of a year as the shallow foundations of the house respond to ground movement as it moistens and dries with the seasons. See Chapter 5.

Larger cracks may indicate possible settlement to the house. Door openings are weak spots: cracking above a door frame, doors that stick badly, or frame linings out of square can all indicate a structural problem in a load-bearing wall. Where an internal wall is badly cracked it may actually be because it is built off a floor, instead of having its own foundations. So if your internal doors are well out of alignment this could be a symptom of a defective floor, and not necessarily a problem with the joinery or walls.

Vertical cracking often occurs at junctions between internal partition walls and the main external walls, due to inadequate fixing at the time of construction between the two or differential movement between different materials. If such cracks are more than about 3mm wide, or the width of the crack varies throughout its height, this may be a clue that the outside wall has bulged out due to a lack of restraint and may need to be tied in. See Chapter 5.

Once the cause of the movement has been rectified, a bolster chisel can be used to chop away the edges of the crack and the loose debris raked out before moistening the plaster and applying the appropriate filler in layers.

Movement in walls often shows around doors.

Patch repairs

In many older houses some areas of plaster are 'live'. The plaster moves when you press against it, showing that it has lost its key to the wall or that the coats themselves may have separated.

Small areas of loose plaster can often be hidden with a heavy lining paper before wallpapering or painting. But if the wall is in a bad way and several areas are loose, it is better to strip all the old plaster off and replaster the wall completely, or to dry-line it with plasterboard (see below).

If there are only one or two weak areas, they can be patched as follows:

- Identify the extent of the damage by rapping the wall with your knuckles – loose plaster will produce a hollow sound. Mark out the damaged area with a pencil.

- Using a bolster chisel and a club hammer, remove the defective plaster by chipping small amounts away, working inwards from the edges so as to keep the size of repair to a minimum.
- Clean the masonry below and dampen prior to applying a backing coat of browning or bonding plaster. This is brought up to just below the surface and allowed to harden.
- Use a thin coat of finishing plaster, levelled off flush to the surrounding old plaster.

Dry-lining

As described earlier, dry-lining walls with plasterboard is a good alternative to plastering, if space permits, with the added benefit of improved insulation. Whereas plastering is a difficult skill to master, fixing plasterboard is a realistic DIY project. See 'Step by Step'.

'Dry-lining' means fixing sheets of plasterboard to an existing wall using dabs of plaster, or by screwing or nailing it to a timber frame. It is a good way of insulating cold main walls to reduce condensation. Some boards have a white decorative face and can be fixed so it's exposed for direct painting or wallpapering. But the best option is to use 'thermal check' foil-backed board of the thicker 12.5mm (0.5in) variety, or thicker composite boards ready insulated with slabs of polyurethane foam. Standard plasterboard sheets are available as 2400 x 1200mm (8 x 4ft) or 1830 x 900mm (6 x 3ft), the latter being easier for one person to handle. Joints between panels are filled with jointing compound and paper tape or cotton scrim. Outer corners need a tougher cross-fibre tape or metal angle beads. The easiest finish is to fill the joints and decorate or wallpaper direct to the board surface, or finish with skim plaster 2 or 3mm thick.

New walls

Modern stud walls lined with plasterboard are lighter and easier to construct than those of masonry, although they have relatively poor soundproofing qualities, even if the void is filled with mineral wool insulation. The use of modern concrete blocks is not advisable for dividing walls unless there is adequate support below, eg when replacing a previously removed solid wall.

New blockwork is also very prone to significant shrinkage as it dries out over the first nine months, particularly if damp when laid.

DIY precautions

Drilling holes in internal walls is a common cause of electrocution and flooding, so it's wise to invest in a cable and pipe detector – they're cheap and easy to use. As noted earlier, concrete blocks comprising all kinds of industrial waste materials were commonly used, and asbestos cement sheets may be concealed behind innocent looking plaster surfaces, so it also makes sense to wear a suitable mask when drilling – just in case.

Technical data

Timber frame partition walls are typically constructed with timber stud uprights 100 x 50mm (4 x 2in) at 300–400mm (12–16in) intervals.

Defect: Surface cracks in plaster

SYMPTOMS
Thin hairline cracks in plasterboard.

Cause The plaster has lost its 'key' due to poor adhesion of plaster or vibration

Solution *Carefully check the cracked area for lumps of loose plaster. If the problem area is fairly small, cut out the loose part. Replaster to a flush finish. In severe cases, replace or line with plasterboard. See 'ceiling defects'.*

Cause Plasterboard walls can suffer from thermal movement or shrinkage at joints, or poor quality workmanship

Solution *Rake out and fill joints. In severe cases, rejointing and skimming may be required, or replacement of damaged boards.*

Defect: Movement cracks

SYMPTOMS
Cracking typically at abutment of main walls.

Cause Structural movement

Solution Structural movement is more likely where cracks are more than about 3mm (0.1in) wide or where the plaster on each side is not level. The cracking may be indicative of more serious movement within the structure as a whole, commonly at bays and side walls. Load-bearing internal walls may have insufficient foundation depths and could require underpinning or construction of new supporting brick piers. See Chapter 5.

Cause Differential movement

Solution *Where dissimilar materials in the wall construction have expanded or contracted at different rates (eg lintels over door or window openings), rake out cracks and apply mastic or filler.*
However, if differential movement recurs or is substantial, fitting expanded metal lath or plaster scrims across junctions and then plastering over can isolate the surface from periodic movement cracks. Otherwise, a cover strip such as a timber batten can be fitted to hide the cracks.

Defect: Thin or defective separating walls

SYMPTOMS
Noise transmission.

Cause Inadequate separating walls between dwellings

Solution *The noise-resistance of a separating wall can be poor due to the wall being built of only single width brickwork (115mm/4.5in) with gaps and holes. The solution is to block any holes and to dry-line and insulate the wall for sound. Build up missing party walls in the roof.*

Areas of poor quality bare brick (eg under floors or in the loft) can be rough-rendered and gaps filled with mortar or foam to block air paths.

Ideally, construct an independent new wall of timber studwork and plasterboard over the old wall, leaving a minimum 50mm (2in) gap in between. Use 75 x 50mm (3 x 2in) timbers for the framework, secured at the edges to the walls, floor, and ceiling, but leaving a void so that it is independent from the old wall. Pack with a minimum of 25mm (1in) mineral wool quilt or acoustic board insulation. Board over with two layers of 12.5mm (0.5in) plasterboard with staggered joints, sealed at the joints with scrim, sealant, or coving. In addition, to reduce sound via the roof void fix a new layer of plasterboard over the old ceiling and dry-line the firebreak wall.

STEP BY STEP

Dry-lining a wall

TOOLS REQUIRED

- Pencil, chalk, and tape measure
- Spirit level
- Long straight edge rule
- Hawk and steel trowel
- Sharp craft knife

MATERIALS

- Plasterboard and direct-bond adhesive

Photos courtesy Lafarge Plasterboard Ltd.

Dry-lining is a great way to get a smooth new surface on old internal walls or ceilings or for insulating cold main walls. You also get the added benefit of improved sound and fire resistance, and you can hide new electric cables and pipes (suitably protected). Select 'thermal check' foil-backed plasterboard for bathrooms and kitchens, to protect against condensation. Old walls must first be free from damp.

The traditional method of dry-lining is to construct a framework of treated timber 25 x 19mm (1 x 0.75in) battens built onto the wall. The boards are then fixed to the framework with special non-rust screws or clout nails. Alternatively, 'quick to fit' metal frame kits are available.

The 'direct-bond' method can be used to cover solid walls that are reasonably true. Here, the boards are secured directly to the wall using dabs of plaster adhesive, so any large areas of old loose wall plaster must first be removed.

CUTTING PLASTERBOARD

Having measured the wall and marked the board accordingly, score along the line fairly deeply use a sharp craft knife and a straight rule, and then repeat. Lift the board off the floor and give it a sharp knock along the cut line so that the waste part snaps away neatly. Cut off any remaining paper, trying to avoid tearing the surface. Awkward shapes can be cut with a saw.

1 The floor and ceiling are marked with a chalked line, allowing for the thickness of board plus at least 10mm ($^3/_8$in) of adhesive.

2 Next, the walls are marked with vertical lines to indicate the positions of the rows of dabs. Use a long straight-edge, spirit level and a piece of chalk, or a chalked plumb line.

3 Mix up the special adhesive plaster and scoop some of it onto a hawk. Then use a steel float to place them on the wall. Dabs should be 250mm (10in) long and 50–70mm (2–3in) wide.

4 Dabs are needed at 600mm (24in) centres, plus 50mm (2in) below the ceiling. A continuous line is needed above the floor. Apply enough for one panel at a time.

5 While being lifted clear of the floor with a foot lifter, the plasterboard panel is pressed firmly onto the dabs of adhesive. Then it is wedged in place at the bottom.

6 Finally, the plasterboard is tamped into place with a long straight-edge, aligning it with the marks on the floor and ceiling. Repeat the process for subsequent panels.

STEP BY STEP

Direct decoration to plasterboard

Plasterboard walls and ceilings are normally skimmed with a finishing plaster to a maximum of 5mm (0.25in) thickness, but they can be decorated or wallpapered direct instead, as shown below. It is best to use tapered-edge boards (rather than square-edged joints), as the shallow recess over the joints can be filled with jointing compound (setting time approx 90 minutes) and scrim tape for an invisible joint.

TOOLS REQUIRED

- **Steel trowel**
- **Taping knives (100 and 150mm)**
- **Feathering sponge**
- **Tin snips (cutters)**

MATERIALS

- **Jointing compound**
- **Air-drying finishing compound**
- **Joint tape or scrim**
- **External corner metallic tape (optional)**
- **Sandpaper (120 grit)**
- **Dry wall sealer paint and emulsion**

Photos courtesy Lafarge Plasterboard Ltd.

USING TAPERED PLASTERBOARD

1 Apply jointing compound to the tapered joint with a 150mm (6in) taping knife.

2 Take a strip of paper joint tape and bed it into the compound. Then cover with more jointing compound so it is flush with the board face.

3 If necessary, the edges can be smoothed with a damp sponge to minimise sanding. Allow joint to dry.

USING SQUARE-EDGED OR CUT PLASTERBOARD

4 When set hard, add a second coat of jointing compound with a trowel and feather it out beyond the first coat, then smooth it off at the edges. When dry, apply a finishing coat of air-drying compound and again feather out beyond the edges of the previous coat. Allow to dry. Rub down until smooth, and it's ready for sealing and decorating with a minimum of two coats of emulsion.

5 After step 1 above, bed the paper joint tape in the compound as before, but apply a 200mm (8in) wide band of jointing compound over the joint tape.

6 When dry, apply a second coat of jointing compound 250mm (10in) wide extending down the edges of the joint tape.

7 When set hard, apply a finishing coat of air-drying compound over the entire joint, covering the tape and feathering out onto the plasterboard face. Repeat stage 3. Rub down until smooth, seal, and decorate.

8 For internal angles, apply jointing compound to both boards using a 100mm (4in) knife then repeat steps 2–4.

9 External corners need a tougher finish. Metallic 'flex tape' is cut to size with tin snips. Apply a 50mm (2in) wide band of fast setting jointing compound each side of the corner. Bed the tape onto the corner so its metal side faces in towards the plasterboard. Then cover each side with layers of joining compound and finish as described above.

FLOORS

Original 1930s parquet or pine floors can look great – but how do you know what dangers are lurking beneath them? If the furniture vibrates alarmingly when you walk past, or crossing the room is an uphill struggle, does it suggest a floor design fault or a DIY disaster?

Serious dampness and rot may have been taking place unseen for many years, but timber floors aren't alone in suffering from significant defects. Original solid concrete floors, often tiled, can develop their own special problems – bulging from sulphate attack or hollowness, cracking and sinking.

If you lived in a fabulous architect-designed villa of the inter-war period, beneath your feet you would most likely find large expanses of fashionable polished parquet woodblock flooring. Other grand designs of this period could boast floors boldly finished in glamorous terrazzo marbled mortar or exotic seamless magnesite.

TOP AND BELOW: Restored parquet. (Photo: Finer Flooring)

But in conventional houses, the floor construction was one part of the building that had evolved only slowly from tried and tested Victorian methods. The typical 1930s house would have the upstairs and much of the ground floor built from traditional timber floorboards on joists, with the kitchen floor (and, more rarely, those of the reception rooms) of solid concrete construction, much like its predecessors – only perhaps built a little more robustly.

Solid or suspended?

The difference is not always obvious, especially if the floors are carpeted or covered, in which case stamping hard on the floor a few times may elicit a hollow sound and a slight bounce or 'spring' to confirm suspended timber construction. Concrete should, of course, feel completely rigid. The existence of airbricks to the main walls near ground level may also verify that the original floors were of timber.

For all their faults, suspended timber boarded floors score highly for practicality and appeal. They feel warmer than concrete, and access to pipes and cables is relatively straightforward, plus they look great when stripped and sanded. And traditional floorboards allow you to work out the structure of the house fairly easily. The joists should span in the opposite direction to that of the floorboards – which often tends to be the shortest width in a room – as indicated by the nail runs. See Chapter 8.

Plain floorboards were normally of softwood such as pine (known as 'deal'). Their widths varied depending on the quality of house but they were typically 125–200mm (5–8in) wide and about 20–25mm (0.75–1in) thick. Some more expensive houses had thicker, interlocking tongued-and-grooved boards, perhaps of beech or maple, or slim oak floorboards over a concrete floor.

If the property has been extended in recent years you may also come across modern chipboard panels, which are not generally liked as they are prone to creaking and can weaken or even disintegrate if they become damp. In addition they cannot be easily lifted or refixed should access be required to hidden pipes and cables.

ABOVE: Oak floorboards.

RIGHT: New solid oak boards. (Photo: Finer Flooring)

BELOW: Painted pine.

How level should the floor be?

Most floors of this age will not be perfectly true and level. Some will have a definite slope that corresponds to the general settlement of the whole building that took place soon after construction. But unless there are signs of recent cracking and movement to the house, this isn't normally a problem and should usually be within 'acceptable tolerances'.

Floor coverings

The modern passion for beautiful stripped and varnished pine floorboards would be an alien concept to the proud first owners of your home. Instead, the original softwood boards might have received a coating of traditional black bitumen-based paint to help protect them, while bedroom floorboards were often finished in a dark 'Jacobean' stained varnish. Expensive hardwood floors were simply waxed and polished. But elsewhere, contemporary art was making an appearance – and being trampled underfoot. By far the most popular covering was linoleum – natural hessian and cork-based 'lino' – which was widely used throughout the house. The amazing thing about lino was the wide variety of sensational patterns in which it came – fashionable abstract art or cool modern jazz images, perhaps, for the bathroom, and more relaxed floral images for the bedrooms.

(From Linoleum **by Jane Powell)**

The Edwardian passion for parquet flooring had continued unabated as a relatively expensive finish to ground floors, and occasionally upstairs floors too. Cheaper alternatives, such as cork tiling in parquet-like patterns, were sometimes used in halls and landings, but both would commonly have oriental rugs or carpet squares spread on top. Kitchens and downstairs bathroom floors were often finished with red quarry tiles (some kitchens had rubber blocks or lino sheets in 'battleship brown' to camouflage dirt, or decorated with patterns simulating tiles, marble, or granite), whereas in 'moderne' homes you risked being ambushed by rugs projecting shocking cubist patterns.

On a more sedate level, this was the dawn of a radical new floor covering regime – the British love affair with wall-to-wall fitted carpets was soon to take off in a big way, but not just yet. Seamless Axminsters were the luxury item at the top of everyone's wish list but, for the time being at least, they were rarely affordable.

DIY disasters

Sadly, many 1930s houses have suffered from inappropriate modern DIY alterations, such as laminate flooring of a non moisture-resistant type in bathrooms and kitchens, and ceramic floor tiles on suspended timber floors, where the flexibility in the floor structure has caused the tiles to crack or damp has seeped down through the joints, causing hidden decay to the floor timbers. To be suitable for tiling, floors must be very stable. The tiles should be placed over an oil-based hardboard layer laid with the rough side up (to provide a key for the tile adhesive).

Even apparently normal plain timber floors may not always be quite what they seem: pine floorboards were sometimes nailed to treated timber battens resting on the surface of solid concrete floors – a popular method of floor construction in some local authority housing – while expensive parquet floors were often laid over a base of plain floorboards.

The worrying thing is where new floorboards have been subsequently laid over the original ones. To spot this, check

if the surface boards butt against the skirting rather than under it, or if floor levels are higher in one room than another. This can be a recipe for trouble as the reason for covering them over may have been to hide rotten or beetle-riddled old boards, and you can't tell their condition without lifting the new ones. If there's no significant amount of spring to the floor and the walls aren't damp and the airbricks are clear, you may be OK. Otherwise the painful process of lifting the newer boards and replacing defective timbers may need to be carried out.

Insulation and soundproofing

A good flow of air under timber ground floors is essential to disperse damp, but can make things a bit draughty if there are any gaps to the boards. Floors in 1930s houses were not insulated, so heat loss can be a problem if you want to retain the original boards. One solution, if you are willing to go to the trouble of lifting and refixing all the boards, is to place polystyrene or quilt insulation between the joists (over battens or netting) and then reinstate the boards. Or if you plan to fit a carpet, a thin layer of insulated plywood or hardboard can first be fixed directly on top of the boards to smooth out irregularities and provide some degree of insulation, although the resultant raised floor level may then necessitate adjustments to doors and fittings. Plain concrete floors can be covered with suitable laminate or timber flooring over a layer of insulation, although the floor levels will again be raised.

Noise transmission can be reduced by either fitting special acoustic floor panels over existing surfaces, or by

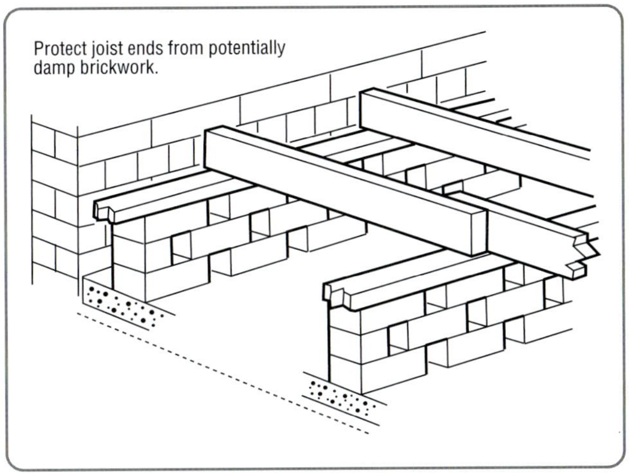

Airbrick provides ventilation under a timber ground floor.

constructing an insulated suspended ceiling below. Houses with older style lath and plaster ceilings can absorb a greater degree of sound than ceilings of plasterboard, as they have a far greater mass.

Timber floors

GROUND FLOORS

Pine (deal) floorboards are normally fixed across timber joists with special flat nails called brads. The floorboards should be laid with their ends resting over the centre of a joist for support. The joists in turn are supported on thick lengths of wood known as wall plates, bedded in mortar along the top of short hidden brick 'sleeper walls'. These 'sleeper walls' are needed because the maximum unsupported joist length ('span') can be as little as 1.8m (6ft). (See technical data at the end of this chapter.)

Lift up a floorboard, and under the coating of dust and debris you should be able to make out the ground below.

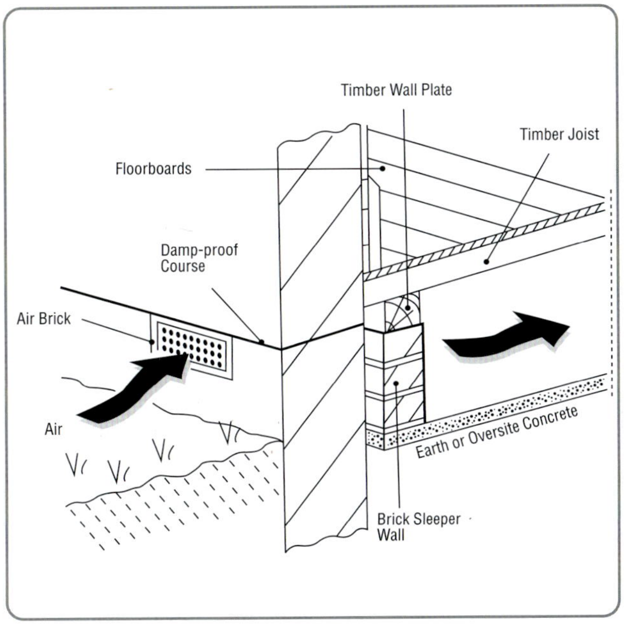

The space under the floor was normally at least 300mm (12in), but deeper 'undercrofts' to houses on sloping sites sometimes allowed this cellar-like area to be used for storage, with access via an external door. Normally there would be a thin layer of 'oversite' concrete (a mixture of cement and 'pit ballast' or similar waste aggregate) laid over the bare earth below the floor to restrict moisture rising upward.

Most problems with floors at ground level arise from dampness of various kinds, which can cause decay in adjacent timbers. So ventilation is provided by airbricks on the lower outside walls to help moisture evaporate before it can cause decay to timbers. There should be a sufficient number of airbricks on each outside wall to maintain a good cross-flow of air under the floors – typically at least two or three in each external wall for an average house. There should be enough to prevent stagnant pockets in corners, for example near solid kitchen floors. Airbricks were mostly of terracotta or iron and any broken ones should be replaced, as they provide easy access for vermin – the space under timber floors is a favourite nesting place for rodents!

The hidden sleeper walls supporting the floor joists are normally built on rubble 'foundations' in a honeycomb pattern with gaps so as not to inhibit airflow. Internal partition walls should likewise have vents in them below floor level.

> **TIP**
>
> **When lifting floorboards, start close to the skirting at one side of the room, leaving the first boards in place under the skirting. When nailing or screwing boards down, be aware of plumbing or electrical cables concealed just below floor level. A metal and cable detector is a very useful gadget.**

UPPER FLOORS

Upstairs floors are of suspended timber construction but are less likely to suffer from damp problems than timber ground floors. The joists often bridge wider spans and tend to be larger and more closely spaced (typically at 300–450mm/12–18in centres). Also you're more likely to find bracing – in the form of small diagonal 'herringbone' bracing struts, or scraps of wood – between upstairs joists, at

RIGHT: Upstairs timber floor with trimmer joist.
ABOVE: New timber ground floor.

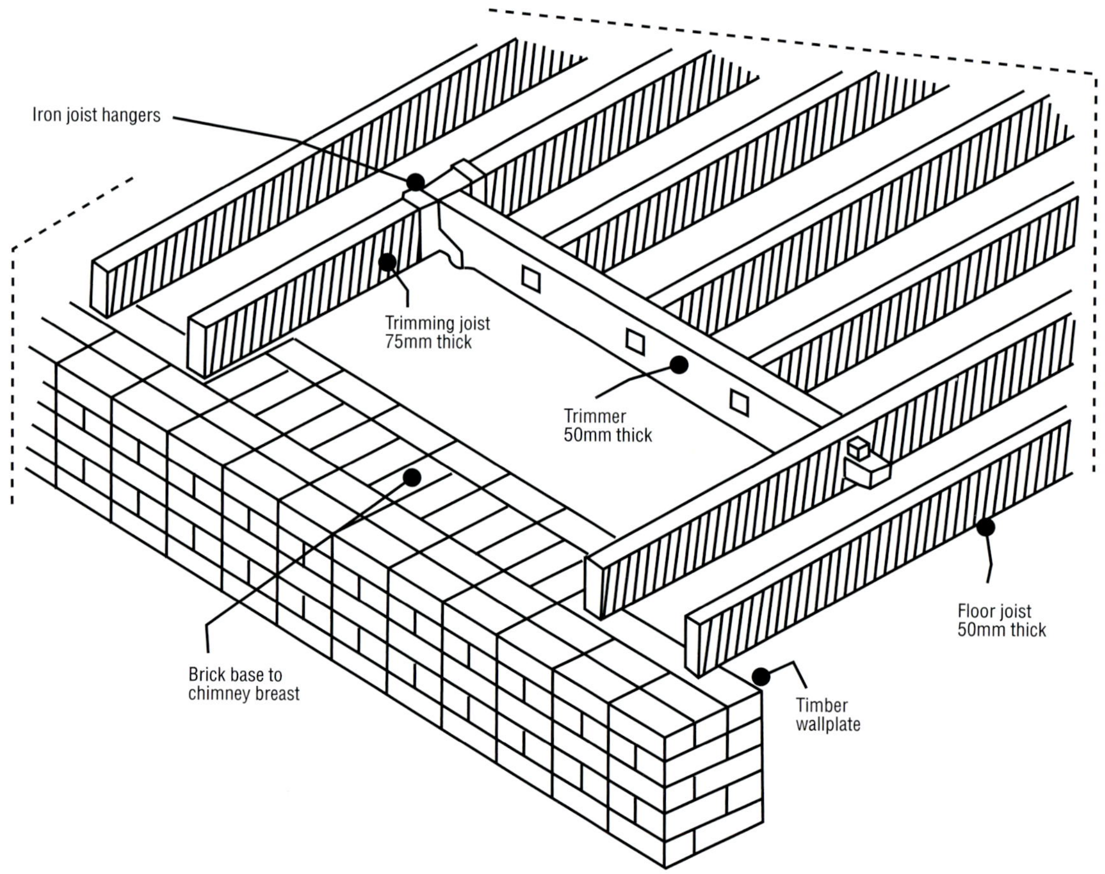

about 1.5m (5ft) intervals, to help prevent bowing or twisting.

The upstairs floor joists are supported with the joist ends either built into the main walls or resting on protruding brick ledges called corbels. The old-fashioned method of building the joists into the wall makes them a potential target for damp and rot, particularly if the walls are of solid brick, and today these methods have been superseded by the use of metal joist hangers. Upstairs floors often rely on internal walls below for additional support, which is one reason why the demolition of internal walls can be such a dangerous pastime. See Chapter 8.

Structurally, the upstairs floor joists do more than just hold the floor up: they also help tie in the main walls.

In some cases the upper floor may also need to provide support for a dividing wall in an upstairs room where there's no wall below it. Here, two specially strengthened 'doubled up' joists may be bolted together directly below the wall, or a steel RSJ might be used. Similarly, where floors had to incorporate openings for stairs and fireplaces/chimney breasts, a frame was made around the opening by butting the ends of the floor joists with thick 75mm (3in) wide 'trimmer' timbers – except, of course, if the builders were slapdash. See next Chapter

Defect: Loose or damaged floorboards

SYMPTOMS

Loose, twisted, and shrunken boards; draughts from gaps in floorboards; creaking boards; uneven floors.

Cause **Poor workmanship or timber shrinkage leaving draughty gaps**

Floorboards that have been cut for DIY fitting of cables and pipes may not have been refitted too cleverly. If a board has been cut at the side of the joist rather than in the centre, there may now be nothing supporting it, so it dips alarmingly when trodden on. Properly fitted boards should have few gaps.

Solution

- Lift the boards and check their condition and screw them securely – woodscrews are more effective than nails at pulling a warped board back against its joist.
- The surface of twisted boards can be levelled by planing or by using a floor sander once the nails have been driven well below the surface.
- Where the board ends aren't supported, lift the defective board to reveal the joist. Firmly nail or screw a batten alongside the old joist to extend it under the unsupported board. Replace and screw down the floorboard.
- Gaps between boards are a source of draughts and can be sealed with a bitumen-based mastic (gun applicator) or by cutting small timber wedges to fit the gaps. You don't want gales blowing up your floorboards, but don't try to solve this one by covering up the airbricks – they are there for a purpose.
- Draughty gaps at skirtings may have since been exacerbated by settlement. Fitting beading at the base can provide a neat solution. See 'step-by-step'.

Cause **Incorrect nailing after lifting boards can cause creaks**

These can also be caused by joists settling, or by warping and shrinkage. Annoying, but not normally dangerous.

Solution *Creaking boards usually just need screwing down or nailing in with brads.*

Make sure the boards are secured at every joist – screws are preferable if there is movement between the fixing nails and the timber. If the surface is very poor, the boards can be replaced with new matching tongued-and-grooved boards and insulated at the same time, or simply covered with hardboard prior to carpeting.

Cause **Rot or beetle infestation can cause floorboards to become soft**

Woodworm (beetle) is recognisable by its distinctive boreholes in the wood. In bad cases, boards can collapse underfoot. See Chapter 6.

Solution *The source of damp must first be eradicated and badly affected timbers cut out and replaced.*

In most cases the damage is very localised and can be treated by spraying with timber treatment fluid available from DIY stores, taking suitable safety precautions. Good airflow to the boards and warmth from central heating will both help defeat the woodworm beetle, which prefers cold, damp, stuffy conditions.

Defect: Sloping floors

SYMPTOMS

Uneven floors; floor surface out of true; gaps to skirting boards; a distinct ridge to floor; the floor in the upstairs bay significantly out of kilter with the room.

Cause **Settlement**

Internal walls that support floor joists often settle, causing floors on all storeys to slope down towards a particular partition which has settled.

Solution *If the settlement is old, no attention may be necessary. A typical example is the spine wall. See Chapter 8.*

Cause **Floor joists twisted or bowed as shrinkage occurred in the timber**

Solution *Fit noggings (bracing struts) between joists at mid span. Screw down any loose boards.*

Cause **Structural movement to main walls**

eg settlement due to insufficient foundations on clay soils or movement to a bay window following renewal of windows.

Solution *Once defects to the bay itself have been remedied, localised making good to bay joists and boards may be required. See Chapter 7.*

Cause **'Humping' of a floor surface**

Often as a result of poorly planned alterations – eg due to a steel beam in the floor structure, where the joists have settled either side of the beam.

Solution *This is not normally a serious problem but can be improved by lifting the boards and packing the joists to make them level.*

Defect: Excessive floor 'spring'

SYMPTOMS

Pronounced deflection to the whole floor in a room when walked on, so that nearby furniture and ornaments vibrate. Floors may sag.

You expect a small amount of spring in most suspended timber floors, particularly upstairs. Apart from rot related causes (see below) there are two main causes of excessive springiness:

Cause **Design fault or a settled sleeper wall**

Inadequately sized timbers are more likely to be found in cheaper houses. The defect in the original design appears to have been particularly aggravated by the weight of furniture. Joists may have warped or deflected under the weight but failed to recover when the load was removed. Settled sleeper walls supporting ground floor joists may, in extreme cases, need to be rebuilt.

Cause **Bad DIY**

Undersized or unbraced joists may have been further weakened by notches cut in them for pipes and cables. Structurally, the depth of a joist gives it greater stiffness than its width, so a basic rule for cutting is that it should not exceed one-eighth of the depth of the timber. Any joists cut more than this must be suspect.

To avoid weakening joists (and to reduce the risk of damage to pipes from floorboard nails), rather than cutting it is better to drill holes for cables centrally (or at least 50mm/2in in from the top of the joist) and not within the first 300mm/12in from the joist ends.

Another problem is incompetent removal of structural walls, which may have left floors unsupported. See Chapter 8.

Solution *Fit 50 x 38mm (2 x 1.5in) noggings as bracing struts between all joists at mid span. Strengthen the floor joists by bolting new timbers to them. In severe cases it may be necessary to build in additional joists. If the joists are weakened by holes drilled for DIY pipes, localised strengthening with metal plates or noggings will help. If any supporting walls have been taken out, structural repairs may be needed.*

Defect: Rotten or infested floor timbers

SYMPTOMS

Soft, damp, or spongy floorboards in localised areas; floorboards collapse underfoot; damp smells; slugs coming up through floorboards.

Dampness aggravated by a lack of sub-floor ventilation to ground floors is the most common cause of decay in timber floors. See Chapter 6.

Cause **The joist ends may have been built into the brickwork of damp external solid walls**

Better-built houses had joists resting on projecting inner leaf masonry corbels. Nowadays it is not permitted to build timber into external or party walls.

Rotten joist ends in main walls are usually found in ground floors, but damp can penetrate walls even at higher levels, particularly in an exposed position (eg facing open land) or where the pointing is old and porous. Leaking downpipes are a common cause of damp to walls. These conditions can cause an outbreak of rot that can spread, as upper floors were not designed with through-ventilation.

Solution *Lift boards over joist ends and check condition.*

If walls are damp, joist ends must be protected from damp with a DPC, or re-hung from modern steel joist hangers. But first check for rot in the timbers by prodding with a screwdriver. Attend to the causes of dampness and treat any decayed timbers and joist ends with preservative. See Chapter 6.

Cause **Damp sleeper walls**

Sleeper walls or brick piers help support ground floor joists. There should be a DPC to keep the timber joists dry and free from decay, but there may be none. Such defects are not common, as the under-floor area should be dry. The sleeper walls themselves are usually trouble free, but on rare occasions damp or subsidence can cause them to disintegrate.

Solution *Check the condition of the ground floor sleeper walls by lifting floorboards near the centre of the room.*

If there is no DPC, the joists may have to be raised so that a plastic DPC sheet can be placed under the timber wall plate. If the brick sleeper wall or pier has disintegrated it will need rebuilding.

Cause **Blocked airflow**

There may be insufficient numbers of airbricks for air to flow freely, or they may have been blocked or rendered over in a misguided attempt to prevent draughts. They must be kept clear, or dampness can lead to rot. Where the house has an extension with a modern concrete floor, there should be ventilation ducts extending through the new floor from the new outside wall.

Solution *Clear blocked vents, replace damaged vents, or fit additional terracotta or plastic airbricks (typical size 215 x 140mm).*

Vents are needed in all walls to prevent 'dead spaces' with no airflow near adjoining solid floors. Soil from flowerbeds must be kept clear of vents. If the concrete floor in your extension has blocked off the old airbricks, it may be possible to improve airflow by fitting extra vents to a side wall. Alternatively a 'periscope' vent can be fitted and channelled to the exterior using extractor ducting.

Cause **Dampness from hidden leaks**

Beware kitchens and bathrooms with suspended timber floors. Hidden leakage from pipes and sinks, or from extreme condensation, can cause rot under units that is only revealed when the units are replaced or the floor collapses while you're doing the washing up!

Water supply pipes are often run in from the street under the house to a kitchen or bathroom at the back. Hidden central heating pipes also pose a risk. A leak in your supply, or next door's, may go unnoticed for years, causing the earth to become saturated, affecting the stability of sleeper walls and structural walls alike. Symptoms include slugs appearing through the floorboards!

Solution *Lift a few boards and check for any dampness under the floor.*

Repair leaks in water supply and waste pipes. Leaks are often close to the sanitary fittings. Even quite minor leaks can cause severe rot if they remain unnoticed over time. Cut out and replace defective timbers and treat the immediate area as described above. Check also that outside surface rainwater is draining away from the house, particularly near doorways. Downpipes discharging by the walls should be redirected. External surface water from the garden may require an additional gulley to improve water dispersal.

STEP BY STEP

Overhauling and sanding a timber floor

TOOLS REQUIRED

- Claw hammer and jemmy to lift boards
- Screwdriver
- Spray for timber treatment fluid
- Hire a belt sander and edge sander for floor stripping plus dust mask, gloves, goggles, and ear protectors
- Jig saw or hacksaw
- Tape measure and spirit level

MATERIALS

- Rot and woodworm fluid (wear protective clothing)
- Floor lacquer or varnish

Once the cause of rot to old softwood timber floors has been remedied (eg damp and lack of ventilation) the floor timbers will need to be overhauled. The boards can then be sanded to produce an attractive, hardwearing, natural finish.

1 Damage to floors often occurs near external doorways and walls. Start by removing all rotten or damaged floorboards to at least 600mm (24in) beyond the area where decay is visible. The lines of the joists below can be seen from the nail runs. A good place to start is at an existing joint between the ends of boards. Insert a jemmy or claw hammer and prise the boards up. With tongued-and-grooved boards, the tongues can be cut using a circular saw or flooring saw along the length of the board. Remove any nearby skirting that obstructs access.

2 If there are no convenient joints at board ends to start from, a board can be cut. Ideally it should be cut directly over a joist, so that relaying it will be easier. But it is normally simpler to cut it at the side of the joist and when relaying to fix a batten to the side of the joist to support the board end. Beware of pipes and electric cables, which often run under the centre of floorboards.

3 Now the extent of any hidden damage to the floor timbers can be checked. If joists have to be removed, cut them just wide of the wall plate supporting them.

4 If there is any rot to the wall plates under the joists, these must also be removed. This can be done by supporting the joists and levering the wall plate out in sections, cutting nails with a metal saw as necessary.

5 Remove old rotten timber. Clean the area and treat nearby timbers with rot fluid (take care!).

6 Apply wood preservative to all new timbers, which should also be of the pre-treated variety.

7 Prepare a strip of plastic DPC and place it under the new wall plate (ie on top of sleeper wall or pier).

8 Having positioned the DPC, slide in the new wall plates, making sure they are level. To adjust the level, use a wooden wedge to prop up one end and pack any gaps (eg with slate or mortar). Remove any temporary joist supports.

9 Fix joists to wall plates by skew nailing through the joist sides.

10 Overlap new joist ends next to the existing ones for extra strength. Skew nail joints or bolt overlapping joists together.

11 The new floor structure should extend well past the initial area of rot. Check air vents are clear.

12 Refix any sound boards or replace with new. Use brads or 20mm No. 8 screws, and reuse old nail holes to help prevent hitting a cable or pipe.

13 If small areas of replacement board are too thin, pack with some sheet wood.

14 Gaps to old boards of more than 5mm caused by shrinkage can be sealed with tapered timber strips (wedges) glued in place. Use a flexible floor sealant or papier mâché for smaller gaps.

15 Punch in all protruding nail heads before sanding and fill small holes with wood filler, or they will tear the sanding belt.

16 Large belt sanders can level rough floorboards, but can be difficult to control, so take care! Ensure the abrasive sheet is tightly fitted. Tilt the machine back slightly, switch on, and gently lower it to the floor. Work in a straight line in slow diagonal sweeps across the grain. Start with medium or coarse sheets.

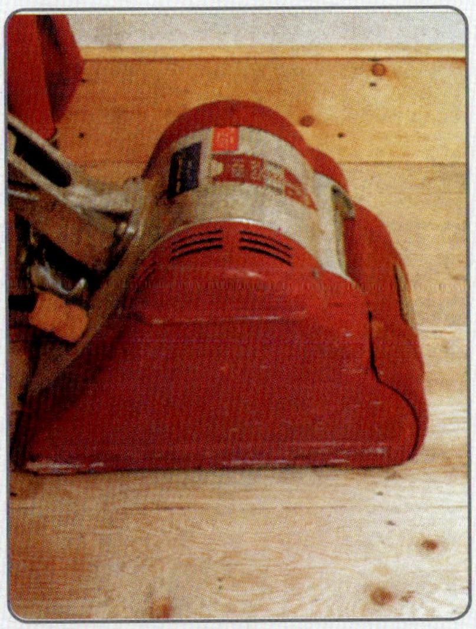

17 Make the second run with fine or medium sheets at 90° to the first, then finish off with a third slow run along the grain using fine sheets.

18 Use an edge sander to get into corners and for warped boards. An orbital sander can be used to finish.

19 After vacuuming all loose dust, apply two or three coats of varnish, the first coat thinned and sanded when dry.

Solid floors

Ground floors to kitchens were normally of solid concrete laid over a bed of rubble hardcore. More rarely reception rooms and halls were also built with solid floors, and this method was soon to become the norm in much post-war housing. Upstairs floors of reinforced concrete are extremely rare but are sometimes found in blocks of flats or flat-roofed 'moderne' houses. See Chapter 2.

Solid floors allowed a more extensive choice of finishes. As noted earlier, buyers of more upmarket properties had a certain fondness for expensive wood block parquet flooring (perhaps to match the oak panelled walls) in hallways and reception rooms. Oak parquet flooring was normally bedded in a layer of bitumen and maintained by sealing and polishing. An expansion joint, such as a cork strip under the skirting, would be left at the edges to give the blocks space to expand (eg on absorbing moisture from the atmosphere).

The most common defects in parquet flooring are:

- Unevenness from unequal wear, which can normally be cured by planing or sanding.
- Loose blocks caused by shrinkage or expansion and subsequent loss of key, cured by resetting the blocks in adhesive.
- Dry rot caused by damp penetration, requiring the removal of the infected blocks, treatment of all adjoining flooring, and renewal with treated blocks on a bed of bitumen.

Another upmarket floor surface was terrazzo, an expensive screed finish of marble chips set in mortar, found in many of the more exclusive bungalows of the period. Lavish marble tiles were also sometimes used.

BELOW: Terrazzo floor. (Photo: South Western Flooring Services)

BELOW: Marble flooring (Photo: South Western Flooring Services)

But strangest of all was magnesite, a magnesium-oxychloride based cement screed that produced an attractive jointless ground floor finish. Unfortunately it was often made using sawdust as a filler, and was also slightly porous, so if it absorbed any water vapour there was a risk of rot, causing the magnesite to expand and break up. It is weird stuff. Normally coloured coral pink or bluish-green with a mottled or grained finish, a small lump will glow brightly when held in a gas flame – the only floor able to perform such party tricks!

Original magnesite may well have now become discoloured and damaged beyond repair, requiring complete removal and replacement with a screed of three parts sand and one part cement, or with timber boarding selected to match floors elsewhere.

In mainstream housing, however, the most common solid floor surface was plain red or black clay quarry tiles, 150mm (6in) square, or occasionally cheap granolithic screed made of 40mm deep cement mixed with stone chippings. With age, old clay tiled floors can become uneven so that the loose and cracked tiles need to be hacked out and replaced. Tiles can also fail if expansion joints have not been provided around the edges of the floor.

To keep dampness at bay, solid floors often relied on a thin coat of asphalt or bitumen adhesive (applied hot and molten) as a basic moisture barrier. But the bitumen base can become brittle with age, causing blocks and tiles to come loose. Some cheaper floors dispensed with the luxury of damp-proofing altogether, relying solely on the impervious nature of the quarry tiles or concrete slab, but without some

Technical data

Suppliers of repro 1930s period floor coverings can be found at www.ThirtiesHouse.co.uk.

Building Research Establishment (BRE) guidelines are specified in the Building Regulation tables at www.ThirtiesHouse.co.uk.

Floor joists are usually a minimum of 150 x 50mm (6 x 2in) thick but can be 8 x 2in, 7 x 3in or 5 x 3in, spaced about 12in or 16in (300–380mm) apart depending on span and spacing. Upper floor joists vary from 150 x 50mm (6 x 2in) to 280 x 75mm (11 x 3in).

Ceiling joists are typically spaced 400, 450, or 600mm apart (16, 18, or 24in centres), usually at 350–450mm (14–18in) centres for upper floors.

Ground floor joists may span no more than 1.8m (6ft) without support, and upper floor joists 2.44m (8ft). The span that a joist can safely cover without support depends on the joist size, and how many joists there are supporting the floor.

Air bricks: total surface area of all vents must be 500m^2 for every 1m^2 of floor area, placed within 450mm of floor corners, spaced no more than 2m apart.

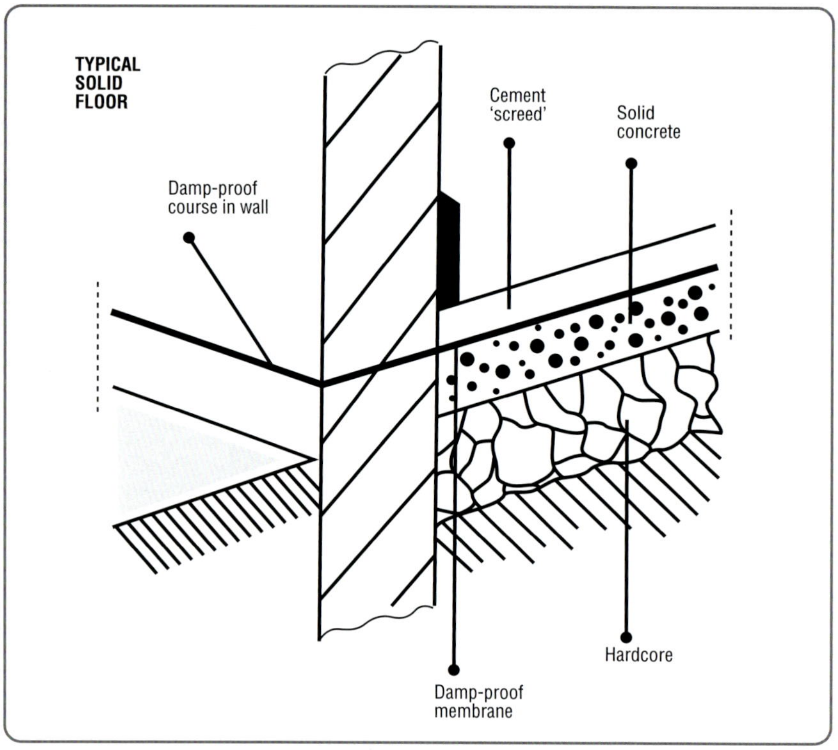

kind of protection there is always the risk that moisture might emerge through the floor as rising dampness. Cold solid floors will also attract damp from condensation, and lino-covered solid floors were well known for feeling cold or damp during winter.

Modern solid concrete floors are constructed of at least 100mm compressed ('compacted') hardcore levelled with sand ('blinding') and covered with approximately 150mm of concrete and insulation to form the 'slab' base. Sandwiched in the concrete is a damp-proof membrane (DPM), usually a thick 1200 gauge plastic sheet to prevent dampness from the ground coming through. The membrane should extend up the sides of the slab and join up with the DPC in the walls. It is normally finished with a levelled sand and cement screed typically 65mm (2.5in) thick.

Defect: Damp floor

SYMPTOMS

Wet floor surface or damp under vinyl; floor tiles lifting or cracked; tiles sound hollow as damp collects below the surface of flooring.

Cause **Leaks from defective plumbing**

Copper pipes embedded in concrete floors are very prone to corrosion and leakage unless protected with tape or run in ducts. Leakage can occur for a long time before failure is detected.

Solution *Break up sections of the floor to expose suspect pipes.*

Defective pipework in floors needs to be hacked out and replaced, and the damaged floor screed and coverings made good. Screeds that are too thin over buried pipes will break down. Where practical, it is better to run new pipes along wall surfaces rather than burying them in concrete.

Cause **No damp-proof membrane**

There may well be no DPM in the original floor, or it may have been punctured where pipes and services run. Kitchen floors were often built bridging the DPC in the walls.

Solution *If the floor is damp, complete relaying may be the most effective remedy.*

If it is otherwise structurally sound a waterproof screed can be applied, but this necessitates raising floor levels and then adjusting levels to adjoining rooms, kitchen fittings, doors, etc, and assessing the adequacy of the remaining floor-to-ceiling headroom.

Cause **Condensation**

Cold floors, particularly in kitchens and bathrooms, will attract condensation as hot air and steam condenses against it. This is fairly common and may look like leakage or even rising damp.

Solution *After levelling out the floor surface (with a levelling compound), a warm covering such as a suitable moisture-resistant timber or laminate fitted over a layer of insulation material will help to prevent dampness caused by condensation. Then provide extractor fans to improve ventilation.*

Defect: Sinking, cracked, or bulging concrete

SYMPTOMS

Uneven floors; cracked floor tiles; floors sound hollow when stamped on; doors stick; walls out of true; gaps below skirtings.

Cause **Poor mixing of the original concrete, or screed that is too thin, can cause floors to sink**

Clues to defective floors include internal walls that are badly cracked due to being built off a floor instead of having their own foundations, and internal doors that are out of alignment. Gaps at skirtings are another indication of floor problems. Look for irregular dips in the floor of more than about 13mm (0.5in), which may indicate localised settlement.

Solution *Some unevenness and slight settlement is not unusual in older solid concrete floors. If the settlement is not excessive, the simplest solution is to lay a levelling screed over the existing concrete.*

However, a severely dropped floor slab may need complete relaying. If the problem is acute but localised, concrete can be pumped into the gaps that have formed in the floor by 'pressure grouting' through holes at 1m (40in) spacing in the slab – an expensive, specialist job.

Cause **Poor compaction**

As well as being of dubious origin, the hardcore was not always compacted too well before being covered in concrete. One problem that can occur is that parts of the hardcore base under the concrete can start to self-compact many years after construction, so the floor sinks and cracks (see BRE definitions of cracking in next paragraph). Typically this is evident around the edges or corners of rooms. Check near door openings, where there may be a slight hump because the wall has a solid foundation and the floor does not. It is more common on sloping sites, where the floor can literally move downhill, albeit at the stately pace of a few millimetres per century.

Solution BRE definitions of cracking tell us that small floor cracks (up to 1mm) and gaps below skirting (up to 13mm) are defined as being 'slight' or 'negligible'. As a rule of thumb, once you get cracks over 5mm (0.2in), or large localised gaps below skirting (more than19mm/0.75in) where the floors are obviously sloping, these count as 'moderate to severe' and are likely to require significant remedial work, as described above.

Cause **Sulphate attack**

This is a chemical reaction that can occur between the concrete and some types of hardcore (eg old clinker from fireplaces or shale), causing the concrete floor to expand and push upwards with cracks and a bulge in the middle of the floor.

Solution *This is not a common problem. It shows by the floor humping upwards in localised areas. In severe cases the concrete will need to be broken up and renewed.*

BELOW: Nice new wood or laminate coverings can hide defects.

FIREPLACES AND FLUES

Here we come to one of the most rewarding renovation projects – adding some glamour and value to your home by restoring disused fireplaces. But the practical challenge of getting the smoke to rise efficiently up the chimney flue is more complex than you might imagine. We investigate common problems such as air starvation, downdraughts, and poor burning, as well as dangers from poisonous fumes and unsupported chimney breasts.

Fireplaces

A house isn't a home without a fireplace. But therein lies the classic dilemma for the 1930s homeowner: what style best suits the architecture of the house? To stick a Georgian fireplace in a suburban semi is to miss a terrific opportunity to fit something really interesting – and appropriate for the age of property.

Here's a little secret: if you know where to look, there are some superb 1930s repro designs now available, as well as salvaged originals, that can transform the feel of a house. Depending on your taste, there is an untapped wonderland of art deco and mock-Tudor pieces just waiting to be rediscovered. But first, let's take a look at how things were built in the beginning – and how it all went so horribly wrong.

Despite the fact that developers in the 1930s frequently advertised new homes as 'all electric', each reception room had its own open fire. However, very few people troubled with the extravagance and hassle of keeping two fires going. Memories were still fresh of voracious Victorian fires that required teams of servants for endless coal carrying. Fireplaces were also often provided upstairs in the bedrooms, since the chimney breasts were there anyway

LEFT: Tiled bedroom fireplace. (Photo: 20th Century Fires)

RIGHT: The height of sophistication – flush-fitted electric fires.

(for the flues from the rooms below to pass through), but these were generally only used for ventilation. Instead, heating could be provided far more easily with freestanding electric fires. Only truly modern houses would have flush-fitting, built-in electric fires, perhaps set within tiled surrounds.

STYLE WARS

Dropped shoulders, angled sides, ribbed openings, geometric motifs, and castellated tops. This isn't Vivienne Westwood's latest creation, but the language of pure 1930s fireplace chic. The choice of styles had become considerably sexier since Victorian times:

All photos: 20th Century Fires

- **All-tiled fireplaces:** these were all the rage, and builders normally offered a choice of colours. Tiles were often mottled, featuring art deco motifs and a fireproof, glazed, kerbed hearth. Very modern. Very practical. A classic deco design might consist of dappled brown tiles with beige inserts and a stepped opening. Or perhaps pale cream and grey or coral coloured tiles set off with a chrome trim. Stimulating stuff.
- **Hardwood mantels:** these had a sense of tradition about them, unlike those young tiled upstarts. For the homeowner with oak-panelled walls, a grand solid oak 'Jacobean' mantel could be just the job. But art deco knew no limits and pervaded even this bastion of tradition, creating all manner of contemporary streamlined mantels designed to fit snugly around – horror of horrors – tiled deco inserts complete with fluted openings. In truth this was really just another Olde Worlde meets 'moderne' compromise, evident in much of the architecture of the period.

- **Traditional brick:** this could be relied upon to not get too trendy, and sure enough, small purpose-made brickette 'Tudor' fireplaces were a popular alternative for the customer with more conventional tastes, culminating in large cottage-style brick inglenooks at the premium end of the market.
- **Cast iron:** even mundane old cast iron had been given a radical makeover and was no longer a stranger to the exotic. Fireplace inserts and mantels would now frequently be enamelled for an ultra-modern look – typically in pewter or flecked blue and cream colours. Odeon-style bedroom fireplaces appeared on the scene resplendent in their enamelled mottled cream finish. Or how about vitreous enamel in flecked blue with bowed centres? Wow.

Only in the bedrooms of some cheaper houses did old-fashioned, slim, black, Victorian-type cast iron fireplaces survive, designed to burn the minimum amount of coal.

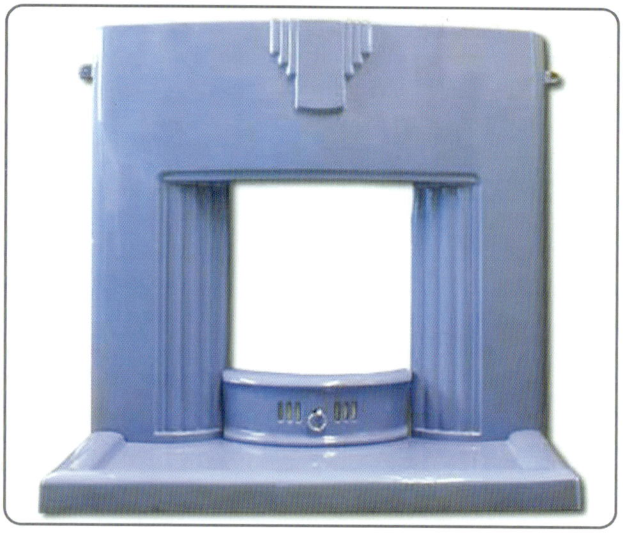

Enamelled cast iron fireplaces. (Photos: 20th Century Fires)

(Photo: 20th Century Fires)

Meanwhile, up at Rich Mansions, the ultimate in art deco fireplaces had arrived, constructed in a radically new wide, horizontal style from rich-veined Canamma green marble and embellished with sumptuous cream-coloured Onyx blocks. A true celebrity amongst fireplaces, guaranteed to blow the pants off incredulous guests. But the excitement wasn't to last…

SO WHAT WENT WRONG?

The story of the sad demise of the fireplace is well known. Tastes changed, and with the widespread introduction of central heating from the 1960s the fireplace was seen as nothing more than an outmoded, dirty, and unnecessarily troublesome anachronism that simply had to go. The fashion-police decreed that they should be ripped out or boarded up and bulky chimney breasts removed to make space. After a period facing near extinction, the revival of all things Victorian since the 1980s has led to a popular resurgence, to the extent that some DIY store designs have now become rather clichéd. Fortunately the world of 1930s gems is still relatively unexplored territory, presenting an intriguing opportunity for the owners of houses of this period.

The real thing

In most houses, it's a fair bet that the originals were discarded long ago. The best guide to tracking down the beauties that may have formerly graced your residence is to find an original fireplace in a neighbouring house of similar age.

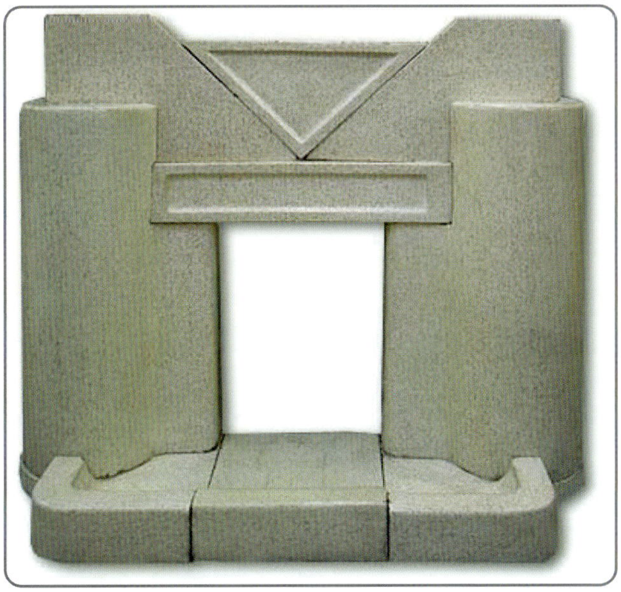
(Photo: 20th Century Fires)

As far as the 'nuts and bolts' of lighting a fire in a 1930s house were concerned, freestanding grates on small legs (with removable ashpan trays underneath to collect the ashes) were rapidly replacing old-fashioned fixed grates. These could be set lower, neatly hidden away behind the 'fret' (ashpan cover). Frets were generally of enamel or lustreware and are still sold today as an authentic period touch in houses built between 1930 and the 1950s. The firebacks that held the grates were often moulded from one piece of fireclay (or of ceramic fibre), which can be replaced with a modern two-section type so that it may be possible to install it without removing the entire fireplace. See Project below.

Some side or rear stacks (mostly now disused) that normally served the kitchens were capable of rather a neat trick when built on external walls. Many were constructed with external soot doors to aid sweeping, or sometimes an outward-facing ashbox, which could be lifted out and emptied from outside, so that the fire did not have to be extinguished when emptying the ash. It also helped to avoid mess in the house. This was a particularly useful feature for 'Baxi' type solid fuel back-boilers, since the hot water supply may have depended on keeping the fireplace back-boiler going 24/7 and some ashpans were large enough to only need emptying every two or three days.

Construction

The fireplaces and flues are a fairly complex part of the building's construction, with each fireplace needing a separate flue right to the top. Where possible, fireplaces were usually built within the party walls, which helped insulate one semi or terrace from next door as well as saving on materials.

Of all the parts of a property, this is one where the Building Acts were at their most rigorous, specifying (but not always enforcing) the method of construction of the chimney breasts, the flue widths, minimum angles for turns within flues, and minimum chimney heights. The Building Acts also strictly stipulated that all fireplaces should have a fireproof 'constructional hearth' built within the floor at a minimum 450mm (18in) to the front and 150mm (6in) either side.

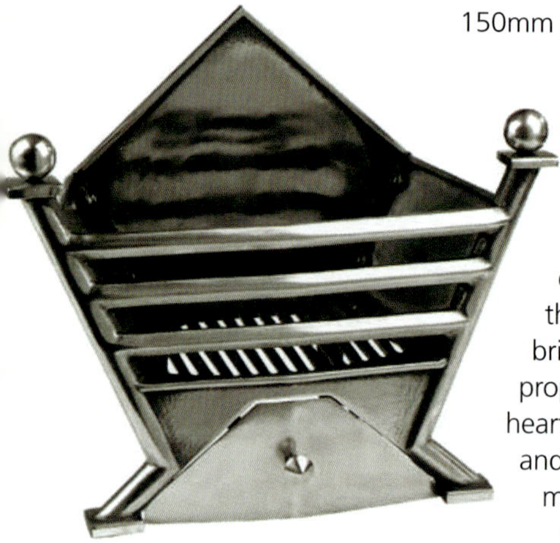

(Photo: 20th Century Fires)

However, should you detect the smell of scorched timber when lighting a fire in a long-disused fireplace, be aware that floor joist ends have occasionally been discovered actually resting in the hot chimney breast brickwork, instead of being properly trimmed around the inert hearth. This is clearly unacceptable and potentially dangerous, and may not be visually obvious if the surface concrete of the hearth was spread over the tops of the joists to conceal them (although the lack of a trimmer joist may give the game away – see Chapter 9).

Opening it up

There is something wickedly enjoyable about excavating an old boarded up fireplace in the hope of revealing a splendid period feature. But more likely all you'll find is an old opening half filled with rubble, soot, dead birds, and chunks of old mortar.

If you propose to reuse an old flue, then before starting you'll need to check that: (1) the chimney breast in the room above and/or in the loft is still there; and (2) that the chimney stack hasn't been taken down. It may have been capped or cowled to protect it from rain, but it should not have been completely sealed.

To open up fireplaces that have been boarded over may simply require the application of a little brute force, but for those blocked off with masonry (normally concrete blockwork) you may need to hire a Kango type power-breaker. But don't get too carried away – take care not to demolish any of the original brickwork that forms the 'builder's opening' (the large square opening in the brickwork of the chimney breast into which the fireplace is fitted), as the top is usually formed with a brick arch holding up the chimney breast above.

If you take a look up the flue from the fireplace (wear eye protectors!) you may be able to see, amongst the sooty old brickwork, how the flue narrows past the throat (aka the 'gather'). It should look like an upside down funnel, smooth all the way up from the fireplace to the flue itself. If you see a flat concrete slab with a hole, or stepped brickwork, this may cause combustion problems for open fires. A simple way to check the flue's efficiency is to light a twist of paper in the opening. If it burns well and the flame is drawn inwards and upwards, the flue is clear. Smoke pellets should also give a useful visual indication. But even if all is well, you still need to get a chimney sweep to clean and inspect the flue before lighting fires.

Refitting a fireplace

Before installing a new fire or heating appliance, you need to first consider how this will affect the flue, because a flue designed for a gas-fired appliance, for example, may not be suitable for a different use, like an open fire. Gas appliances must, in any case, be installed by a competent CORGI registered engineer, who can assess whether your existing flue is appropriate. And if it's the divine aroma of pine logs crackling away in the grate you're after, be aware that

(Photo: 20th Century Fires)

burning wood or coal on an open fire is legally prohibited in smokeless zones, which includes most urban areas – Local Authorities can advise on the status of specific areas.

Not unreasonably, current Building Regulations stipulate that fireplaces must have a sufficient supply of air for combustion and be constructed from non-combustible materials that allow the safe escape of exhaust gases to protect the building from catching fire. Also, the hearth to the floor at the front of the fireplace must also be made of non-combustible material (brick, stone, or concrete) and be at least 125mm (5in) thick. These are usually intact in old houses, most requiring only a little patching with mortar. But some may be cracked excessively due to settlement of the floor and in severe cases may require hacking out and reforming with new concrete.

Removed chimney breasts

Taking out a chimney breast to make more living space is a common, though usually inadvisable, structural alteration. The trouble is that such works are very often done without providing proper support to the remaining masonry and the stack above – with potentially lethal consequences. Structural alterations like this must be approved by Building Control.

Consider this: your party wall with next door may be only one brick thick – about 230mm (9in) – sometimes even less. Sitting on top of it is the full weight of the chimney stack

PROJECT: Replacing a fireback

It is not uncommon for an old fireback to have developed cracks, and as a consequence it may be dangerous to use the fire.

If the cracking is relatively minor it should be repairable with fire cement. Once all the soot has been brushed away, the crack should be raked out using the point of a trowel, undercutting it slightly then soaking it in water. Fire cement should then be trowelled well into the crack, which can be given a smooth finish by going over it with a brush soaked in water.

If there are large cracks in the fireback, or a piece has broken off, the only safe solution is to install a new one. This is best done with the mantel and fireplace insert removed.

1 First break up the old fireback with a bolster chisel and club hammer and clear away. Then remove the old rubble infill behind to expose the original brick 'builder's opening'.

2 Measure the opening of the old defective fireback to ensure you have the right size replacement. Firebacks are normally installed in two sections to allow for expansion.

3 Place the lower section centrally onto a bed of weak mortar, making sure the sides are vertical.

4 Fill the void behind with a mix of weak mortar and rubble, separated from the fireback with a small expansion joint created by first placing a sheet of corrugated cardboard behind the new fireback (it will later burn away, leaving a gap).

5 Once the infill is dry, carefully fit the upper part of the fireback in place on a bed of fire cement. Then point up the edges of the fireback with fire cement. Smooth the joints with a wet paintbrush. Finally, fill behind the top section with more mortar and rubble, then trowel it off to a smooth inward slope at about the same level as the front fireplace lintel (to prevent soot accumulating). When the fireplace insert itself is later fitted, two lengths of fire rope will provide a small expansion joint between the fireback and the fireplace insert, this gap allowing for movement as the fireback gets hot.

structure, a huge amount of masonry supported below by the chimney breasts on either side. Suppose one owner decides to take out the upstairs chimney breast. Unless properly supported, the stack and the masonry below it could become unstable. If the neighbours then decide to do the same on their side, it's probably time to evacuate the building!

BREAST CHECK

To see if any chimney breasts have already been taken out in your house, start by taking a look outside at the chimney stacks. Most semis and terraced houses have a main stack over the party wall in addition to smaller ones on the rear or side walls. In the roof space the main stack usually divides into two chimney breasts that continue into the bedrooms below and then down into the front and rear living rooms on the ground floor.

If there is no chimney breast in these rooms, the question is, what's supporting the remaining masonry above? Look for telltale signs such as a leaning stack, or a cracked, badly patched ceiling next to the party wall where the chimney breast used to be. There may also be some brown ceiling stains where rainwater has dribbled down the old stack. These are small clues that there might be tonnes of unsupported masonry balancing menacingly just above your bedroom ceiling.

The minimum requirement for support to this remaining masonry is in the form of metal 'gallows brackets', or preferably a steel joist (RSJ), which should be visible in the

loft or within the floor above (if it's there at all). Unless consent was obtained at the time of the works, Building Control will need to inspect and retrospectively confirm the adequacy of the method of support. Apart from the obvious health and safety issue, unless satisfactory approvals have been obtained, when you come to sell the house the surveyor and solicitors will raise awkward questions likely to scare away buyers.

Flues

A 1930s house may not feel complete without its fireplace, but behind those exuberant art deco inserts and mantles deadly hidden dangers may be lurking.

The purpose of chimney breasts is to safely enclose the flues. They were traditionally built up in brick with a hole (the flue) left in the middle. As it progresses upward, this structure develops into a fairly complex network of adjacent but separate flues serving different fireplaces in different rooms, which in a semi or terrace would include next door's as well.

But today even experienced builders can be caught out trying to guess the precise routes of old flues. There is the cautionary story of the Building Control officer who one day received an emergency phone call from an irate owner of a 1930s semi. The caller was extremely alarmed to discover showers of bricks raining down into his living room fireplace. It transpired that the builders next door were busy removing a bedroom chimney breast but hadn't bargained for the bizarre method of flue construction. Instead of the party wall neatly separating each property's flues on either side as normal, these flues were instead run in a central line, one in front of the other! Other houses were built with flues wrapped around each other to aid the 'draw' of the fires. Moral: think twice before tackling such a job (and see earlier comments regarding the Party Wall Act).

REALITY TV

A more familiar problem is the risk of rain and sleet pouring straight down onto the fire. To prevent this and to check downdraughts, flues were normally constructed of corbelled brickwork in a gentle curve – which is why you shouldn't be able to see daylight when looking up a flue. The normal flue size for an ordinary fireplace was roughly one brick square, or about 230 x 230mm (9 x 9in).

As the flues and chimneys were being built, the masonry would normally be rendered internally with parging (see Chapter 3) to make them smoke-tight. However, over the years rain from unprotected chimney pots has often combined with soot and acidic gases from coal fires to degrade the parging and the mortar joints. Loose lumps of parging can fall off and collect on ledges within the flues, and if the flue isn't swept to remove this debris it can act like a sponge and soak up polluted water that eventually seeps through the chimney breasts. Worse, the thin wall of brickwork between flues can deteriorate, enabling smoke and fumes to pass from one flue into another. Feeling sleepy? You may be inhaling the poisonous fumes from next door's gas fire.

Symptoms of 'parging failure' include debris in the fireplace, blocked flues, and smoke escaping into other flues. CCTV cameras of a similar type to those used to investigate hidden damage in drains can be used to help detect flue defects such as masonry flaws, faulty linings, fire damage, dampness, and birds' nests. The solution is normally for the flue to be relined. In fact, lining is necessary for all active flues of this age, particularly those serving gas fires and boilers, and will also help prevent other problems, like staining on chimney breasts. It is not always easy to see if a flue is already lined; the most obvious clue is normally where you can see a metal terminal or cowling at the chimney pot.

Older floor-standing boilers, on the other hand, often have very visible 'naked' flue pipes, typically of steel or asbestos cement. These often run up through the house until entering a chimney breast. Such flue pipes must be properly supported and periodically checked for signs of scorch marks, cracking, or gaps at joints, and there should be at least 25mm (1in) clearance with surrounding floorboards, joists, etc. Modern wall-mounted boilers are less cumbersome, with small balanced flues that project through an external wall. See Chapter 12.

Technical data

See Building Regulations Part J. For full details of specialist suppliers and trade associations, downloadable Building Regulations, and further advice, please visit www.ThirtiesHouse.co.uk. See also the solid fuel association website at www.solidfuel.co.uk.

The ratio of the flue diameter to the fireplace opening cross-section should not be more than 1:8. Most grates are no more than 450mm (18in) wide by 500mm (22in) high, and are suitable for a flue as small as 185mm (7.5in). The flue for a solid fuel appliance should be at least 4.5m (14.75ft) high. See BS 5440 for other fuels.

Staining and damp

Ugly stains on chimney breasts can result from old acidic, tarry dampness in flues seeping through eaten-away mortar joints and into the plaster. Dampness on upstairs chimney breasts may also be due to problems at roof level such as defective flashings, rain coming down pots, or eroded brickwork and pointing to the stack. See Chapter 3.

But there's another, more insidious kind of dampness. Over the years, the unholy alliance of rainwater in the flue and water vapour from condensation (due to a lack of ventilation), combined with the toxic combustion gases from coal fires (tar acids, ammonia, sulphates etc), can cause damp to find its way into the surface plaster of the chimney

Goodbye toxic mould

If unused chimneys are boarded up but are not ventilated they will suffer from condensation and damp staining. In the 1970s, houses built without chimneys but fitted with double-glazing became so hermetically sealed that serious problems occurred with condensation and toxic mould. See Chapter 6. Disused fireplaces can provide an ideal solution by helping to ventilate the house. They should be ventilated at both top and bottom to get a through-flow of air to disperse unhealthy stagnant moist air. There are two things to check:

1 If fireplaces are boarded up there should be an open vent or airbrick built in, to allow a flow of air up the stack (unless the stack has been removed, or taken down into the loft).

2 The redundant chimney pot should be protected with a hood, so that rain doesn't get in, but vented so that there's still a draught to ventilate the flue. There are several suitable pots and caps available (see Chapter 3). An alternative method is to reduce a redundant chimney in height, fit airbricks in the sides of the brickwork and cap off the top, for example with a suitable concrete paving slab bedded on mortar. Flues must first be swept to prevent the risk of soot coming into the room through the vent.

breast. And that damp may well contain our old friends hygroscopic salts, which contaminate the plaster (see section on 'Rising damp' in Chapter 6). In fact they can appear anywhere that damp has previously got into the house (eg from leaking flashings).

Even when you've solved the cause of the damp, it can be infuriating to see patchy dampness on the plaster reappearing. Each time the air in the house becomes a little humid the salts absorb it and liquefy, doing an excellent impersonation of penetrating damp. But when the atmosphere is dry (or when you get the builder round to check it) the damp has mysteriously disappeared!

When plaster is heavily stained or contaminated by salts, the best remedy is to hack off all the affected plaster, wash down and seal the exposed brickwork (which may contain further salts), and replaster with a 1:3 cement/sand base coat and a 'Multifinish' plaster topcoat to at least 300mm (12in) beyond the old staining. This is the same remedy as for plaster affected by rising damp. Alternatively, stained plaster may be sealed and dry-lined with foil-backed plasterboard.

Defect: Combustion problems – fires burn poorly

SYMPTOMS

Fire becomes choked and struggles to burn.

Cause **As described opposite for a smoky fire, but with less obvious symptoms** – eg a fire may burn well for a while, but a poor airflow or downdraught means the fire chokes on exhaust gases that are not fully dispersed. Downdraughts are complex because the house itself can act like a big chimney, being full of warm air that naturally rises, sometimes with immense suction.

Solution *As for a smoky fire.*

But there may be a simpler solution. A poorly fitted loft hatch or draughty upstairs windows will compete with the chimney to suck air (and smoke) upwards, so check these first. In very windy conditions, an air vent on the downwind side of the house can create 'negative pressure' that literally sucks the smoke back down the chimney.

Also, extractor fans, cooker hoods, other fires and boilers all need air to work; if they have a stronger pull than the chimney, they win! So extractor fans should not normally be positioned in the same room as an open-flued boiler (ie one that's not a balanced flue through the wall) or an appliance such as a 'living flame' gas fire.

Combustion problems may also be caused by unsuitable inserts fitted to chimney pots by roofers (eg to prevent ingress of rain), and by the wrong type of flue terminal.

Defect: Smoky fires

SYMPTOMS

Smoke doesn't go up the chimney but billows into the room.

Cause Air starvation – insufficient air to carry the smoke into the flue

There are several possible causes of smoky fires, but a lack of air is the most common. Like a car engine, a fire needs fuel and air for combustion. Cut the air supply and an engine will splutter and the exhaust becomes heavy with unburned fuel. An open fire needs at least six changes of air in the room per hour to burn well. Air is drawn into the fire from the room, which in turn needs to be replaced.

Solution *Check by opening a door or window – if the smoke clears, the problem is likely to be air starvation.* Install vents or underfloor ducts, or fit a small pipe direct from outside to feed the fire. Rooms must not be completely airtight.

Cause Unsuitable size of flue

Too large a flue (more than about 230mm square) can cause smokiness because it never really gets warm. Too small (less than 185mm square) can choke the fire. Flues should be the same size all the way up.

Solution *Line large flues with suitable lining, such as special concrete or fireclay pipes.*

Cause Poor chimney draught caused by defective construction

(eg sharp bends in the flue) or air leaks at mortar joints

Solution *A chimney sweep can check the run of a flue with rods. If severe, open up the front of the chimney breast and rebuild defective areas.*

Cause Adverse flow conditions due to poor design

Anything in the flue that is not smooth and symmetrical can affect the aerodynamics of the flue gases leaving the chimney in gusty weather. If the throat over the fire is too large, the escape of smoke and gases is slowed. Or if the fireplace opening is too large in relation to the flue (ie more than six times larger), or too high (more than 610mm/24in), smoke may enter the room.

Solution *Fit a throat restrictor.*
(or wedge a thin sheet of metal across the front of the throat) to reduce the entry zone to about 100 x 250mm (4 x 10in). To lower the fireplace opening, fit a metal canopy or place a thin piece of metal 75–100mm (3–4in) high across the top of the opening to reduce height to 510–560mm (20–22in).

Cause Unsuitable chimney pot

A round pot base fitted over a square flue, for example, may cause an obstruction to the flow. Cowls or guards on pots may look clear from ground level but could actually be sufficiently blocked to affect the burning of the fire.

Solution *Replace with suitable chimney pot for flue. Check cowls are clear.*

Cause Downdraught causes smoke to blow back

There are several causes of downdraughts. Typically the chimney is not high enough above the ridge, or wind currents near chimney tops create a 'high pressure zone', caused by high buildings, trees, hills etc nearby.

Solution *Extend chimney with 'long tom' pipes, or build up the stack. Fitting a special draught-inducing cowl or circular deflector should also help.*
Alternatively fit a concrete capping at the top of the chimney supported by small piers at each corner with gaps in between.

Defect: Chimney fires

SYMPTOMS

Hot chimney breasts; smell of burning. Fires in flues may burn unnoticed until structural damage is caused or fire spreads to the main house.

A build up of soot and tar or straw from nests can catch fire, causing hidden fires that are hard to extinguish. A chimney fire can burn at over 1000°C, causing metal liners to collapse.

Cause **Inefficient combustion due to poor air supply, or to the same causes as for smoky fires, listed above, or to excessive soot (see below)**

Solution *Improve air supply.*

Flues need to be swept at least twice a year to remove combustible soot deposits and blockages, especially if burning wood or peat, which are particularly aggressive fuels and produce a rapid build up of tar and deposits. Sweeping with a brush and rods is still the best method. Sweeps should be NACS or HETAS approved or members of the Guild of Master Sweeps.

Defect: Blocked chimneys

SYMPTOMS

Smoke blowing back; feathers, straw etc in grate; flies attracted by decomposing dead birds.

Cause **Flue blocked by debris, soot, nests, dead birds, etc.**

Solution *Ensure chimney has been swept.*

Some old flues have voids and bends that can harbour birds' nests, which drop off and cause blockages. Debris may be from damaged parging or from slipped bricks that separate one flue from another (known as 'bats' or 'mid-feathers'). The flue will need to be lined.

Excessive soot may be due to using unsuitable fuel. To check the flue is clear, a metal 'coring ball' can be lowered down the flue. Check the size and position of fireplace throat and lintel. (See technical data box.)

Defect: Birds entering the house via the chimney

SYMPTOMS

Feathers, sticks, straw, and soot in grate; bird ingress.

Cause **Unprotected chimney pots allow nesting and bird access**

Solution *Fit a special protective ' bird guard' to the pot.*

Defect: Smoke and fumes leak into other rooms

SYMPTOMS

Obvious smoke leaks. Fumes and carbon monoxide cause drowsiness and can be fatal.

Cause **Air leaks through defective brick joints or cracked parging can allow toxic smoke and fumes to leak into rooms**

They can also have the effect of cooling the exhaust gases, reducing the draught and affecting combustion.

Solution *Do a smoke bomb test (available from DIY stores) and trace leaks. Make good defective joints and line the flue (see below).*

Installing flue liners

If you want to reuse an old fireplace it is important that the flue is impervious to poisonous combustion gases. But flues of this age won't be. The solution is to line the flue.

The danger with old slow-burning coal and gas boilers is that of excessive condensation of gases in the flue. Old brick flues must be lined, to prevent this condensation from attacking and eating away at the mortar and brickwork. New flue liners also need to be insulated, particularly if the chimney is located against a cold outer wall.

There are three basic types of flue liners: stainless steel liners, poured concrete linings, and rigid clay or concrete pipes.

STAINLESS STEEL LINERS

Solid fuel, wood, or gas 'living flame' effect fires require a flexible double skin liner (Class 2). They have a smooth inner skin and corrugated outer surface and are installed by being pulled either up or down the old flue by an attached rope. The ends are then fixed in position – the top is secured by a sealing plate bedded on the stack top before a metal terminal is added. To reduce the risk of condensation, the space around the liner is usually back-filled with mineral insulation such as vermiculite.

Wood burning stoves need special rigid metal liners (minimum of 1mm thick), as they generate extreme heat in the flue. These are installed in sections with joints secured by clips. Again, the space around the liner is insulated by being back-filled. Oil-fired boilers also need a special insulated lining due to their high operating temperatures.

Closed gas fires and boilers may only require a lightweight single skin flexi liner (Class 1). The life of some steel liners is limited to only about 10–15 years, so if an old gas fire is replaced with a solid fuel stove or an open fireplace the liner will probably need to be changed also.

POURED CONCRETE IN SITU LININGS

Linings can be made on site by pouring concrete down the flue around a special inflatable thin rubber tube, which is later deflated and removed to leave a smooth new flue. A standard 225mm (9in) square flue will accommodate a 185mm (7.25in) cast lining, which meets Building Regulations requirements. But there are some potential drawbacks – it may require opening up chimney breasts at bends to position the tube correctly, and the large amount of water used can cause dampness.

SOLID LINERS

Rigid pipes of clay, concrete, or terracotta come in ready-made sections that slot together, but installing them is only really feasible where the chimneys are large and fairly straight or where they are being rebuilt.

Old kitchen boilers often have flues lined with clay pipes, asbestos cement pipes, or concrete pipes.

(Photo: 20th Century Fires)

INTERNAL JOINERY, KITCHENS AND DECORATIONS

If you enjoy the idea of being a house-detective, where better to start than in your own home.

It's surprising how much of the history and status of a pre-war house can be revealed from the internal joinery and finishes, and how hidden clues may indicate the presence of potential killer defects that can be safely eradicated if spotted early enough. From the complexity of staircase construction to common faults with internal doors and skirting, all is revealed.

If you think 'status anxiety' is a purely 21st-century phenomenon, a trip back in time might tell a different story. The entrance hall and front room were traditionally the places to show off your taste and affluence to guests and callers, as they had been for the Victorians. The quality of the internal fittings and finishes here were designed to project the most prestigious image within the available budget. Most people didn't yet own cars with which to parade social status, so in all but the cheapest houses the lavishness of the visible joinery, glazing, and floor coverings bore an enhanced significance, often becoming plainer in rooms out of the public eye.

Having been suitably impressed by the stained glass and leaded lights around the porch and front door, upon entering the hall the visitor would, in grander homes, be treated to a vision of baronial England – 'Jacobean' oak panelling, false beams to ceilings, and even retro inglenook fireplaces. But it was the simple country cottage look that was the most popular mainstream choice for interiors, despite the existence of 'modern movement' design influences.

Fittings sometimes varied from house to house in the same road to the extent that it is not unusual to find different sizes of skirting boards, architraves, doors and handles in adjoining properties. This, however, was probably less to do with status and more to do with the materials that the builders had to hand at the time, which depended on the deal they could negotiate with the local builders' merchant.

Nonetheless, it is these features, along with the windows and fireplaces, that chiefly gave houses their character, and which, if still surviving, can add to the value. In their own way, 1930s houses are design classics; it is unfortunate (although understandable) that many previous owners made the mistake of spending good money sanitising them into featureless boxes. The challenge now is to up the value by restoring original features or installing new fittings appropriate for the age. If the old interiors have been stripped out there may still be clues as to what was there originally, such as the evidence of old fixing holes or hardboard covers on doors, and neighbouring houses of a similar age and style may retain some original features.

The vogue for light stripped pine is of relatively recent origin – in the 1930s softwood was regarded as very ordinary timber, to be painted or darkly varnished, whereas better quality hardwood such as mahogany banister rails would

RIGHT: The country cottage look was a popular interior style. **(Photo: Greg Stevenson)**

normally be polished. As a general rule, the more expensive the house the more exposed areas of hardwood (panelling, stairs, floors etc) were left visible. In most homes, however, the woodwork would have been painted, often in colours such as brown, dull white, or cream, or painted in a grained pattern to resemble more expensive oak.

Stairs

From a decorative viewpoint today, staircases can present an attractive opportunity for stripping the wood to fully display their innate quality and style. Because this was one of the largest assemblies of timber in the house, 1930s builders could enhance the appeal to buyers by creating something as fashionable as possible within the available space and budget, perhaps by hinting at the grandeur of staircases from days of old. So, depending on the size of the hall, the stairs would ideally incorporate a quarter turn near the base and another near the top, some with an intriguing glimpse of an upper galleried landing.

By now, old fashioned turned-wood spindles and ornate newel posts were rather despised and hence had largely disappeared in favour of simple square-section posts and 'stick' balusters, often arranged in groups of three. An alternative 'streamlined' modern treatment was to fully enclose the bannisters with boarded panels, a style which, because of its cost-saving possibilities, was enthusiastically adopted by some Council architects. Handrails were typically of painted plain softwood or of more expensive polished hardwood, being oval or 'toad's back' in section.

Standard staircases were formed from four basic elements: treads, risers, strings, and carriages. The steps (treads and risers) slotted at each side into rebates cut into the strings (the long lengths of timber running top to bottom); a close fit was ensured by driving in thin hardwood wedges at the joints with the strings, and small triangular blocks were glued under the treads at the joints with the tops of the risers. Finally, additional support was provided by

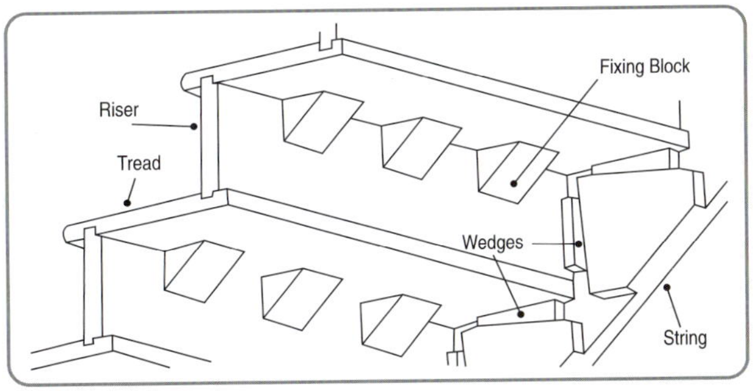

two or three carriages (thick lengths of timber running along the underside).

The main staircase normally had just one straight main flight. The turns in the stairs, known as 'dog legs', were built with fan-shaped steps called 'winders' radiating out. The main difference between a modern staircase and an older one is the pitch. Some originals have relatively narrow treads and high risers to achieve what would now be an illegally steep angle, so modern replacement staircases may not actually fit the available space. It is therefore usually better to repair existing staircases than to rip them out.

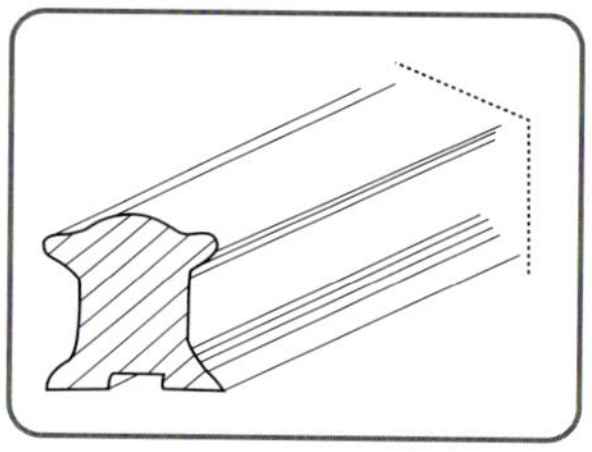

Today, the design of stairs is controlled by the Building Regulations (see website), and constitutes one of the more complex parts of the legislation. Briefly, stairs must have a clear minimum width of 800mm (31.5in) and must not be steeper than 42°. Stair 'goings' ('goings' are the treads without the small projecting front 'nosing') must be not less than 220mm (8.7in) deep and risers no more than 220mm (8.7in) high. There must be clear headroom of at least 2m (6.5ft) and an unobstructed landing space at the top and bottom, so you cannot have a doorway directly adjoining the stairs. A balustrade at least 840mm (33in) high is required at the side of the stairs and the gap between spindles must be less than 100mm (4in).

Streamlined modern bannister – made of old-fashioned lath and plaster.

Although the staircase is a complicated exercise in joinery it is fairly easy to carry out basic maintenance such as refixing loose blocks or wedges under the treads (where accessible) and replacing wooden spindles. Staircases are surprisingly susceptible to attack from beetle and rot, as they often adjoin damp outside walls and most under-stairs spaces can be poorly ventilated – ideal conditions for timber decay. But mild beetle attack is not normally serious. If it is still active, with signs of wood dust around the bore holes, it will require treating with an appropriate insecticide. See Chapter 6.

Defect: Wobbly bannisters/balustrades

SYMPTOMS

Loose handrails and spindles.

Cause **Loose joints, eg between newel posts and handrails, or loose balusters**

Solution Handrails are joined to newel posts with mortise and tenon joints that can be dismantled and reglued. If the joints between different lengths of handrail are loose, look on the underside of the rail for a small timber plug, which conceals a bolt or screw that can be tightened to pull the rails together.

If balusters are loose, the simplest repair is to reglue the loose joints and diagonally screw through the end into the tread or handrail.

Worn nosings (in front of the riser) can be cut or prised off the front of the tread and replaced in matching new timber, glued and screwed into place.

Defect: Gaps to the walls, movement, sagging stairs

SYMPTOMS

Loose newel posts; unstable stairs.

Cause **Inadequate support to staircase. Staircase has come loose from wall**

Solution *Check how staircase is supported. The main string may be inadequately fixed to the wall: refix with plugs and screws or use masonry bolts.*

Cause **Rot or woodworm**

Solution *Check for rot, especially at the base of the newel post at ground floor level, and for woodworm under the stairs. Cut out and renew affected timber and treat remaining timbers.*

Cause **Defects in wall: bulging, damp, etc**

Solution *See Chapters 5 and 6. Repair wall and refix staircase.*

Defect: Loose treads and risers

SYMPTOMS

Squeaks, creaks, and soft treads.

Cause **Loose fixing blocks under treads or loose wedges**

Because the timber has shrunk or the old glue has weakened some of the joints between stair components may have opened.

Solution *Securely refix loose blocks and wedges with glue (from underneath).*

Check how treads are supported and refix with timber packing if necessary. Where stairs are plastered underneath, the plaster will need to be removed to gain access. To avoid this, it may be sufficient to simply refix the small triangular blocks under the rounded front edges of each step (the nosings).

Internal doors

One of the most distinctive features of 1930s houses is their trademark 'one over three' internal doors. These are a design classic with a large square upper panel over three thin vertical panels (or more rarely two or four panels). For the design elite, strictly modern architecture demanded 'clean' doors, totally flush without panels. Although these were few and far between, they did spawn some copycat DIY improvements in later years, with hardboard panels concealing the original panelled doors. Variations on the theme included the more 1940s style 'ladder' panelled door with four or five equal oblong panels.

The typical panelled door of Douglas fir or pine has a solid frame about 32mm (1.25in) thick, with thin solid timber infill panels, secured with discreet decorative mouldings. Dearer houses had doors in hardwoods such as oak. Locks or latches were mortised into the outer edge, except where older surface-mounted rim sash locks were sometimes used to avoid weakening thinner doors.

Another 1930s classic is the opaque glazed door, which was used to good effect in many more fashionable houses and apartments. Doors with panes of striped 'reeded' glass are very much of this era, with glazing beads sometimes dividing the panes horizontally into a staggered brickwork-like pattern on double doors to living rooms (Poirot fans may recognise this). Note that much original full length glazing is

close to floor level and is now generally quite brittle and will not comply with current safety standards.

The handles were of classic oval-shaped Bakelite (some with separate handles and key fobs) or deco-patterned metal, or merely of old-fashioned plain brass and cast iron designs. Modern angular chrome handles were the preserve of those living in modernist villas.

Door frames were concealed conventionally with timber architraves (moulded cover strips) which today may be difficult to match exactly. Plainer, smoother styles were now generally preferred to the older Victorian ogee shape for both architraves and skirting.

Internal doors were invariably painted. If you plan to strip them, cold dipping is preferable to the hot dip process (which can loosen joints and split panels) or flame guns (which can leave ugly scorch marks). Alternatively use a hot-air gun and a scraper, or a poultice, or solvent-based stripper.

Common defects are similar to those described for external doors in Chapter 7, including warping, split panels, and sticking in frames. Serious defects are rare, as the doors are not usually exposed to damp. Panels can sometimes be removed by carefully prising off the moulding that holds them in place and replacing the damaged panel.

If an old door has been cut too short – perhaps to accommodate old carpets since removed – a matching piece of wood can be cut and spliced in using wood filler to mask the joint. Door catches may require easing and adjusting. Keys can be made up for old locks by locksmiths, and repro rim sash locks and ironmongery are widely available. Doors that stick can be remedied by adjusting the door stops or removing the door and planing it down, unless the problem is due to deflection in the frame caused by structural movement in the wall. See Chapter 8.

Original reclaimed doors are still widely available. However, selecting new replacement doors can be a little tricky as old openings may be of non-standard sizes and doors were sometimes custom-made on site. Door heights varied between 1905–2030mm (75–80in), although door thickness would often be equivalent to today's standard 35mm (1.37in). A rough guide to typical original door widths is:

Airing cupboard	610mm (24in)
Bedroom doors	686mm (27in) or 711mm (28in)
Ground floor doors	762mm (30in), 787mm (31in), or 812mm (32in)

This compares reasonably well to modern 1981mm high manufactured doors, which are available in common widths of 686, 762, and 838mm (27, 30, and 33in), and some in larger standard sizes of 724 x 1968mm (28.5 x 77.5in) and 813 x 2032mm (32 x 80in). If all else fails, a good joiner can make new matching doors – at a price.

Replacing an internal door is not always as easy as it looks, as in older houses there may be a slight bow at the head of the doorframe. This can be planed, or the top of the door trimmed. Holding the new door up to the frame allows you to pencil around the perimeter so that any undulations in the frame can be allowed for by planing the door to match (working inwards from the corners, to prevent splitting). The gap at the bottom should be 3mm (0.125in) above the floor covering.

If the hinges or the inner edge bind on the frame, this can often be solved by sanding the corners to a slightly bevelled finish. Hinges should be positioned about 150mm (6in) from the top and about 200mm (8in) from the bottom. The screws shouldn't all be driven home until the door closes correctly.

Fitting a new door lining will inevitably damage the surrounding plasterwork, but is rarely required unless making a new opening in a wall. Door linings of planed softwood are sold in stock sizes to take standard doors, but can be adjusted.

Linings are secured to the surrounding masonry by screws, fitted in pairs to prevent twisting. Thin packing strips need to be placed behind the lining timbers to achieve a straight edge. Once fitted and the plastering completed, the door can be hung and the architraves mitred and nailed in place over the joints.

ABOVE: Lavish deco oak veneer. **(Minchinhampton Architectural Salvage Co)**

Skirting

Skirting was either made from timber mouldings or, sometimes, constructed from boards which could be bent to curved shapes (eg at the top and bottom of the stairs). Plain modern chamfered styles or simple moulded *ovolo* or *lamb's tongue* patterns were now very much in vogue. Skirting was fixed into wooden plugs in masonry walls or was sometimes nailed to breeze blocks. As with architraves, matching original skirting exactly is often impossible today due to the number of local variations in styles.

Small gaps at skirtings often date from the time of construction, but may have since been exacerbated by settlement. One cosmetic solution is to fit timber beading at the joint to the floor. However, larger gaps may sometimes be an indication of problems with the floor itself – irregular dips in the floor of more than about 14mm (0.5in) may indicate localised settlement. Defects to the skirting boards themselves are usually down to rot or beetle, caused by dampness near outer walls, or poor DIY alterations – look for signs of filler at joints.

Other joinery

There was a clear hierarchy in the world of wall finishes. The cheapest houses may only have had painted brickwork in bathrooms, WCs, and kitchens. The next best thing was painted plaster, or preferably wallpapered plaster, which was the most common wall covering. Superior to this was old-fashioned painted wooden wainscoting (lower-wall panelling), or polished hardwood panelling, perhaps made from oak-faced plywood with traditional pegged joints.

But if you wanted to be achingly cool, and had a few quid to spend, art deco style light oak panelling with beautiful inlaid veneer was simply the cat's pyjamas. This was likely to be found in the luxurious residences of some super rich celebrities and captains of industry.

In conventional houses, Victorian dado rails had now all but disappeared. Picture rails, however, were still widely fitted running above door level, creating a traditional decorative frieze to the upper wall between the picture rail and the ceiling.

The main risk to timber panelling, or any wood adjacent to external walls, is from attacks of rot or woodworm due to damp in the walls and poor ventilation. See Chapter 6.

Traditional picture rails remained popular...

...even moderne curvy ones.

Kitchen units

By modern standards kitchens were extremely cramped. Even larger kitchens were only typically about 12 x 10ft (3.6 x 2.5m). Nonetheless, they were still advertised as having 'every modern device' – a major selling point. As well as a gas or electric cooker (or an enamelled range – Agas date from 1929) there would also often be a black or enamelled iron boiler for hot water (also useful for incinerating rubbish). Typically, an *Ideal* coke boiler would stand on a quarry-tiled base in a corner. But somehow these compact kitchens also managed to accommodate a kitchen sink and draining board, a wringer, and a storage cabinet – not forgetting space for the kitchen door, the garden door, a larder, and a window – and sometimes a coal fired copper for washing clothes!

Freestanding modern cookers were a massive advance over temperamental Edwardian ranges. They were enamelled inside and out to make cleaning easier, and often had controllable three-position taps and a thermostat. Being raised up on legs allowed easy access for cleaning, and the enhanced height reduced the need to stoop. Fridges, on the other hand, were a hugely expensive luxury, far beyond the means of most homeowners. A tiled larder was provided instead, ideally north-facing, with a gauze window to keep food cool.

The smaller suburban house did not have the space to provide both a large kitchen and a dining room. Thus the kitchenette or 'dinette' was created, which was little more than a rear reception room with a tiny kitchen space that was partially partitioned off.

Some more expensive houses had the luxury of futuristic fitted kitchens, complete with folding seats and a pull-down ironing board. But for most, modern worktops and units had not yet arrived. Private builders preferred to supply cheaper freestanding kitchen cabinets or a fold-away drop-down work-table, whereas Council house designs laid more emphasis on providing built-in cupboards and stores. Crockery was stored on a dresser, rack, or movable cupboard. The kitchen sink, flanked by a teak draining board, was a traditional white-glazed earthenware 'Belfast' or butler's sink, often with modern chrome-plated taps.

Today, kitchen units are usually of the flat-packed kit variety. Common defects are poor joints to worktops, loose hinges and fittings, hidden leakage or damp from condensation behind units, and poor DIY workmanship generally. It is often simpler to replace complete units with standard-size new ones than to contemplate lots of minor repairs.

'Good Housekeeping' 1937: futuristic fitted units. (Photo: Greg Stevenson)

Decoration

There are many publications providing in-depth coverage of interior design, decorating techniques, and art deco styles. Space does not permit a full account here, but more information can be found at the www.ThirtiesHouse.co.uk website.

As we have seen, the most fashionable finishes were expensive oak-panelled walls and hardwood parquet flooring. But both were beyond the budget of most homeowners, who decorated their houses by wallpapering or painting the walls, and added curtain pelmets made from stepped plywood over the windows.

Wallpapers with strong colours such as blues, yellows, and purples on dark backgrounds were very 'in'. Oriental landscapes and exotic plumed birds were also popular, with floral patterns common in bedrooms. But perhaps the most frequently recurring motif was the Chinese lantern.

Some wallpapers also served to imitate more expensive finishes – for example, antique wood-effect wallpaper, or anaglypta that resembled Jacobean plaster ceilings. Design inspiration was often drawn from the movies, whence the vogue for palm trees and desert scenes. But many preferred the more subdued 'Olde English' style, keeping walls plain beige, with textured wallpapers offset by decorative borders. Where walls were painted, bright pastel colours like cream, apple green, light grey, and powder blue were fashionable.

In kitchens and bathrooms tiling was very desirable, but it was expensive, so 'half-tiling' became the norm. It was considered essential around the food preparation areas – ie the stove and sink. Normally cream or white tiling was carried up from the floor to waist height and topped with a narrow dado band of black-and-white chequered tiles or plain cream tiles. The remaining upper wall space between the tiles and the ceiling was painted in gloss, oil, or enamel paint for ease of washing, or else lined with wallpaper which was then varnished. Wallpaper in a tile pattern was a popular, cheaper alternative. Some Council houses made do with basic gloss-painted brick.

Ceilings in kitchens and bathrooms were also painted with gloss paint to protect them from steam. Alternatively traditional chalk and water-based whitewash was sometimes used, but this tended to crack and flake with condensation unless the ceiling had been lined with paper prior to whitewashing.

LEAD PAINT

Although modern titanium and plastic paints and synthetic colourants were developed in the 1930s, many oil paints were still made traditionally from white lead, linseed oil and ground pigment. Old lead-based paint is not normally harmful unless it is disturbed – dust from sanding or scraping can be dangerous since lead is toxic when absorbed through the skin or by ingestion. So wear a respirator and keep children away when working. Even chemical strippers generate fumes that may carry lead. Blowlamps and hot-air strippers aren't ideal either since they also produce smoke and dust. The best advice is to use a poultice type paint stripper, obviating the need for scraping or dangerous fumes. After completing the work, clean the area with a vacuum cleaner and wash down the stripped surfaces and flooring nearby with detergent. Bag up all clothes and wash them thoroughly, separately from other clothes.

THE SERVICES, BATHROOMS, PLUMBING AND HEATING

Today, there are some important issues with the services that owners of 1930s homes should be aware of. There are potential dangers from such things as defective electrics, old lead piping, corroded water supply pipes and faulty flues emitting poisonous carbon monoxide. Concerns about vermin infestation or dead birds contaminating your cold water supply are not as fanciful as you may think. Even those small annoyances such as low water pressure, dripping taps and knocking pipes are investigated.

A services revolution transformed British homes in the 1930s. To get some idea of the magic this new era brought to people's daily lives, you'd have to first imagine how it felt growing up in a world substantially lacking in the services we now take for granted – heating, hot water, decent artificial lighting, and the convenience of instant electric power. For this had been the experience of most of the homebuying public about to be seduced by glittering new suburban houses offering such wonders as porcelain bathroom suites with hot water on tap, instant electric fires, warm airing cupboards, and thermostatically controlled enamelled cookers. This was the first generation to discover the irresistible appeal of a fully plumbed-in bathroom and an indoor toilet – something not to be sniffed at!

Often overlooked, the services can nowadays appear to be a relatively unexciting part of the property – until you consider how fundamental warmth, light, and sanitation are to our existence. Yet even for many property professionals, this remains a subject as mysterious as Shinto Buddhism. Nevertheless, a staple topic of dinner party conversation seems to comprise spine-chilling tales recounting the devastation caused by malicious power cuts or malevolent boilers packing up, and the staggering size of the resulting bills. So with this financial incentive in mind, it may be worth spending a little time exploring the electricity, gas, water, and drainage systems in your house.

There follows a brief description of the history of the services in houses of this age and some of the more common defects encountered. However, each area is very specialised and this chapter can only provide an outline. Before undertaking any work it is essential to refer to appropriate specialist manuals.

Instant art deco electric heat.
(Photo: Minchinhampton Architectural Salvage Co)

(Photo: Middlesex University MoDA)

Electricity

Electricity is the biggest killer in the house. At least a thousand fires and more than 50 deaths each year are due to electrical faults. Wiring usually lasts only about 30–35 years and should be tested at least every ten. Most houses have electrical systems that are unsatisfactory in some way, either due to badly executed alterations or just through sheer age. Electrical DIY work is restricted by the Building Regulations (see website for details), so before tackling any electrical work it is essential to consult a specialist guide. If in any doubt, always consult a qualified NICEIC electrician.

In the 1930s, electricity was regarded as a clean and exciting modern power source. It was supplied to new homes, many of which were advertised as having 'all-electric kitchens', but its use was largely confined to lighting plus a few small appliances like electric fires and irons, since most houses contained only a small number of power points. Although kettles, toasters, and vacuums had begun to appear in the shops, electrical appliances were primitive, expensive, and inefficient, and were not very widely used. One serious problem was that electricity supplies could suffer inconsistency, with different suburbs in the same town sometimes having incompatible AC and DC currents.

Early cables used rubber to insulate the live wires and were sheathed in cotton braid or an outer casing of lead. Early two-pin plugs and round-hole sockets (later changed to three pin types) did not have fuses. Modern plastic-insulated cable and 13amp square-pin sockets appeared in the 1950s but effective earthing was only widely introduced from the mid-1960s. Modern white or grey PVC cabling has a live of brown and a neutral of blue. The bare earth cable needs to be covered with yellow and green striped plastic sleeving when connected.

ABOVE: Old fuse box – still working.
BELOW: Rewireable fuses – now obsolete.

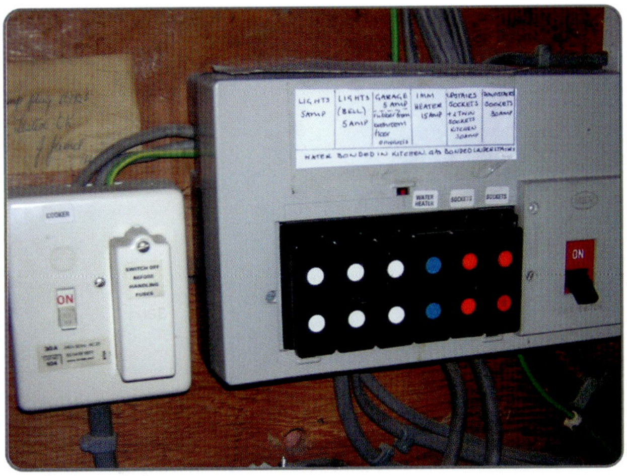

The main supply entering the house terminates in a fuse near the meter. These belong to the electricity company, and should not be tampered with – everything else is yours. Another pair of cables then runs from the meter to your consumer unit (fuse box), often located at high level in the hall or else in an outside meter box. Most supplies come in underground, but some are from overhead cables carried on poles and are connected to the house via insulated terminals at high level.

If the fuse box is made of metal, wood, or Bakelite (hard dark plastic), or has old rewireable fuses, it means the system is dated and likely to need replacing. Modern consumer units have MCBs (miniature circuit breakers) for each individual circuit. These are special fuses that automatically switch off when they sense a fault or overload, thereby potentially saving lives (as well as saving messing around with old rewireable fuses in the dark). Modern 'split load' consumer units provide additional RCD (residual current device) protection for the more vulnerable circuits (showers, outdoor sockets, external lighting, etc).

The power circuits that supply the socket outlets in the walls are arranged as 'ring mains', usually with one circuit per floor. The 2.5mm^2 'twin and earth' cable connects from the 32amp MCB in the consumer unit, looping round all the 13amp socket outlets on one floor in series and then back to the MCB. One circuit can normally serve a floor area up to 100m^2 (an average semi has roughly 50–60m^2 floor area per storey). The kitchen, being a high demand area, has its own circuit. Also, electric cookers and immersion heaters have separate 45amp and 20amp MCB fuses respectively but use 'radial circuits', where a single cable is run from the MCB direct to the unit – which is the way all circuits used to be wired until about 50 years ago. Cables run to outdoors should have separate RCD protected circuits.

HOW MANY SOCKETS?

Depending on room size, a modern household needs about three or four double-switched socket outlets (DSSOs) for each bedroom, five or six each for kitchens and living rooms, and a couple for halls and landings. It is possible to add an extra socket by extending from one of the existing sockets on the ring using suitable cable. This is called a 'spur' – but no more than one spur is normally permitted from any socket.

DANGER SIGNS

Be concerned if you see any of these: old fuse boxes with rewireable fuses, roundpin plugs, radial circuits to sockets, rubber sheathed cable, frayed flex, brittle PVC cable or burn marks.

Also check for DIY surface-mounted sockets on skirtings, surface-run cables, power points in damp walls, insufficient numbers of sockets (evident from lots of 'spurs' and multi-

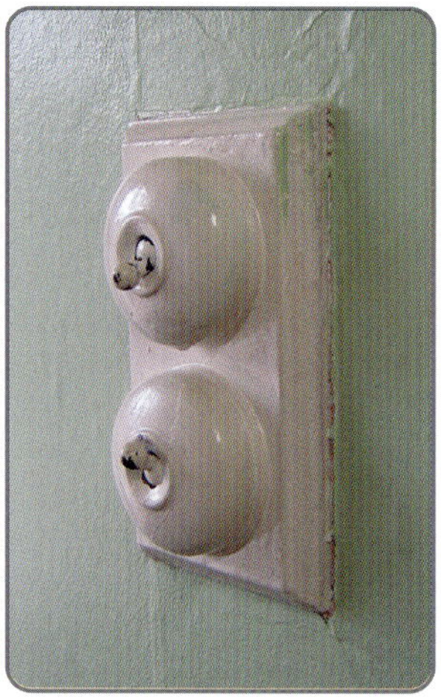

outlet plug adaptors) and any switches and sockets positioned close to sinks, basins and showers, or with loose covers.

Cables should be run in protective plastic trunking, or, when laid within plastered walls, in oval plastic conduit tubing or behind a flat steel shield. Any outdoor cables should be run in special protective conduits. Contact with polystyrene insulation (eg in lofts) should be avoided, as it can react with and soften the PVC sleeving.

Electricity will always head for earth, taking the easiest route (normally along its circuit). But in the event of a fault, leaking current could pass to earth through you, the floor, and the walls, and particularly through anything wet or metallic. So to protect against electric shock, all metal components should be connected with an earthed wire (green and yellow sleeved) so that they can't retain any current and no dangerous shock current can flow. The requirement is to bond metal items such as incoming service pipes (eg mains water, gas, oil), metallic waste pipes, central heating pipes, hot and cold water pipes, metal baths and heaters, etc. Pipework run completely in plastic shouldn't normally need to be bonded. Bathrooms and kitchens are high risk areas, so nothing electric should be touchable where a person could simultaneously be in contact with water. Only specially protected fittings are allowed in bathrooms, and bathroom light switches should either be of the pull-cord type or else located on the wall outside the bathroom door.

You can buy 'plug testers' which plug into sockets and have indicator lights that may help identify some deficiencies. But if the consumer unit doesn't have a sticker showing when your system was last tested, it means it should now be checked by a qualified electrician. Any electrical alterations should also be professionally checked.

LIGHTING

It is hard to over-estimate the impact of modern artificial lighting, which started to be widely introduced in the 1920s and 1930s. New cheap, bright, and reliable electric filament lamp bulbs transformed homes. It may be an exaggeration to suggest that dingy candlelit hovels suddenly blossomed into radiant palaces of light, but that's how it must have felt to the occupants. Some 'moderne' homes even had newly invented strip lights and stylish art deco uplighter wall brackets.

In many houses, ceilings sprouted pendants with fashionable hanging 'fruit bowl' shades made of glass or new materials like perspex and alabaster. Kitchens were carefully lit so that the whole room was illuminated and the housewife didn't stand in her own light, with lamps fully enclosed in spherical opal shades to prevent steam or dust gaining access.

Some distinctive 1930s designs are today making something of a comeback, with repro versions of deco uplighters, rounded Bakelite-style switches, and chromed square units with thin bulbous-headed flick switches.

Modern lighting circuits are normally arranged with a separate circuit for each floor. The 1.0mm^2 or 1.5mm^2 'twin and earth' cable connects from the 6amp MCB in the consumer unit, joining up all the ceiling rose lights in turn. The switches are wired directly to each rose via a single cable. To get access to the cables you normally need to work from the floor or loft above.

Defect: No power at socket or unit. Sparks at switches

SYMPTOMS

Fuses keep blowing; scorch marks around 'plug holes'; plug flexes get hot.

Cause **Blown fuse in plug or unit**

Solution *Check and replace plug and unit fuses and/or the MCB itself.*

Cause **Cable too small for load. Damaged cables**

Solution *Fit new ring main.*

Cause **Faulty switch, plug, or socket**

Solution *Identify and replace.*

Cause **Faulty circuit (overloaded or incorrectly installed), or loose cables/connectors inside socket or appliance**

Solution *Check fuses are of correct capacity. Check all connections. Check there are separate circuits on each floor, and for the kitchen, the cooker, and the heaters, etc.*

Tip: Always remember to switch power off at the consumer unit before starting any work!

Gas

This was a time of intense competition between gas and electricity companies. From as far back as the 1880s, when penny slot meters were introduced, gas manufactured from coal had been popular, mainly for lighting. But in new 1930s houses the lighting was now electrically powered, and houses in urban areas were generally supplied with gas for cooking (and gas fridges for the better-off), since cooking with electricity was very slow and therefore less popular. The cooker was at the heart of the kitchen, and new freestanding enamelled models such as 'New World' gas cookers were particularly sought-after.

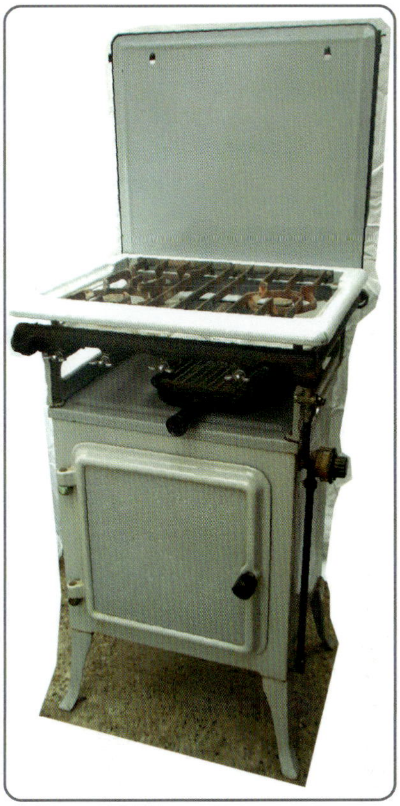

Original mains gas supply pipes were of cast iron. But iron can rust and become paper-thin or clogged up, causing poor pressure, so suppliers have recently undertaken a major programme of replacement with modern yellow polyethylene plastic underground pipes, which should normally be trouble-free. The incoming mains gas service pipe terminates at a stop valve by the gas meter. Meters are often tucked away under the stairs or, more recently, located in external meter boxes, but meter cupboards should always be well ventilated and free from damp. Modern above-ground supply pipe extensions are often visible running externally along the wall near ground level, usually in copper pipes. As a safety precaution, gas pipework should be kept more than 25mm (1in) away from electricity cables.

Natural gas is not poisonous; the main risk is that of explosions. Hence work on gas appliances and pipework must, by law, only be carried out by qualified GAS SAFE registered engineers. If you smell gas, first turn off all gas appliances and the supply at the meter, open windows and doors to disperse the gas, and do not switch any lights on. Then phone British Gas. Sometimes a leak may be traced simply to an unlit pilot light or faulty gas cooker burner. The best advice is to have all gas appliances serviced annually under a maintenance contract.

Technical data

NB Before undertaking any work on any services, it is essential to refer to appropriate specialist manuals.

To calculate British Thermal Units, and for full Building Regulations, see www.ThirtiesHouse.co.uk.

Original art deco taps. **(Victorian Plumbing Ltd)**

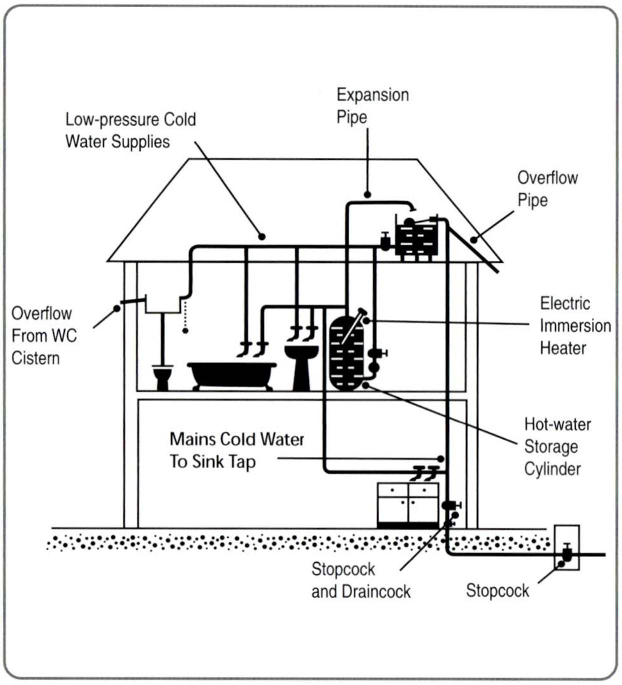

Water

PLUMBING AND COLD WATER

Water is piped into the house from the main below ground level in the road via a stopcock in the pavement or front garden. As with most services, pipework beyond your boundary is the responsibility of the provider. Underground water pipes should be at least 750mm (30in) below ground level to avoid damage from frost.

Pressurised cold water supplies were originally run in pipework of cast iron or lead. As with iron gas pipes, iron water pipes may suffer from corrosion, and the rust can then restrict the flow and turn the water an unpleasant brown colour. Lead pipes are a potential health issue in soft water areas but are generally considered acceptable in hard water areas, as the pipes will have become lined internally with protective limescale. If you still have original supply pipes, contact your water company as replacement with modern heavy duty blue polyethylene plastic pipework may be advisable. There should be a second stopcock inside the house, typically in the kitchen or downstairs cloakroom, which can be shut off in an emergency. As it enters the house, the supply pipe must be lagged to prevent freezing and bursting, particularly if run under cold floors or along cold main walls.

The incoming mains supply runs through the house direct to the kitchen sink (suitable for drinking water), and the 'rising main' then usually continues up to a cold water storage tank in the roof space.

COLD WATER TANKS

The purpose of the cold water tank (storage cistern) is to store water for washing and for WCs in case the mains supply is cut off. When needed, this stored water flows back

LEFT: Original lead rising main. RIGHT: Redundant galvanised steel cold water tank (right).

down to the taps by gravity, so the water pressure in the bathroom is governed by the height of the tank (known as the 'head').

Tanks typically store at least 230 litres (50 gal) and need to be located high up, usually in the roof space. Like toilet cisterns, overflowing is prevented by a ball valve that automatically shuts off the incoming water supply when the tank is full. As the water level rises so does the floating

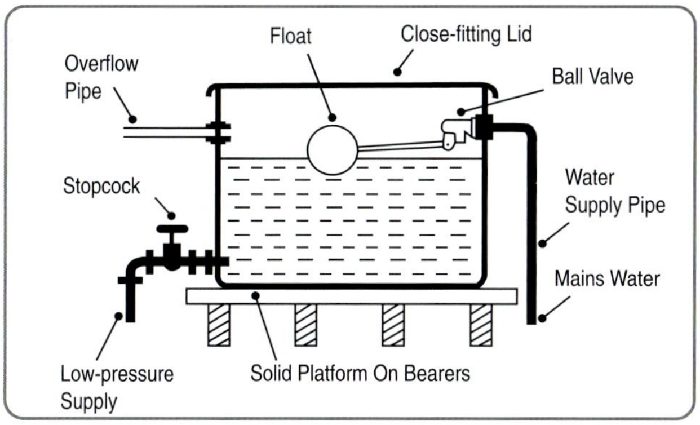

plastic or copper ball, causing its arm to push the water inlet valve closed. Just in case this fails, water tanks and WC cisterns have overflow pipes sticking out through the walls.

Basically, if your tank is made of anything other than modern plastic there is a good chance it will soon need replacing. Redundant tanks of riveted galvanised iron or steel or asbestos cement can be a problem to remove, and are often left sitting in lofts. Tanks full of water can weigh over 250kg (equivalent to three adults) and must be well supported, ideally on a thick exterior-quality plywood deck resting on at least four timber bearers designed to spread the weight over several joists to a supporting wall below.

Tanks need insulation jackets to stop condensation dampness forming and soaking down to the deck and the ceiling. Loft insulation below tanks is usually omitted to help take the chill off the immediate area and prevent freezing.

Asbestos cement cold water tank.

(Photo: Middlesex University MoDA)

And if the tap water in your bathroom has been tasting a bit gamey recently, make sure your tank has a fitted lid: it is not unknown for decomposing pigeons or rats moulding away in water tanks to spread disease.

INTERNAL SUPPLY PIPES

Most modern pipework is run in either 15mm or 22mm copper. But in unmodernised houses you may find original iron pipes, which if combined with copper can react. Should any iron or lead remain, it will need to be replaced.

Mixed steel and copper pipe.

Steel tubing has occasionally been used as a replacement, but copper + steel = corrosion. Today, plastic piping is becoming common, even for hot water pipework, and can be safely used with other materials.

Any unlagged pipes in the roof space will be at risk of bursting during winter freezes (as the frozen water expands). Pipe lagging should be provided at the earliest opportunity, as it is a cheap and easy way to prevent the damage and mayhem caused by such leaks.

Be aware that some original pipes or flues may have been insulated with asbestos quilt insulation (often held in position by chicken wire). This is a soft whitish material, and the health risks posed by this type of asbestos are potentially high. If seen, it should be avoided until specialist contractors can arrange its safe removal.

Sanitary fittings

In the 1930s a fully plumbed-in bath and an indoor WC were extremely enticing luxury features for most house buyers. Properties on privately developed new estates were now being built with interior bathrooms and separate toilets, usually adjoining the rear first floor bedroom.

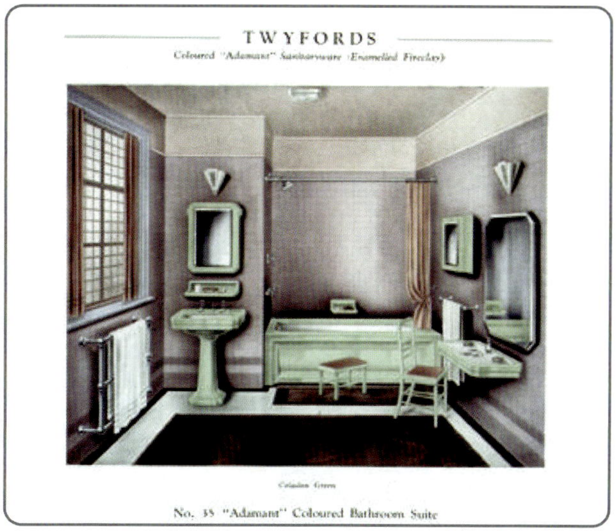

RIGHT: Art deco bath. (Photo: Drummonds Architectural Antiques Ltd)

FAR RIGHT: (Photo: Greg Stevenson)

A Modern Bathroom by Harrods

Not everyone could stretch to a 'Harrods streamline moderne' bath in cool art deco style with its zigzag motifs, but nonetheless, many of the new bathrooms were both practical and stylish, with chunky pedestal wash basins, coloured porcelain enamel baths fashionably boxed in with side panels, and chrome-plated hand-shower mixer attachments (rather than plain old-fashioned nickel-plated taps). Features like chrome towel rails ingeniously heated by pipes from the hot water cylinder were advertised as luxury fittings, but were not that unusual.

A large expanse of hygienic wall-tiling was desirable – the higher the tiles reached up the wall, the greater the social standing of the owner. Many were advertised as having 'walls tiled to dado height', with the black-and-white dado tiles breaking up the bathroom's sanitary white.

Today, streamlined design is not normally considered a priority for toilets, but newly introduced low-level toilet cisterns, some with chromed pipes and handles, were then the height of fashion. To be really cool, however, your loo seat and cistern could be made from new Bakelite plastic, or even lightweight asbestos. The less exciting reality for most toilet-users was the traditional choice of a wooden

seat in plain deal, or perhaps more expensive mahogany or walnut; and in much bog-standard housing, old high-level pull-chain cisterns harking back to the previous century continued to be the routinely fitted piece of kit.

Common defects to look out for with modern sanitary fittings include: leakage at the edges of fittings (especially around bath-seals), particularly where hand-shower mixers are used; damp seeping through wall tiles; and poor DIY tap and pipe connections. Shower trays are very prone to leakage and may have minimal access for maintenance. Check also that bath feet are properly supported over joists, not just on loose floorboards.

Photo: Adrienne Chinn Design Co Ltd.

Defect: Insufficient water supply

SYMPTOMS

Low pressure at taps.

Cause **Low water pressure at the kitchen cold tap may be due to a corroded supply pipe or because the supply is shared with other properties (worse at times of peak demand)**

Low pressure to upstairs taps can be due to insufficient height ('head') of the water tank above the bathroom.

Solution *Renew incoming supply. Relocate cold water tank at least 1m (3ft) above taps or fit a pump to boost shower pressure.*

A weak flush from WCs may fail to fully discharge waste, in which case the ball valve in the WC cistern should be adjusted to ensure it refills fully.

Defect: Water overflowing or dripping

SYMPTOMS

Dripping overflow pipes and taps; knocking noises.

Cause **Overflow pipes leaking due to defective ball valves. Taps dripping due to faulty or worn washers**

Solution *Replace ball valve to water tank or WC cistern. Renew tap washers or the complete mixer/tap unit.*

Cause **Knocking noises in cold pipes can be 'water hammer' caused by high pressure**

Solution *Reduce pressure from tank, eg by fitting a larger float of at least 150mm (6in) diameter.*

Heating

The subject of heating, hot water, and boilers would justify a large book in itself, so the following can only serve as a very rough guide.

Central heating was virtually unknown in the 1930s, so electric fires and gas or paraffin heaters provided room heating (if any), along with a traditional open coal fire in one of the reception rooms (with the majority of the heat disappearing up the chimney). To feed the fire, a typical house would store a tonne or more of coal or coke in a bunker near the back door (rather than the old custom of keeping it under the stairs or in a cellar). Only if you lived in an expensive modernist villa would you be likely to experience the miracle of underfloor heating.

The first modern electric fire (complete with kettle and toast rack) had been produced by Belling in 1912, and this was developed during the 1920s to become the popular glowing coal-effect electric fire. Fitted electric fires slowly began to replace open fireplaces, their surrounds sometimes 'slabbed with the best English mottled tiles' in assorted colours. Even in bathrooms, advanced electrically heated towel rails began to appear.

Today, there are two basic types of conventional heating system (regardless of the type of fuel used). With a simple direct system, water is heated by the boiler or immersion heater and stored in the hot water cylinder until used at the taps. With the more common indirect system, the boiler's hot water is kept separate for the central heating (primary circuit). The water piped to the hot taps is from the cold-water tank, heated in the hot-water cylinder (secondary circuit). Both systems have an emergency expansion pipe leading up to the small 'feed and expansion' tank in the loft. But there is a third, simpler alternative: a modern sealed system such as a combination boiler that takes water straight from the mains and provides all hot water and central heating on demand – see section on 'Hot water' below.

In terms of safety, it is open-flued heating appliances, like gas fires, that are potentially the most dangerous to occupants, as they get combustion air from the room. Those with an input rating higher than 7kW and all decorative 'living flame' gas fires, as well as those with back-boilers, require additional room ventilation in the form of a 230 x 230mm (9 x 9in) airbrick in the wall. They are only suitable for properly vented reception rooms, not bedrooms.

CENTRAL HEATING

Central heating (CH) was not generally installed in new houses in Britain until as late as the 1960s. Only some more expensive pre-war houses had a few bulky cast iron radiators gravity-fed via large iron or steel pipes.

Modern CH systems pump hot water from the boiler to steel radiators in each room via pipework which comprises separate parallel 'flow and return' circuits, usually in 15mm copper pipe. The 'flow' circuit feeds the hot water to each radiator and the 'return' circuit takes the old cooler water back to the boiler. The temperature output is controlled by wall thermostats – see 'Controls' below.

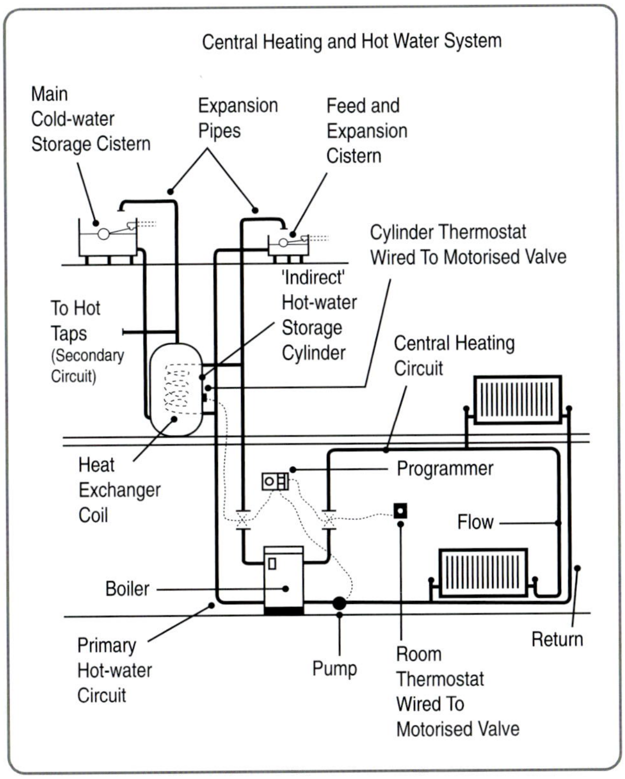

Before installing radiators, you need to calculate the required size of radiator to heat each room in BTUs (British Thermal Units), and to be sure that the boiler is man enough for the job. For optimum room warmth, radiators tend to be located on outer walls, often by the windows where the room is coldest.

Common defects to look for are: poor DIY workmanship with irregular 'bendy' pipework; thin 8mm microbore pipework, which can be relatively prone to blockage; pipes unsupported, with insufficient clips; leaks at radiator valves; rusted radiators; unprotected pipes run in concrete floors; and badly refitted floorboards.

Central heating systems need periodic maintenance, including flushing through to reduce limescale, and ideally should be checked annually under a service contract. Pressurised combination ('combi') type systems require more frequent 'bleeding' to release built-up air.

Electric heating is quite common in areas without a gas supply, typically comprising fixed storage heaters that take cheaper off-peak electricity at night, store it in special bricks, and release the heat the next day. They need separate electric circuits with switched fused outlets to the heaters. Older ones are very bulky and there's relatively little control – once the bricks have been heated up you can't then decide you don't want them 'on'. Popular alternative fuels in areas without a mains gas supply are oil, bottled LPG/Calor gas, and solid fuel (coal, coke, wood, etc).

BOILERS

Cast iron coke boilers were commonly fitted in kitchens (finished in a choice of 'classic' black or natty modern enamel), producing hot water that was circulated to a cylinder in the airing cupboard upstairs (some with an immersion heater for summer use). These floor-standing boilers had vertical flues running up through chimneys, sometimes lined with asbestos cement. Where boilers have been boxed in, it is not unusual for the cupboards to be protected with asbestolux insulation panels (see earlier warnings regarding asbestos).

Alternatively, many houses had back-boilers built behind the living room solid-fuel fireplace. Such boilers normally take their air for combustion direct from the room, so vents must be provided in the walls as described for open-flued gas fires. Solid fuel and oil-fired boilers in particular must have a permanent supply of air.

Flue too close to plastic pipe.

Today, wall-mounted gas-fired boilers, with balanced flues projecting through the wall, are popular. These are normally 'room sealed', taking air from outside and expelling exhaust gases externally through the same flue, which is sometimes fan assisted.

The rules governing the location of balanced flue terminals are complex, but generally they should be at least 300mm (11.8in) away from gutters, windows, doors, eaves, airbricks etc (though fan-assisted flues can be closer), and should obviously not discharge into enclosed areas such as side passages.

The preferred location for boilers is within kitchens or utility rooms, rather than bedrooms or bathrooms where they can only be of a 'room sealed' type with balanced flues. Boilers that are boxed-in (enclosed within cupboards etc) need external wall vents unless they are of a room sealed type that can work safely at higher temperatures.

Modern boiler systems are either 'conventional', with a small 'feed and expansion' tank in the loft and a hot-water cylinder, or 'sealed systems' (such as combination boilers) that don't require separate tanks. As noted earlier, combis provide both heating and instant hot water but they may have a relatively short lifespan (some not much more than 12 years, compared to more than twice that for conventional boilers, depending on maintenance). The most efficient modern boilers are condensing boilers, which are designed to extract extra heat from the flue gases.

Like cisterns, boilers have emergency overflow pipes to the outer wall, the difference being that faulty boilers can expel boiling water under pressure. Not surprisingly, regulations now require these pipes to be directed downward to ground level against the outer wall surface as a safety measure.

CONTROLS

Traditional room thermostats sense the air temperature in the room where they are installed but need to be positioned 1.5m (5ft) above floor level to work accurately. Adjustable thermostatic radiator valves (TRVs) fitted to each radiator are a better solution, as they allow a custom temperature to be set for each room.

You need to be able to control heating and water separately and most makes of boiler now incorporate clocks and programmers and a built-in thermostat control dial that shuts off when the water gets to a certain temperature. Old systems relied on gravity and convection to move water around, but modern boilers have integral pumps. Larger houses may require additional electronic pumps to improve flow.

HOT WATER

Another interesting 1930s appliance was the wall-mounted 'Ascot' type gas (or electric) water heater, placed next to the kitchen sink or the bath to provide hot water on demand. But these were less popular than the more commonly fitted hot water systems operated by the boiler in the kitchen, or by back-boilers, which supplied hot water to bathrooms, sometimes via a copper storage cylinder in the airing cupboard. Some houses had a 'wash-boiler', a large enamelled drum on legs with a lid and a tap at the bottom,

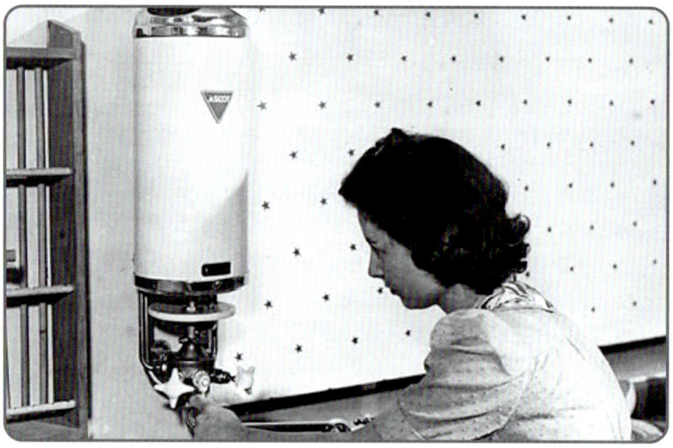

heated either by gas or electricity. This was more versatile than its coal-fired predecessors and besides boiling clothes could heat water for baths.

Today, unless your house has a sealed system such as a combination boiler where water is heated on demand, hot water is normally stored in a cylinder in the airing cupboard, usually incorporating an electric immersion heater to boost the hot water when needed (some combined cylinders incorporate a small cold water tank). Cold water

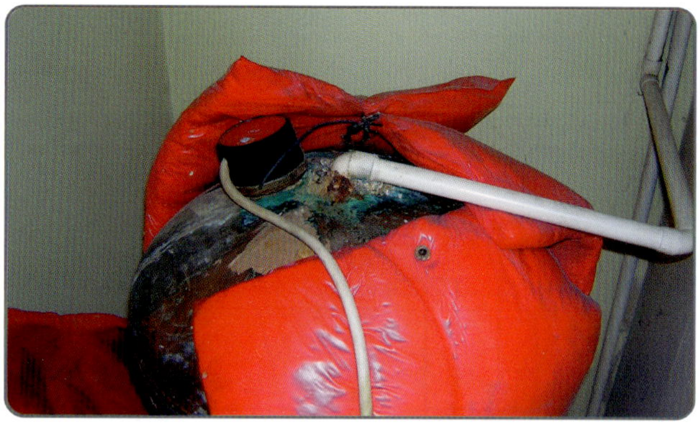

from the large storage tank in the loft refills the cylinder as hot water is drawn off at the taps. You may see a spaghetti of copper pipes in the vicinity, one of which is an emergency expansion pipe from the cylinder up to the tank above. If the hot water is still fed through old steel or cast iron pipes these could be subject to corrosion, causing the water to become rust coloured, and they will need to be replaced.

Modern cylinders are manufactured covered with integral polystyrene foam insulation: those with old lagging jackets are likely to need replacing shortly.

Drains

We tend to take drains for granted until a foul stench alerts us to a hidden problem. And problems don't get much more serious than foundation movement caused by leaking underground drains. This is especially likely where, as in 1930s semis, the drains often run alongside the main side wall. But even apparently minor defects such as damaged gulleys can cause localised structural problems.

WASTE PIPES

So what exactly does happen to all that waste water from baths, sinks, and showers after you pull out the plug? Answer: the water first discharges via a U-shaped trap directly underneath the plughole. The trap prevents nasty sewer odours coming back up the pipe, the smell being unable to get past the water 'trapped' in the bottom of the U, which forms a seal – one of the great plumbing inventions, simple but highly effective.

The waste water from upstairs bathrooms then discharges out through the wall via pipes that either link directly to the main soil stack or simply discharge into a hopper – a small, open collection box on top of a downpipe over a gulley. Hoppers, however, are prone to blockage, since being at high level they tend to be neglected, often leading to overflowing and damp problems.

At ground level, waste water from kitchens and bathrooms usually discharges through pipes run out through the wall and down into a gulley. Gulleys are often enclosed with a brick surround and should have gratings to stop old hair, fat, bits of vegetables, and general yuck from clogging them. The gratings consequently need to be cleared periodically. Modern

Defect: Poor discharge of water

SYMPTOMS

Smells; gurgling noises from plugholes.

Cause **No trap or blocked trap**

Solution *Fit new trap or clear and refit existing trap.*

Cause **Not enough fall, or pipes are sagging**

Solution *Relay the pipes set to a decent slope. Fit clips every 750mm (2.5ft).*

Cause **Overloaded blocked hoppers or blocked drains**

Solution *Clear out hoppers. Clear drains (see 'step-by-step').*

Cause **The small amount of water that should remain in the trap as a seal is getting sucked out by a vacuum further down the pipe**

If the pipe is very long and too small in diameter, or serves several sanitary fittings at once, the sheer volume of water will cause a vacuum.

Solution *Replace with larger bore pipes, or fit a special 'anti-siphon' trap or 'bottle trap', which retains more water in its seal and has a one-way air valve that lets air in to prevent a vacuum but stops smells getting out.*

back-inlet gulleys have jointless pipes that connect below the grating and traps that can be easily cleared. See Chapter 4.

Original kitchen and bathroom waste pipes were usually made of cast iron (or sometimes of lead or asbestos cement) and may still be OK, unless rusted, split, or leaking. Modern plastic pipes are relatively trouble-free if properly installed with sufficient support-clips and suitable falls – plumbers seem to sometimes forget that water runs downhill. External pipes are usually run in grey plastic which is UV-resistant (ie it shouldn't become brittle as a result of ultra violet sunlight). Internal white plastic waste pipes and fittings are push-fit, being either 32mm (1.25in) for basins, or 40mm (1.5in) for baths, showers, and sinks.

SOIL AND VENT PIPES (SVPs)

Soil stacks, or 'stench pipes', are large-bore (100mm/4in diameter) external vertical waste pipes with branches for upstairs WCs and bathrooms. They are vented at the top to prevent siphonage and must project at least 900mm (3ft) above the windows so as not to alarm residents with foul odours, normally terminating well above eaves level. The tops should be protected (eg with a wire balloon) to stop them becoming blocked with birds' nests etc. As noted earlier, upstairs bathroom waste pipes normally connect into the SVP. 'Branch' pipes connecting into the side of the SVP should be no longer than 3m (10ft), with provision for rodding access (to clear blockages), and must be properly supported. In contrast, some old ground floor WCs may have been built with their own soil waste pipes that run down through the floor internally and out through the wall underground, at foundation level, where they are particularly prone to cracking.

Original cast iron SVPs will now be of some age and unless regularly maintained (painted) may suffer from rust and require replacement with modern plastic fittings. They are very heavy, so watch out for loose support brackets and minimal fixings – it's not unknown for top lengths of pipe to come crashing down – a terrible way to end your days. Check for rust and limescale 'tide marks' at joints, indicative of leaks and possible blockages. If old asbestos SVPs are defective they will need to be removed by licensed contractors. Modern houses have internally-run SVPs to protect them from frost, but because they are boxed in they sometimes have very restricted access. Where you need to install additional bathrooms or WCs you don't have to go to the trouble of fitting another SVP. Instead 'air admittance valves' (aka Durgo valves or stub stacks) terminating within the bathroom or loft can be used, as they have a special one-way valve (like anti-siphon traps), but they must be located above the flood level of the highest sanitary fitting in the house.

Signs of leakage.
ABOVE: Iron SVP
BELOW: Plastic SVP

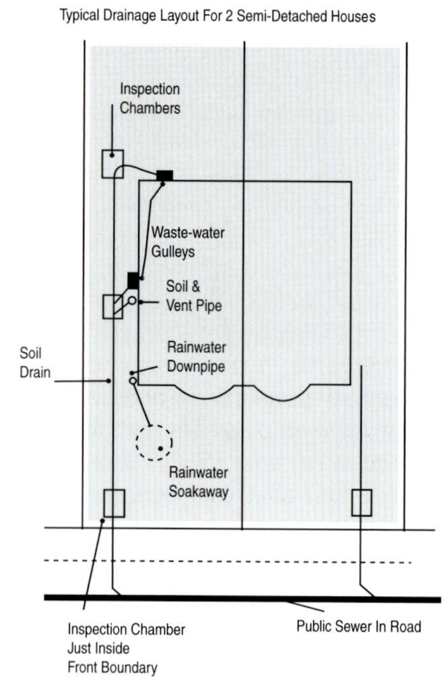

DRAINS AND SEWERS

The requirements for drainage systems are explained in the Building Regulations, and no work should commence until formal approval has been obtained from Building Control.

There are normally two separate drainage systems. Bathroom and kitchen 'foul' waste goes to a water treatment works via the sewer, and this is kept separate from relatively clean rainwater drainage. The reason for this is that in heavy storms a deluge of rainwater could otherwise overwhelm the sewers, causing waves of liquid sewage to rise up and flood. As described in Chapter 4, rainwater often discharges instead to soakaways in the garden, or to nearby streams. So don't be tempted to connect waste water from, say, a washing machine to a handy nearby drainpipe, or your lawn may start flooding and bubbling with detergent – and the Environment Agency could prosecute.

In actual practice many pre-war houses and properties in larger cities often had combined systems in which rainwater and foul waste used the same pipework. One clue to this is where you see hoppers taking bathroom waste pipes as well as rainwater from downpipes. Also, modern back-inlet gulleys (eg serving kitchens) are permitted to take some run-off water from the surrounding ground surface.

Underground pipes can also be a bit of a legal minefield. For example, did you know you could be responsible for the repair of drainage pipes beneath someone else's land?

Drains are pipes that carry waste water from just one property, and are the responsibility of the owners up to the point where they join a drain from a different property. At this point the drain becomes a sewer, and sewers can be private or public. Private sewers are the joint responsibility of each of the properties that drain into it, up to the point where they join a public sewer maintained by the water authority, which is normally beyond your boundary.

GOING UNDERGROUND

Underground foul drains connect to the public sewerage system, or in some more remote areas to a cesspit or septic tank. Most pipework was traditionally made from clay (salt-glazed stoneware), connected at 'spigot and socket' joints sealed with mortar. Over time these can be prone to cracking. Since the 1950s there has been much variety in pipe materials: pitch fibre, asbestos cement, concrete, and now plastic, all with their various pros and cons, but pitch fibre is particularly prone to problems. Modern plastic underground pipes with flexible joint seals (collar couplings) were introduced in the 1960s. Adaptors are available for joining most types of dissimilar pipes.

Main underground waste pipes were typically 100mm (4in) or 150mm (6in) in diameter, laid in a trench to a gradient or fall no flatter than 1:40 and bedded within 100mm (4in) depth of gravel or concrete, and then covered with 300mm (12in) of soil. However, it was not uncommon for rogue builders to bed pipes directly in the earth, so that over time settlement in the surrounding ground has imposed stresses on the rigid pipes, causing the joints to fracture.

Drains run at any depth less than 900mm (3ft) need to be protected from loads (eg by reinforced concrete). In a typical 1930s semi or detached house, it is common to find a much shallower drain run parallel to the side of the house. Because this area sometimes doubles as a parking space with a thin concrete hardstanding, the pipes can be particularly vulnerable. Clay pipes are easily fractured by loads from foundation settlement or vehicles, so it is advisable to avoid parking here. Another major cause of damage to shallow drain runs is from people obliviously bashing metal fence posts into the ground.

All parts of the drainage system must be watertight otherwise effluent will leak out, contaminating the ground. Conversely, if the water table is high, water from the surrounding soil can enter the system and your pipes will act in reverse, like a land drain. However, old pipe joints can often leak, and some species of trees – particularly willows – are highly efficient at seeking out moisture through even the tiniest cracks, ultimately choking the pipes with giant root balls.

Leaking drains are a common cause of structural movement in houses. Over time, the wet ground below a house can become more and more marshy and unable to support the foundations. This may go unnoticed for years as the wall may span a small 'soft spot'. But if it happens at a

BELOW LEFT: Inside a cracked sewer pipe.
BELOW RIGHT: Root ball alert (Photos: Dyno)

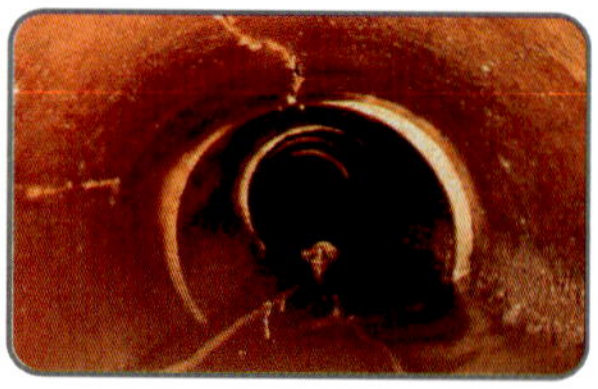

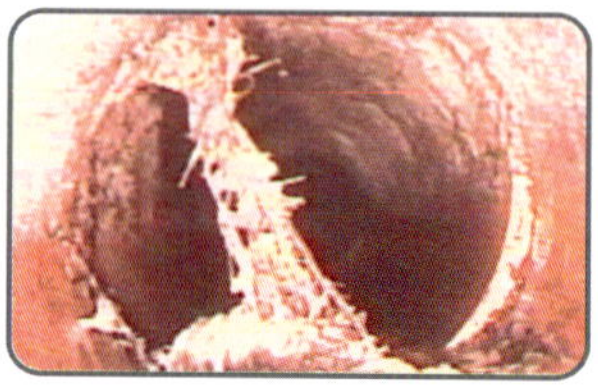

New underground plastic rainwater pipes, laid in shingle to a suitable fall.

corner, cracking and collapse is more likely. Leaking drains can be checked with specialist smoke or water tests or CCTV cameras, or you can hire equipment to test if the system is airtight. The procedure involves sealing off sections of pipe at inspection chambers using inflatable 'bungs' and pumping in air; a pressure gauge then measures if the air pressure drops (it shouldn't). Pipes can sometimes be repaired internally using special pressure grouting equipment or by inserting a new pipe inside the old one, but in severe cases localised excavation and replacement may ultimately be the only solution.

One advantage of building semi-detached houses rather than terraces was that they avoided the old problem of needing to lay drain runs directly below the house. In a typical semi, the WC would commonly be served by underground drainage pipes run down the side and out to the sewer in the road. But even terraces of this age were commonly built with integral passageways providing a 'foundation-free' route for underground sewer pipes.

Inspection chambers are needed for gaining access to clear blockages, and there should be one at every change of direction of the drain, typically at the corners of buildings. Needless to say, in reality many older houses have only one chamber (or none at all), and construction of a new chamber around an existing pipe is a complex operation. Chambers are normally built of brickwork – either 230mm (9in) thick, like main walls, or else only of 115mm (4.5in) thick rendered brick – and have a concrete base covered with mortar 'benching'. Chamber sizes are rarely less than 750 x 600mm (30 x 24in). The original covers were of thick cast iron with an airtight seal (more modern covers may be of concrete, steel, or plastic). By lifting the cover it should be easy to spot any damaged benching or render, which must be restored to a smooth finish to prevent blockages. In order to facilitate emergency access it is important that inspection chambers are not obstructed or obscured. Unfortunately the temptation is often to 'tidy them up', and many are now hidden under patios or paving. Some may even have had extensions built over them, for which special consent should have been obtained.

Today, ready-manufactured chambers may be of concrete or pre-formed plastic set in concrete, or there may instead just be small access points with screwed covers through which drain rods can be inserted ('rodding eyes'). Common causes of blockage include nappies flushed down WCs and hot liquid fat poured down kitchen sinks, which then solidifies. See 'step-by-step'.

PRIVATE DRAINAGE

In rural areas houses may not be connected to a main sewer. Instead, you may encounter cesspits – large watertight underground chambers – usually made of brick and covered with a concrete slab. Cesspits need to be pumped out periodically into a mobile tanker to prevent overflowing. Septic tanks are similar to cesspits but have two or more interconnected chambers like mini sewage works with outlets in nearby fields to disperse treated liquids, so they need less frequent pumping out. Obviously, in order to prevent overflowing rainwater pipes must not be connected. These tanks can often leak with age, requiring lining or rebuilding.

Defect: Blocked drains

SYMPTOMS

Water not running away.

Cause **Blocked main sewer in road**

Solution *If neighbours' drains are also blocked the problem may be in the main sewer – call the Local Authority.*

Cause **Tree roots in the pipes or debris from collapsed underground pipes**

Solution *A specialist CCTV inspection will confirm extent of any structural damage, but first notify your insurers as the cost may be covered.*

Cause **Grease or solid matter in the chamber or pipe**

Builders' rubble often gets washed down during works, as does loose render from inspection chamber walls.

Solution *Clear with drain rods as per 'step-by-step', or try flushing with a high-pressure water jet. Caustic soda can help clear light blockages (take care!).*

STEP BY STEP

Photos and text:
Ian MacMillan

Clearing a blocked drain

If your bath water doesn't drain away, or the loo fills up when flushing, or if a gulley outside the house starts to overflow, it's likely that you have a blocked drain.

Most blockages can be cleared quite easily if you have access via inspection chambers (small manholes). You will need a set of drain rods, which can be hired or purchased from DIY stores. An alternative method is to use a high pressure water cleaner with a special drain cleaning attachment. Some have retrojets so that a cleaning unit will advance along the pipe unaided. The pressure created by one of these machines may be sufficient to clear some blockages.

TOOLS REQUIRED

- **Set of drain rods**
- **Pressure washer (optional)**
- **Jemmy and large screwdriver or drain keys**
- **Claw hammer**
- **Trowel**

MATERIALS

- **Protective clothing, gloves etc**

Older house drains are normally 100mm (4in) or 150mm (6in) diameter pipes made from salt-glazed stoneware, laid in straight lines. At every point where the pipes have to change direction there should be (but often isn't) an inspection chamber.

Most houses should have more than one inspection chamber. The first one nearest the house is the highest. If this is full of waste water, the blockage is further out. It is always the chamber directly upstream of the blockage that will be full, whereas the one downstream of the obstruction (away from the house) will be empty. It is better to start rodding the blockage downstream from the empty inspection chamber. The Local Authority is normally responsible for maintenance where blockages occur in pipework beyond your boundary.

1 Locate the empty downstream inspection chamber. The inspection chamber upstream of the blockage will be full of water and solids. Clear the area around the cover to prevent any stones etc lodging in the rim and stopping the cover from sitting back in the frame properly. Clean out the key holes and use a drain key to lift up one edge of the cover, or else use a jemmy and a large flat screwdriver to prise the cover up and a claw hammer to finish lifting – and to prevent damaged fingers if it slips. Put the cover safely to one side. Place a piece of board against the far side outlet

(downstream) so that when the blockage comes loose it will not then enter the next length of pipe.

2 Connect your rods. These are a series of slightly flexible sections that are screwed together to make a much longer rod that can reach the obstruction.

3 There are a number of different end fittings. The first to be used is the 'worm' or 'corkscrew'.
(N.B. If your pipes are of more modern pitch fibre material, these fittings could potentially damage the soft surface of the pipes.)

4 In this instance one of the branches is blocked. Push the rods up the drain, remembering to constantly turn them in a clockwise direction – otherwise you risk unscrewing the rods and leaving one up the pipe. Push and turn the rods until you meet resistance, then keep going for a short distance further.

5 Pull the rod back, and keep turning clockwise (resist the temptation to change to anti-clockwise turning when you pull the rod back). Some of the obstruction should now be cleared, coming into the chamber – be prepared for a sudden gush of effluent when the blockage is shifted. A flush of the WC can help wash the remaining soil further down and out of the pipe.

6 The second attachment can now be used, the flexible scraper. This is pushed into the drain and passes over the remaining obstruction. When pulled back, it should bring the solids with it. Having dislodged the obstruction, remove it from the manhole with a trowel.

7 The third tool to use is the rubber plunger. Locate the upstream chamber (If there is one) and push the plunger back down the drain to ensure the obstruction is well and truly clear. As a precaution, check any other branch pipes that enter both manholes with the rods and rubber plunger. The scraper can also be used to clear any sediment that may have solidified on the bottom surface of the chamber and pipes. Wash the drain through, flush the toilets, and make sure that all is working properly.

8 Wash down the drain and the benching (the concrete surfaces).

9 Replace the cover after greasing the edges to prevent rusting and to make it easier to gain access next time. Thoroughly clean all the equipment used.

THE SITE

If you're into gardens and garages, these were the glory days. But no matter how charming they appear, gardens may conceal potential dangers to the property and occupants alike. They can also be a legal quagmire, with adverse rights, flying freeholds, and peculiar liabilities. As you will see, it pays to not let things run amok in the great outdoors. We show how to seek out and eliminate the dangers in your own back yard.

How about this for a garden makeover? Crazy paving leading to a fantasy rockery adorned by garden gnomes and a concrete wishing well; a neatly striped lawn with perimeter flowerbeds, integral water feature (pond), and organic veggie garden. TV gardeners might squirm, but these were once major features of the suburban dream.

True, tastes have evolved somewhat since the days when garden gnomes were considered really cool. But what hasn't changed is the importance of the area immediately surrounding the property to the wellbeing of the house. Neglect this, and many of the defects in the preceding chapters will thrive.

Garden history

In marked contrast to Victorian front gardens screened behind railings, walls, and high hedges, the new suburban semis had low brick walls or white picket fences that allowed passers-by to easily see over. Even where walls were topped with chains loosely hung between posts, the front garden was now on public display so that the quality of your roses could be inspected and commented on by complete strangers.

Garden on display – fashionable from late 1920s.

Entry to this suburban horticultural show was typically through a timber front gate, perhaps incorporating a sunray motif, and along a crazy-paved path to the front door, flanked by a small patch of lawn with tidy flower borders. Social pressure on owner-occupiers ensured front gardens were neatly maintained.

In contrast, back gardens were private places screened by high, boarded fences, and were frequently put to good use producing plenty of fruit and veg. Gardens were often generously sized by modern standards – anything from 24 to 60m long (80–200ft) – and frequently organised with Germanic precision.

A typical layout would be divided into two main sections. The space nearest the house, by the French windows, was for family recreation – a crazy-paved patio and a lawn/play area with decorative borders (kitchen windows were deliberately large and wide so an eye could be kept on the kids playing in the back garden). Furthest away would be a separate vegetable patch and a greenhouse at the far end, often tucked away behind a privet hedge. Most homes also had a shed or small workshop. Some cheaper garden fences, however, were only of basic softwood, or chicken wire strung between metal stakes.

The rise of the semi as the most popular new house type permitted space for a hardstanding to the side (over the drain run) and usually a side gate, something rather appealing after the endless lines of terraces that had predominated in previous decades. This allowed garden equipment and building materials to be carried through without messing up the house.

Garages

A strange and mysterious thing was happening to the country's menfolk. Headlines of the time featured the 'Bentley boys' and British land speed triumphs, so although car ownership was negligible many aspired to the status symbol of owning a house with single garage.

However, new houses built with garages were the exception – many had nothing. 'Garage space' was nevertheless sought by many forward-looking purchasers. The lucky few who could afford one were free to escape for long, pipe-smoking hours, tinkering happily in those small shrines to the automobile and motorcycle.

The fascination about (what we now see as) purely utilitarian buildings is evident in some of the architecture, with its incredible attention to detail. It was the 1930s that gave us the classic double garage-door design, with its distinctive twin layer of six small panes per door. Generally speaking, there were three broad types of garage: the upmarket integral garage (some of them with a stylish bedroom porthole window above); the detached 'cottage' with its neat brick walls and pitched tiled roof; and the small attached garage (often in a block of two or three) with its modern-looking brick parapet wall above the doors, hiding a flat roof. Garage walls were typically of single width brickwork supported by attached brick piers (columns) every 2m (6.5ft) or so. Some, however, were just glorified timber garden sheds on wonky concrete slabs. Regrettably, garage design has been pretty much all downhill since these glory days.

Garages are usually just about the most neglected part of the property, and by now most will require a good overhaul or even replacement. Garages constructed more recently are commonly of prefabricated concrete and asbestos or of flimsy amateur blockwork. If the asbestos doesn't get you, the criminally insane electrics surely will. See 'Outbuildings' on page 208.

Houses at risk

As noted above, neglect to the garden around the house can, over time, lead to serious problems in the house itself. Common danger signs to look for include:

- Over-enthusiastic garden makeovers that have heaped piles of earth and flowerbeds against the walls.
- Paths and drives built up in layers over many years, submerging the damp-proof course.
- Subsiding paving slabs sloping drunkenly towards the main walls instead of draining away.
- Rainwater downpipes that discharge pools of water next to the house.

Previous chapters have stressed the need for external ground levels to be at least two courses of bricks below the damp-proof course (or about 200m/8in below floor level) to prevent damp getting inside or damaging brickwork. Airbricks must be kept clear of accumulated earth, plant growth, and paint, which can block them and thereby hasten rot and beetle attack to floor timbers.

If your garden slopes down towards the house or is relatively high, the earth should be cut back so that there's about 1m (3.3ft) of flat, paved ground next to the walls. Or

Correct Position Of Paving Next To External Wall

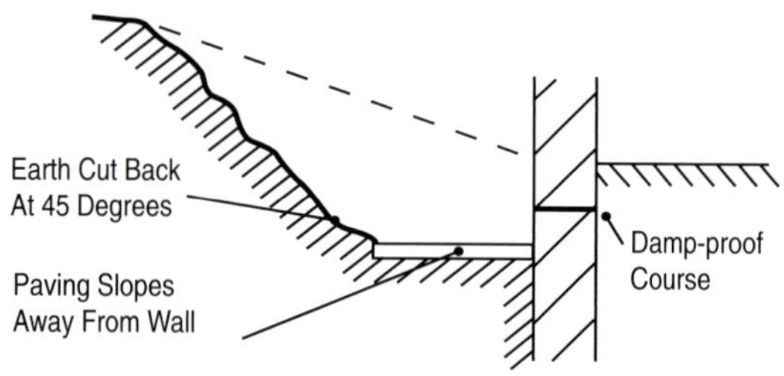

rather, not completely flat, as the paving should tilt away slightly towards the garden. In severe weather, rainwater from a sloping site can come cascading in the direction of your living room and so needs to be channelled away. Larger paths and drives need proper drainage, with channels or gulleys leading to soakaways to prevent water ponding near the building.

Bear in mind also that paving over previously bare earth next to a building can cause the ground to dry out and shrink, so it's worth leaving permeable gaps with sandy joints between slabs.

Downpipes should discharge into gulleys protected with kerbs around the gratings, to prevent water seeping back to the walls or pouring through airbricks. In winter, puddles of ponding water can turn to dangerous black ice.

Drains are a major cause of structural movement to houses – look for the telltale signs of leakage from drains, like extensive moss on paths and tide marks up side walls.

Anti-personnel devices

If such risks to the house weren't bad enough, there is another more serious danger – to yourself and your family. This is all the more worrying since the garden is the last place you expect to be maimed or killed. But even the most innocent-looking suburban gardens often contain dangerous structures and other potentially fatal pitfalls waiting to ambush the unwary. Consider some of the usual suspects:

- Unprotected DIY electric extension cables run to outside lighting and outbuildings (often half-buried in flowerbeds or dangling merrily in the breeze like high voltage washing lines).
- Rusted ice-thin drain cover 'mantraps'.
- Old underground air-raid shelters, often camouflaged under rockeries.
- Concealed stagnant ponds or forgotten wells.
- Slimy, slippery paths and decking.
- Decrepit rotten sheds and garages.
- Unstable ornamental brick arches, and loose coping stones or ridge tiles.

But perhaps the chief offender on the danger list has to be that innocent-looking garden wall. Some original garden walls that appear to be made from stone may actually comprise unwholesome, reconstituted blast-furnace waste, used to create a 'rustic' stone effect. Yet that may be the least of your worries. Many garden walls are self-built with little or nothing in the way of foundations. As we saw with bay windows, even the smallest walls need foundations of at least 450mm (18in) depth to clear seasonal movement in the ground. And if built with a DPC they may be even more unstable, since the DPC can weaken the bond of the mortar joint. Pushing walls over can be lethal child's play.

If a garden wall is leaning or you can make it move by pushing, it will need to be rebuilt with decent foundations before a gust of wind blows it over and the neighbours unleash a pack of slavering lawyers in your direction. Long stretches of wall also need expansion joints every 6m (20ft), as modern cement mortar is not tolerant of thermal movement and will crack. If a wall is low enough that you can step over it, it should be OK being built of single 115mm (4.5in) width brick; any higher and you need to build it 230mm (9in) thick. It is also easy to underestimate the cost of construction. But remember that with boundary walls there may be legal notices that first need to be served under the Party Wall Act 1996. Even if you're on chummy terms with the neighbours, this should always be checked out.

'No problem,' you may say. Go for the option of a nice new fence instead. It would certainly be a cheaper alternative, although relatively short-lived (the concrete post and base type will last longer, but requires simple foundations). But a word of warning before you wield the mallet: as noted earlier, serious damage to underground drains is frequently caused by enthusiastic fence-erectors banging in metal spikes along boundaries. So first spare a thought for the location of the drain run, which can be worked out from the position of inspection chambers or from plans at the local Drainage Authority.

KILLERS IN THE HILLS

Now we come to the real killers – retaining walls. Technical progress meant that reinforced concrete had started to be used for many major retaining walls expected to hold back large areas of high or unstable ground. But in residential gardens some were cheaply and thinly constructed of brick or stone. In hilly towns, like Ashbourne and High Wycombe, retaining walls are commonplace, but many are now so old or poorly built that they have become a liability, an avalanche waiting to happen.

The place to check first is the upper side – on top of the ground that's being held back. Look for tension cracks and dips in the ground, which may be the first sign of subsidence in the retained earth, leading to bulging or overturning where the foot of the wall is pushed out, causing the top to collapse backwards. The thing that finally pushes them over is usually a build-up of water pressure, sometimes aggravated by the weight of cars parked above. So weep holes near the base are essential to relieve pressure, and these should be checked, as they may well have become blocked. For sufficient strength, retaining walls need to be constructed to a height:thickness ratio of about 3:1, but in reality often aren't.

Outbuildings

Even the most superbly renovated properties can conceal guilty secrets in the form of gruesome old structures festering in their back gardens. All manner of noxious horrors can make their unwelcome presence felt: rotten timber shacks, visibly collapsing coal sheds and, as described above, corroding concrete-panelled garages with roofs of corrugated asbestos sheeting may be waiting to do their worst.

Old outbuildings are naturally a magnet for children, who will inevitably be drawn to something lethal or toxic. The cost of demolition and removal should not be underestimated. Asbestos cement materials are very common and generally not dangerous if left alone (see Chapter 8). However, such roofs are notoriously fragile, and a legal liability should someone unwisely choose to walk on one and fall through, possibly injuring themselves on the razor sharp shards. Council tips can be reluctant to accept some asbestos-based materials and specialist licensed contractors know how to charge.

Beware also of primitive lean-to conservatories and attached garden walls built without any foundations whatsoever, just placed over old paving slabs. They will wriggle around and pull away in tune with the vagaries of the ground and the weather.

Trees

Some of the more exclusive suburban developments were finished with rows of neat forest trees. Avenues lined with plane trees, limes, and flowering cherries helped create the archetypal leafy suburb. But some have now grown to 20m or more.

Fortunately, properties in these more expensive areas tended to be set further back from the road, but that doesn't take account of generations of reckless DIY tree planters in the intervening years who may unwittingly have caused ground conditions to alter drastically.

It is typically after long, parched summers that houses can start displaying symptoms of apparent subsidence – cracks in the plaster, bay windows, and brickwork, and doors or windows not closing properly. At least 15 million houses in Britain are built on shrinkable clay, which is very prone to movement. Insurance companies get an average of 30,000 subsidence claims a year at an estimated cost of up to £200 million.

Any tree or shrub that grows fast, or thirsty broadleaf trees, will extract a lot of moisture from soil and can upset ground conditions. Roots can extend more than one-and-a-half times the height of the tree, so any structure within that 'influencing distance' can be affected. On the other hand, mortgage lenders' legal advisers often insist that valuers insert standard tree-warning phrases at the slightest hint of a shrub nearby, and this can alarm homeowners into a slash and burn mentality and unnecessary bouts of pre-emptive tree felling. The resulting acres of naked concrete may be less threatening technically, but the diminution of 'kerb

appeal' to the value of a property may arguably cost more than any likely remedial works. And unknown to you, trees may be subject to a tree preservation order (TPO), making it a criminal offence to fell one without consent. In conservation areas all trees are automatically protected by TPOs.

So what to do? Opinions vary widely on this subject, to the extent that professional tempers can swiftly become frayed. Some experts believe passionately in tree removal, others that trees are best pollarded (severely pruned) to restrict their growth, since ground 'heaving' upwards as a result of trees that have been removed no longer absorbing moisture can cause as much damage as subsidence. The sensible thing is to first obtain an arboricultural report from a tree specialist before jumping to conclusions. Today, insurance companies are much more likely to monitor cracking over several months and may well conclude that it is due to settlement from cyclical movement, albeit influenced by nearby trees.

A big issue for many people is that of the infamous leylandii (cypress conifer), since these can grow at the rate of nearly a metre per year, reaching over 25m and blocking natural light to all around unless regularly trimmed. The Control of High Hedges and Anti Social Behaviour legislation allows Local Authorities to issue remedial notices enforcing action where trees are in excess of 2m (6.5ft) high.

Flying freeholds and rights of way

It is quite common in inter-war terraces for one of the upstairs bedrooms to be located partly over a shared passageway below. This is known as a 'flying freehold', a phenomenon that solicitors like to mull over at some length. There may indeed be practical issues to consider, such as insulation (gales blowing under your bedroom floor) and the liability for maintenance, in a similar way to flats.

Semi-detached houses may sometimes share a front garden hardstanding, which can include the area between the sides of the houses where the boundaries may not always be clear. Or the plot of one house may be raised up on a stepped concrete slab, with possible implications for surface water dispersal and maintenance. One very common problem is that the space to the side is now often too narrow to permit an average size modern car access to the garage at the rear.

Technical data

Go to www.landsearch.me.uk for land registry title deed checks.

Because former Council houses were originally under the sole ownership of the local authority, individual land rights were not an issue. But as they were sold off individually, legal rights of access would have been drawn up, and these can sometimes appear slightly peculiar, such as rights of way over other gardens. Some properties may also have car access via an unmade-up back lane.

All such land-rights should, of course, be investigated by your solicitor along with the usual pre-purchase checks such as confirming which boundaries are your liability and enquiries concerning any history of flooding, mining, wells, toxic waste, radon gas, or nearby landfill sites.

GLOSSARY

Access tower A movable scaffolding platform allowing access for high level work on roofs etc.
Aggregate Gravel, shingle, or pebbles, etc, used in the manufacture of concrete.
Airbrick A perforated brick or metal/plastic grille used for ventilation, typically in external walls to suspended timber ground floor voids.
Apron A metal strip, usually of lead, fitted at the base of a chimney or under window sills above tile-hung bays, to provide a waterproof joint.
Architrave Moulded wood strip covering the joint at the edge of a door or window frame and the surrounding wall.
Asbestos cement Cement with 10–15 per cent asbestos fibre as reinforcement. Hazardous fibres may be released if it is cut or drilled.
Asphalt Black tar-like substance used as an adhesive and impervious moisture barrier on flat roofs and floors.
Back gutter A metal flashing strip forming a waterproof seal between the back of a stack and its roof slope.
Balanced flue Metal vent that allows gas appliances both to draw air in from outside and to expel exhaust fumes. Some are fan assisted.
Balusters Vertical spindles supporting the handrail of a staircase.
Balustrade A row of balusters/spindles joined to a horizontal rail, typically to a staircase or landing.
Bargeboards Boards placed along the verges of a roof, usually at gable ends, often of decorative timber. Also known as 'vergeboards'.
Battens Thin lengths of timber to which tiles or slates are nailed or fixed.
Back-boiler A tank or series of pipes at the back of a fireplace for heating water. 'Baxi' was one of the best-known manufacturers.
Beetle infestation Larvae of various species of beetle that tunnel into wood causing damage, usually evident as small boreholes. The generic term is 'woodworm'.
Benching Smooth layer of concrete alongside the drainage channel in an inspection chamber. Also known as 'haunching'.
Binder A horizontal timber beam laid across ceiling joists in some roof spaces, to help strengthen the structure.
Bitumen Black, sticky substance related to asphalt. Used in sealants, mineral felts, and DPCs.
Blockwork Walls made from cement-based blocks instead of bricks (usually internal walls in 1930s houses).
Bond The pattern in which bricks are laid in mortar to form a wall.
Bonnet tiles Profiled 'corner' tiles laid along the main hip rafters (to cover the outer edges of hipped roofs).
Box eaves The framing around the edges of the exposed rafter feet just under the lowest course of roof tiles.
Breeze block Commonly used term for various types of concrete building blocks, originally made from cinders ('breeze').
BTU British Thermal Unit.
Cames Strips of lead that hold pieces of window glass together.
Carriage A thick length of timber running along the underside of a staircase.
Casement A window hinged at one edge and designed to open inwards or outwards.
Cavity wall Standard modern (post-1930) main wall construction comprising two leaves of brick or blockwork about 280mm thick, separated by a gap (cavity) of about 50mm which can be insulated. The leaves are secured together with wall ties.
Cement fillet The covering over a junction (eg between roofs and walls) made from mortar instead of a metal flashing.
Cesspit or **cesspool** An underground tank to hold sewage and foul waste, needing regular emptying.
Cheeks The vertical sides of dormer windows.
Chimney breast That part of the chimney flue that projects into a room. The 'stack' is the part above roof level.
Cill Variant spelling of 'sill'.
Cistern A water storage tank (usually to a WC or water tank in loft).
Cloaked verge tiles Purpose-made modern angled roof tiles laid along the sides of a roof so as to cover the verges (at the edges), thereby eliminating the traditional need to point up verges with mortar.
Coke breeze Waste ashes from coke- or coal-fired furnaces, often used as a crude covering to the earth under timber floors, sometimes mixed with sand and cement or lime.
Collar A horizontal timber member that joins and restrains opposing roof slopes.
Combination boiler Modern 'sealed system' gas boiler that activates on demand for hot water or central heating and does not require water tanks or cylinders, being supplied direct from the mains.
Coping Masonry covering laid on top of a wall to stop rain soaking into it, usually of stone or concrete.
Corbel Projection of brick, stone, timber, or metal jutting out from a wall to support a load such as a beam.
Cornice and **coving** Ornamental plaster around the joint of a wall and ceiling. Coving is a curved strip covering the joint.
Cowl A cap to a chimney or vent pipe.
Dado Protective wooden or tiled horizontal strip running along internal walls, about 1m above the floor.
Damp-proof course (DPC) An impervious layer (eg slate, felt, PVC) built into a wall to prevent the passage of dampness.
Damp-proof membrane (DPM) An impervious layer (polythene sheeting, bitumen, etc) within a concrete ground floor slab to prevent rising damp.
Dentil slips Special small pieces of roof tile inserted in the gaps where the top row of wavy pantiles meets the straight line of the ridge tiles.
Distemper Solution of ground chalk and animal glue size used in decoration.

Dormer window A window that projects out from a roof slope.
Dowel Thin timber plugs that hold jointed sections of timber together.
DPC(s) Damp-proof course(s).
DPM(s) Damp-proof membrane(s).
Dragon ties Timbers placed diagonally across the corners of a hipped roof structure at the bottom of the hip slope. These help prevent 'roof thrust' or movement from 'splaying out' as a result of downward pressure from the roof slopes.
Eaves The overhanging edge of a roof near the gutter.
English bond Bricklaying pattern in which courses laid lengthways alternate with courses laid crossways.
Fall The slope or gradient, typically of a pipe run or flat roof, to ensure water run off.
Fanlight A small window above a door or casement.
Fascia Horizontal timber boards that run along the eaves at the base of roof slopes. They often cover the ends of the rafters. Gutters may be fixed to them.
Featherboarding A lining of timber boards laid over the rafters, under the tiles. Fitted to some better quality roofs.
Fibreboard Lightweight board for ceilings or internal walls, made of compressed wood pulp. Now superseded by plasterboard.
Fillet A small strip of cement/lime mortar, timber, plastic, etc, used to cover or seal the junction between two surfaces.
Flashing A thin strip, usually of lead or zinc, used to cover roof joints to prevent leakage (eg to chimney stacks).
Flaunching Smooth contoured cement mortar around the base of chimney pots.
Flemish bond Bricklaying pattern in which the bricks in each course are alternately laid lengthways and crossways.
Flue lining Flues are the 'exhaust ducts' for gases from fires or appliances. Flue linings are long tubes fitted within flues, usually of stainless steel, clay pipework, or concrete.
French drain Shallow gravel-filled drainage ditch.
Frieze The part of a wall above the picture rail.
Gable The triangular upper part of a wall under the verges at the edge of a pitched roof ('gable end').
Gather Alternative name for the throat of a chimney flue.
Granolithic A mixture of cement and stone chippings.
Gulley An opening into a drain, receiving water from downpipes or waste pipes.
Half-round guttering Guttering that is nearly semi-circular in section. The most widely used modern type.
Hangers Vertical beams supporting the roof ridge.
Haunching See 'benching'.
Header The end of a brick, visible in solid walls when laid crossways (see 'stretchers').
Heave The opposite of subsidence. It occurs when the ground swells with water.
Hip The external junction where two roof slopes meet.
Hip iron Protruding galvanised metal straps found on hipped roofs, screwed to the base of hip rafters to help prevent hip tiles slipping off.
Hip tiles Tiles bedded in mortar along the outside edges or 'corners' of a hip slope.
Hopper or **hopperhead** An open-topped box or funnel at the top of a downpipe. It collects rainwater or waste water from one or more pipes.
Inspection chamber A 'manhole' with a removable cover providing access to the drainage channel at its base.
Jack rafters Rafters which butt at their tops against a main hip ('corner') rafter instead of against the ridge like ordinary rafters.
Jamb Vertical side part of a door frame or window frame.
Joists Horizontal structural beams used to construct ceilings, timber floors, and flat roofs.
Lap The overlap of courses of slates or tiles.
Lath Thin strips of wood traditionally used as a backing to plaster.
Leaded light Window divided up into small panes by strips of lead.
Lino or **linoleum** A sheet material floor covering made of hessian, jute, etc, plus a mixture of powdered cork, linseed oil, rosin, and pigment.
Lintel Horizontal structural beam over a window or door opening. Normally made of timber, concrete, stone, or steel.
Louvres Glass or timber slats laid at an angle or hinged so that they can be opened to allow ventilation.
Mastic A generic term for any sealant used in the building process, eg for sealing joints around window openings.
Magnesite A solid flooring material, often white or grey, made with mineral magnesium carbonate.
MCB Miniature circuit breaker.
Mezzanine An intermediary floor, eg between the ground and first floors.
Mortise A slot cut in a section of wood for a corresponding 'tenon' of another section to fit into.
Mullion An upright division of a window such as a vertical bar dividing individual lights.
Newel A stout post at the bottom or top of a stair to which the handrail is fixed.
Nib The projecting lug on the back of a tile that hooks over the supporting batten.
Nogging or **noggin** A short timber batten that fits between a pair of joists or timber studs to add strength.
Nosing The rounded projecting edge of a stair step.
Oriel window A window projecting from an upper floor.
Padstone A stone or robust block laid under the end of a beam or steel joist, to help distribute the load.
Pantiles Large curved roofing tiles with lugs that hook over the battens.
Parapet Low wall along the edge of a flat roof or balcony.
Parging Lime and sand mortar, traditionally mixed with cow dung and ox hair for added strength.
Parquet floor Small strips of wood usually laid on a solid floor to form a pattern.
Party wall The wall which separates, but is shared by, adjoining properties.
Pier A vertical column, usually built in brickwork, used to strengthen a wall or support a weight.
Pitch The angle or slope of a roof, technically the ratio of span to height.

Plasterboard Large thin sheets made of plaster sandwiched between coarse paper, used for ceilings and internal walls.
Plinth The projecting base of a wall, usually of brick or render.
Pointing The smooth outer edge of mortar joints between bricks, stone, etc.
Purlins Horizontal beams in a roof upon which the rafters rest.
Quarry tiles Plain single colour 'geometric' floor tiles made from clay, often red or brown, usually unglazed. From the French word *carré*, meaning square.
Quoin Projecting bricks or stone blocks traditionally used at corners of walls.
Rafter brackets Metal brackets screwed to the ends of rafters to support guttering where there is no fascia board.
Rafters The main sloping roof timbers to which the tiles/slates, battens, and felt are fixed.
Rails The main horizontal timber cross-members of a door, as opposed to the main vertical members called 'stiles'.
RCD Residual current device.
Rebate A recess, groove, or rectangular step cut in the edge of a piece of timber or stone, etc ('rebated' or set back), to receive a mating piece.
Render or **rendering** General term for the finish applied to external wall surfaces of sand and cement/lime (or the first coat of internal plastering). It may be smooth, or finished in roughcast, pebbledash, etc.
Retaining wall Usually a garden wall built to hold back or retain a large bank of soil, rubble, etc.
Reveals The vertical sides of an opening cut in a wall (typically of brick or stone), eg between a door or window frame and the front of the wall (see also 'jambs').
Ridge The top or 'apex' of the roof where two slopes meet, formed from a timber board (the 'ridge plate') joining the tops of the rafters and covered with shaped 'ridge tiles'.
Riser The vertical portion between treads of stairs
Rising damp Moisture soaking up a wall from the ground, by capillary action, or through a floor (see 'damp-proof course').
Rodding access Removable covers at bends in drainage pipes, gulleys, etc, allowing access for clearing blockages.
Roof spread The outward thrust of a poorly restrained roof causing a wall to bow out. (See 'collar'.)
Roof thrust The outward and downward pressure on a wall from the weight of a roof.
Room sealed appliance One that takes its combustion air from outside via a 'balanced flue' and expels exhaust fumes via the same flue. Most modern boilers are room sealed.
Roughcast A rough render finish to external walls, usually incorporating gravel.
RSJ Rolled steel joist used for structural support (eg to walls or floors), usually spanning relatively wide openings.
Saddle piece Middle part of the flashing for a centrally located chimney stack.
Sarking boards Alternative name for battens.
Sarking felt A layer of bituminous felt used for covering roofs before laying battens as a secondary defence against rain. Not normally fitted in pre-war houses.
Sarking timber Timbers laid over the rafters, on which the slates or tiles are laid.
Sash window Two-part, vertically sliding window that can be opened at both top and bottom.
Screed A smooth finish coat on a solid concrete floor slab, usually of mortar, concrete, or asphalt.
Scrim tape A special weaved material for reinforcing the filler concealing joints between plasterboard panels.
Secret gutter Soaker at the junction of a roof obscured by the lap of the slates or tiles.
Septic tank Private drainage system comprising underground tanks where sewage decomposes through bacteriological action. Can require periodic emptying.
Settlement General disturbance in a structure showing as distortion in walls etc. Usually the result of initial compacting of the ground due to the loading of the building.
Sill The lower horizontal member at the bottom of a door or window frame. Externally it should throw water clear of the wall below (of stone, concrete, brick, or timber). Internally it is a shelf at the bottom of a window.
Skylight A window in a roof slope or ceiling to admit daylight.
Sleeper wall A dwarf wall supporting the joists under a suspended timber ground floor.
Soakaway A rubble-filled pit for rainwater dispersal.
Soakers Strips of metal (usually lead, zinc, or copper) fitted beneath tiles to provide a waterproof joint at the junction of a roof with a wall or a chimney. Normally overlain with flashings.
Soffit The underside ('external ceiling') below eaves, balconies, etc.
Soldier course A line of bricks set in an upright position at the top of a flat arch or opening.
Spalling The crumbling of masonry or tiles as a result of weather damage.
Spigot and socket joint A pipe joint where the plain end of one pipe (the spigot) fits into the socket of the other.
Spine wall A centrally located dividing wall which carries a load from the roof or floor above it.
Squareline guttering Modern guttering with a rectangular section.
Stiles The main vertical timber side members of a door, as opposed to the main horizontal cross-members called 'rails'.
Stretcher The side of a brick, visible in walls when laid lengthways (see 'header').
String Long length of timber running from top to bottom of a staircase.
String course A course of brickwork that projects beyond the face of an external wall (or band course).
Struts Timber props supporting purlins, found in roof spaces.
Stud partition Lightweight internal wall, usually of a timber framework faced with plasterboard or lath and plaster, usually non load-bearing.
Subsidence Ground movement, often as a result of clay shrinkage, drainage problems, or mining activities.
Subsoil Soil lying immediately below the topsoil, upon which foundations usually bear.

SVP Soil and vent pipe. Vertical stack taking 'soil' waste from WCs and bathrooms, etc, typically of plastic or iron, and vented at the top, normally terminating at roof level.
Swept valley tiles Purpose-made curved tiles used to cover joints between roof slopes (valleys).
Tanking Waterproof treatment to basements.
Terrazzo Marble chips set in mortar.
Throating Alternative name for a drip groove.
Tie bar Large metal bar passing through a wall to brace a structure suffering from structural instability.
Tilting fillet A timber fillet fixed under the roof coverings above the eaves, in order to raise the edge of the first row of slates.
Tingles Small folded strips of lead or copper used to keep loose slates in place.
Tongued-and-grooved boarding Close fitted boards where the edge of one board fits into a groove of the adjoining board.
Transom Horizontal bar of wood or stone across a window or the top of a door.
Tread The horizontal 'flat' part of a step or stair.
Trimmer A small section of timber joist run at right angles to the ends of the main floor joists to form an opening, eg for stairs or a fireplace.
TRV Thermostatic radiator valve. An adjustable sensor valve next to a radiator allowing its temperature to be set.
Undercloak Extra line of tiles at verges, placed underneath the end slates or tiles to tilt them up and create a neat edge.
Underfelt or **underlay** Alternative names for sarking felt.
Underpinning A method of strengthening weak foundations where a new stronger foundation is placed beneath the original.
Valley The junction of one roof with another at an angle, typically where a bay window roof meets the main roof. Often formed by a strip of lead or zinc sheeting over a timber board base. 'Open valleys' leave the metal strip exposed; 'mitred valleys' have slates over the edges; and 'laced valleys' have rows of tiles over the trough.
Valley gutter Gutter at the bottom of the 'V' at the junction of two roof slopes.
Verge The edge of a roof, especially over a gable.
Vergeboards See 'bargeboards'.
Wainscot Wood panelling or boarding on the lower part of an internal wall.
Wall plate A timber beam placed on a wall, eg at eaves level for the roof rafters, or to receive floor joists.
Wall ties Strips of metal built across cavity walls to join the inner and outer skins.
Water bar A thin metal or plastic strip laid across a threshold or along the bottom of a door to help prevent the entry of rainwater.
Weather board A board fixed to the bottom of a door on the outside to prevent rain driving underneath.
Weatherstruck Style of mortar pointing to brickwork. It slants downwards, projecting slightly from the wall surface, to help disperse rainwater.
Woodworm General term for beetle infestation.

BIBLIOGRAPHY

Barrett, Helena, and Phillips, John. *Suburban Style: The British Home 1840–1960*, Macdonald Orbis 1987.
Building Research Establishment. *Housing Defects Reference Manual*, E. and F.N. Spon 1991.
Colour Library. *DIY and Home Improvements*, Colour Library Books 1986.
Edwards, Dennis, and Pigram, Ron. *London's Underground Suburbs*, Bloomsbury Books 1986.
Melville, Ian A., Gordon, Ian A., and Murrells, Paul G. *Structural Surveys of Dwelling Houses*, Estates Gazette 1964 onwards.
Morris, Ian. *Bazaar Property Doctor*, BBC Books 1989.
Powell, Jane, and Svensen, Linda. *Linoleum*, Gibbs Smith 2003.
Saint, Andrew, and Bowdler, Roger. *London Suburbs*, Merrell Holberton 1999.
Seeley, Ivor H. *Building Maintenance*, Palgrave Macmillan 1987.
Stevenson, Greg. *The 1930s Home*, Shire Books 2003.
Wickersham, John. *Repair and Home Renovation*, Haynes 1995.

Websites
www.bricksandbrass.co.uk
www.c20fires.co.uk
www.lafargeplasterboard.co.uk
www.periodproperty.co.uk
www.propertybooks.co.uk

INDEX

Author:	Ian Rock
Editor:	Ian MacMillan
Project Manager:	Louise McIntyre
Copy Editor:	Ian Heath
Design/layout:	James Robertson and Lee Parsons
Line illustrations:	James at Aztec Design
Index:	Peter Nicholson

Chapter Opener Photos
Simon Clay (chapters 1, 7 and 13)
Edifice (Intro and chapters 2, 3, and 6)
Elizabeth Whiting & Associates (chapters 8, 9, 10, 11 and 12)